Civil War
Museum Treasures

Civil War Museum Treasures

Outstanding Artifacts and the Stories Behind Them

KENNETH D. ALFORD

Foreword by Chris Calkins

McFarland & Company, Inc., Publishers
Jefferson, North Carolina, and London

LIBRARY OF CONGRESS CATALOGUING-IN-PUBLICATION DATA

Alford, Kenneth D.
Civil War museum treasures : outstanding artifacts and the stories behind them / Kenneth D. Alford.
    p.   cm.
Includes bibliographical references and index.

ISBN 978-0-7864-3186-1
softcover : 50# alkaline paper ∞

1. United States—History—Civil War, 1861–1865—Museums—Guidebooks.
2. United States—History—Civil War, 1861–1865—Antiquities.
3. Museums—United States—Guidebooks.
I. Title.
E646.A44   2008   973.7'6—dc22   2007048913

British Library cataloguing data are available

©2008 Kenneth D. Alford. All rights reserved

No part of this book may be reproduced or transmitted in any form or by any means, electronic or mechanical, including photocopying or recording, or by any information storage and retrieval system, without permission in writing from the publisher.

On the cover: *from top left* A lock of Lee's hair; Lee's engraved, five-shot, .28-caliber revolver; Lee's pocket Bible (all courtesy Arlington House); tattered garrison flag (courtesy Fort Sumter National Monument); Grant's leather Grimsley saddle (courtesy U.S. Army Museum at Fort Lee, Virginia)

Manufactured in the United States of America

McFarland & Company, Inc., Publishers
Box 611, Jefferson, North Carolina 28640
www.mcfarlandpub.com

For my grandchildren:
Kate, Amanda, and Luke Thomas;
Kenneth, Andie, and Daniel Alford;
Jacob and Maggie Li Alford

Acknowledgments

I am grateful to the many people and establishments who helped with the research of this book.

Special thanks are due to the rangers of the National Park Service. Their dedication and absolute passion for their profession is unsurpassed, and I express my heartfelt gratitude to Ted Alexander, Antietam; Mike Antonioni, Fort Foote; James Blankenship, Petersburg; Jim Burgess, Manassas; Chris Calkins, Petersburg; Elaine Clark, Andrew Johnson; Janice Frye, Spotsylvania; Rich Hatcher, Fort Sumter; Elizabeth Joyner, Vicksburg; Jennifer McDaid, Arlington House; David Ogden, Gulf Islands; Richard Raymond, Harpers Ferry; Mary Troy, Arlington House; and Joe Williams, Appomattox. An individual appreciation is bestowed to Dean Knudsen, Gettysburg, who exemplifies their finest traditions.

For their generous support and assistance, I owe a debt of gratitude to Daniel W. Barefoot, Lincolnton, North Carolina; Heather D. Beattie, Virginia Historical Society; Dr. Boyd D. Cathey, North Carolina State Archives, Eleanor Clark, Rosenberg Library; Gayla Coates, Simpson County Historical Society; George Collins, Tusculum College; Jeannine Disviscour, Maryland Historical Society; Josh Fox, Soldiers and Sailors National Military Museum; Bruce Robert Graetz, Museum of Florida History; Michael E. Gonzales, 45th Division Infantry Museum; Jack Gumbrecht, Historical Society Pennsylvania; Luther David Hanson, U.S. Army Quartermaster Museum; Mary Laura Kludy, Virginia Military Institute; Greg Lambousy, Louisiana State Museum; Kris Leinicke, Rock Island Arsenal Museum; Cynthia Luckie, Alabama Department of Archives and History; David Martin, Staunton River Battlefield; Dorene Buchanan McElwain, the Historic Cannonball House; Jeff Meyer, Missouri History Museum; Lisa McCown, College of Washington and Lee; Heather W. Milne, The Museum of the Confederacy; Abbie Norderhaug, Wisconsin Veterans Museum; Steven Solomon, National Museum of Health and Medicine; Vaughan Stanley, College of Washington and Lee; Alan Thomas, Prairie Grove Battlefield; and Jane Yates, The Citadel Archives and Museum.

Many thanks to my friends Thomas Sharp, for traveling with me on my many journeys, and Blair Clarke, for advice and unlimited use of his vast library.

I am indebted to my good friend, Larry Bush, of Pensacola, Florida, for his help in reading and strengthening this manuscript.

Last and absolutely not least, I pay tribute to my wife, Edda, for her patience and understanding.

Table of Contents

Acknowledgments — vii
Foreword by Chris Calkins — 1
Introduction — 3
A Quick Look at the Civil War — 5

1. Alabama — 11
2. Arkansas — 15
3. District of Columbia — 18
4. Florida — 32
5. Georgia — 35
6. Illinois — 58
7. Iowa — 61
8. Kentucky — 63
9. Louisiana — 66
10. Maryland — 68
11. Minnesota — 78
12. Mississippi — 80
13. New Mexico — 85
14. North Carolina — 88
15. Oklahoma — 96
16. Pennsylvania — 99
17. South Carolina — 113
18. Tennessee — 118
19. Texas — 125

20.	Virginia	127
21.	West Virginia	199
22.	Wisconsin	202

Appendix: Same Battles, Different Names	213
Notes	215
Bibliography	219
Index	221

FOREWORD

Artifacts, those three-dimensional objects that can be seen, touched, and examined, are the only tangible physical reminders of our past. In Ken Alford's *Civil War Museum Treasures*, these artifacts—consisting of such day-to-day items as articles of clothing, flags, books, letters, and bullets—are transformed into cherished objects because of their unique connection to Civil War history. Alford has assembled fascinating and touching examples, tied to specific events that transpired during that war. The book includes battlefield flags that men fought and died over; a mother's loving poem ripped by the penetration of a bullet; and scores of other captivating mementoes of the American past, each accompanied by an intriguing story. Readers will want to carry this book—assembled by state and location—with them as they travel the country visiting the many battlefield sites and museums dedicated to the understanding of those four turbulent years that shaped our nation.

Chris Calkins, Historian, Petersburg, Virginia

INTRODUCTION

The Civil War was the most devastating conflict in the history of the United States. Over 600,000 people were killed and millions maimed in its colossal battles, and it shaped the country in which we live. This cataclysmic episode is naturally the most documented event in American history. *Civil War Museum Treasures* is not intended as a lengthy description of the conflict itself; countless other books have already plowed that ground. Instead, this book examines museum artifacts that survive as vivid remembrances of that war. Likewise, it was not my goal to compile a definitive study of every Civil War museum treasure, for such an accounting is impossible.

I therefore focused on one-of-a-kind articles. Most of these items in our museum collections are priceless, and the majority of the stories of their origins have remained untold until now. I begin most chapters with a description of a particular museum and how the treasure came to be in that location; I then proceed with a chronological narrative centered on each rare item, relating it to a specific Civil War time line and event. It is my hope that this book offers an accurate and interesting accounting of the many extraordinary objects squirreled away in museums throughout the United States.

I began thinking about this book years ago. "Ah, you home Richmond, Ba-GAN-i-a! Why you no write American Civil War?" asked a good-spirited Chinese archivist on my visit to the Shanghai Military Archives. During years of travel while researching certain events of World War II, I had been asked this question frequently by many of the knowledgeable people I had encountered. I was surprised to learn that so many persons worldwide were aware of the bloodiest and saddest war in our history.

Indeed my home is in Richmond, Virginia, and I am steeped in Southern history; my ancestors fought in battles in what was later referred to as "The Lost Cause." Because Richmond, the former Confederate capital, is a city rich in Civil War artifacts, I decided to heed my questioners' advice. After all, the stage for that defining moment in United States history is in my backyard, and it is a fascinating subject.

This project began with my corresponding with more that 400 Civil War museums and archives and asking them to name the most interesting and/or unique items in their collections. Fortunately, the overwhelming majority responded with great enthusiasm. To my amazement most responded most generously by e-mail with attached digital photographs or with the Internet address of their most treasured items, which included many irreplaceable articles and several battle flags.

During my research, I traveled and read endlessly. My travels included the numerous Civil War locations within a day's trip of my home and continued with journeys all the way to Pecos National Park, near Santa Fe, New Mexico. It was there, for example, that I found a Civil War saber recently returned to Glorieta Pass, New Mexico, by the former owner's great-grandson. By car I followed the early battles of General William McClellan and the later battles of General Ulysses S. Grant. At Fort Monroe, Virginia, I found the information regarding Major General Benjamin Butler's Tiffany-designed mess kit, underscoring Butler's opulent and militarily deficient lifestyle. In a remote section near the Staunton River I saw the Union sword given to nine-year-old Donald McPhail when the officer "appropriated" the boy's pony — an event that leads into an account of the 1864 battle of Staunton River Bridge.

I made a trip to Chattanooga to follow the footsteps of General William T. Sherman and his march to the sea and incursion into the Carolinas. From this trip, I gained a better understanding of why my grandfather had absolutely loathed Sherman, but at the same time I gained an admiration for Sherman's battle strategy of "living off the land." The jewel of this trip was the DuBose Gallery in the Atlanta History Center. I write briefly about this large assortment, but an entire book would be necessary to fully cover this collection. In another engrossing and informative trip, I followed the Confederate Treasury train from Richmond to the village of Washington, Georgia. It was there that I set my eyes on the Confederate treasure chest in the Mary Willis Library, a focal point of several stories concerning the missing treasures of the Confederacy.

The most astonishing books were the 1883 four-volume *Battles and Leaders of the Civil War* and Private Robert Knox Sneden's *Eye of the Storm*. Sneden's observation of the daily soldiering life is detailed and insightful. In his March 26, 1862, entry, he condemns the hundreds of Yankee soldiers who are robbing graves. Burned in my memory now is his April 1 entry in which he writes this: "I picked up half a skull of some infant which I use for a soap dish."

War is cruel and my travels and reading reinforced my previous confirmations that throughout history, wartime looting has been met with a certain unspoken acceptance. Civil War history is replete with instances of plundering, and soldiers from both sides ransacked entire estates. A bit of this "disorderly conduct" is revealed in *Civil War Museum Treasures*, including the snatching of the historic Ordinance of Secession of Virginia, looted from the Confederate Capitol by Union soldier Charles W. Bullis.

I was rather happily surprised to discover that many of the particulars needed for this project had become part of the digital age; an item that I consider my best find was received from Tusculum College in Tennessee by e-mail. The image is that of an elegant nineteenth-century porcelain-and-brass tea and coffee warmer in the form of a locomotive pulling a coal car. It's a unique work that becomes even more intriguing when you know its history: it belonged to Jefferson Davis — a gift from the French ambassador to the president of the Confederacy. Other e-mailed images included the inauguration Bible of Jefferson Davis, the bullet that took the life of Abraham Lincoln, the valiant canine Dog Jack, and Old Abe, the war eagle. The entire official 129-volume *War of the Rebellion* has been digitized by Ohio State University. The Internet has proven to be a remarkable research tool for my particular study of the Civil War, and this book is therefore a combination of three years' worth of museum, archive and electronic research.

I must admit that before I began this project I had been most interested in such figures as Jeff Davis, J.E.B. Stuart, and Robert E. Lee, but this project changed my perspective, and my interests today are Abe Lincoln, U.S. Grant, and the United States of America all the way. I sincerely hope that the reader enjoys and benefits from reading *Civil War Museum Treasures*.

A Quick Look at the Civil War

The Beginnings

When John Brown raided Harpers Ferry in 1859, he set into motion events that led directly to the outbreak of the Civil War in 1861. With the election of the anti-slavery Republican presidential candidate, Abraham Lincoln, the Southern states saw a need for drastic action in order to protect what they perceived as their own interests. On December 20, 1860, a secession convention met in South Carolina and adopted an "Ordinance of Secession from the Union." Mississippi, Florida, Alabama, Georgia, Louisiana, and Texas quickly followed suit. These states subsequently sent delegates to Montgomery, Alabama, and on February 8, 1861, they adopted a provisional constitution for the newly formed Confederate States of America. Jefferson Davis was chosen as president for a six-year term of office. The constitution by which the permanent government of the Confederate States of America was formed was reported by the committee and adopted by the Provisional Congress on the March 11, 1861, to be submitted to the states for ratification. All states ratified it and conformed themselves to its requirements without delay. The constitution varied in very few particulars from the Constitution of the United States, preserving carefully the fundamental principles of popular representative democracy and the confederation of co-equal states. A month after the beginning of the Civil War, Virginia, Arkansas, and North Carolina also joined the CSA.

Following in chronological order are the eleven states that constituted the Confederacy: South Carolina — December 20, 1860; Mississippi — January 9, 1861; Florida — January 10, 1861; Alabama — January 11, 1861; Georgia — January 19, 1861; Louisiana — January 26, 1861; Texas — February 23, 1861; Virginia — March 17, 1861; Arkansas — May 6, 1861; North Carolina — May 20, 1861; and Tennessee — June 8, 1861.

Climaxing decades of bitter wrangling and pitting vast sections of a young and vigorous nation one against the other, war bursts upon the American landscape like a lightning bolt out of a darkened sky. Confederate strategy in the early months of the war is mainly defensive in the face of Federal efforts to, one, retain control of the slaveholding so-called border states of Delaware, Maryland, Kentucky, and Missouri; two, to tighten a blockade of the Southern coastline; and three, to regain control of the Mississippi River from Cairo, Illinois, to the Gulf of Mexico. With high spirits and the naiveté of youth, both North and South begin the war in earnest after the attack on Fort

Sumter. The first large-scale battle comes in mid-July as Union troops under General Irvin McDowell clash with Confederate soldiers under General Joseph E. Johnston and General P.G.T. Beauregard on the plains of Manassas, Virginia. A sweeping Confederate victory in what Southerners call the First Battle of Manassas (the North calls it Bull Run) both inspires the federal government to renew its efforts and makes the South overconfident. For the rest of the year the contending armies remain static between Manassas and Washington, giving Union General George B. McClellan plenty of time to organize and train his new Army of the Potomac.

In Missouri, in a lightning-like campaign, General Nathaniel Lyon crowds the Missouri State Guard into the southwestern part of the state; at Wilson's Creek in August he becomes the first Union general killed, and his army is defeated. The Missouri State Guard moves on to besiege and capture Lexington, but retires into southwest Missouri when threatened by federal columns converging from the east and west. A Union army is also defeated at Belmont, Missouri, early in November — the first test of battle for a rising young brigadier general named Ulysses S. Grant. Along the Southern coasts, Federals cling to several forts and employ their power afloat to seize and establish additional fortified enclaves at Hatteras Inlet, North Carolina; Port Royal Sound, South Carolina; and Ship Island, Mississippi. These enclaves not only provide bases for blockading squadrons but serve as springboards for future amphibious operations.

All of 1861's actions combined do not equal in scope a single day of the famous battles fought later in the war.

1862 — The Opening Battles

By early 1862, McClellan has succeeded in turning the Army of the Potomac into a formidable fighting force. He plans to approach Richmond by way of the peninsula between the York and James rivers, and Lincoln consents only on condition that adequately strong forces are left to guard Washington. General Joe Johnston's Confederates abandon their long-held lines around Manassas in early March and withdraw toward Richmond. McClellan's Army of the Potomac moves by water to Fort Monroe and Newport News at the tip of the Virginia peninsula and prepares to march on Richmond, some seventy miles to the northwest. In March, 1862, the Confederate ironclad *Virginia* (the old *USS Merrimac*) raids the Union fleet and would have destroyed it save for the timely arrival of the Union ironclad *Monitor*. This first battle between two ironclads is to revolutionize naval warfare.

McClellan's Peninsular Campaign begins in April, but his progress is slow and he is criticized for over-cautiousness. Even before McClellan begins his advance, Confederate General Thomas J. "Stonewall" Jackson appears in the lower Shenandoah Valley, and in a series of brilliant actions defeats or confounds the guardian Union armies. Having accomplished his purpose, that of causing Lincoln to withhold reinforcements from McClellan, Jackson returns to the peninsula.

Confederate delaying tactics and heavy rains slow McClellan's advance, and it is nearly two months before he comes within sight of Richmond's steeples. When a Southern offensive at Seven Pines on May 31–June 1 fails to dislodge the Federals, and Johnston is wounded, Robert E. Lee becomes commander of the Army of Northern Virginia. The celebrated team of Lee and Jackson now grows to be the center of Union attention. McClellan complains that he lacks the power to advance, and when Lee strikes in the Seven Days' Battle of June 25–July 1, McClellan is forced back as new commander Lee drives the Union troops away from the Southern capital. The threat to Richmond is ended, and McClellan is relieved of his command.

While the evacuation of the peninsula by Union forces is under way, Lee moves north and at the Second Battle of Manassas, August 29–30, defeats an army that has been brought together under John Pope. McClellan is once again restored to command and quickly reorganizes the demoralized army, which now tracks Lee, who has crossed the Potomac to invade the North.

Stonewall Jackson scores a victory at Cedar Mountain and Lee wins at the Second Battle of Manassas, pushing the Federals back to the outskirts of Washington. Within nine weeks, Lee has transferred the war from his own capital to the edge of his enemy's. A Confederate offensive across the Potomac is halted, however, and then turned back after battles at South Mountain and Antietam, Maryland, in mid–September. On September 17 the armies meet at Antietam Creek near Sharpsburg, Maryland. Although Lee's forces stand their ground and repel McClellan's charges, they are nevertheless exhausted by the effort and have to retreat to Virginia. Because he fails to pursue Lee, McClellan is once again relieved of his command even though Lee's first invasion of the North has been stopped. Lincoln takes advantage of Antietam to announce that on January 1, 1863, he will, under the aegis of his war powers, emancipate all slaves held within the Confederacy.

The final action of the year ends in Federal disaster when McClellan's successor Ambrose E. Burnside crosses the Rappahannock to attack Lee's entrenchments at Fredericksburg, and is severely defeated.

When Ulysses Simpson Grant opens the Tennessee and Cumberland rivers by capturing Fort Henry and Fort Donelson in February 1862, he becomes the outstanding Union general in the West. Not long after, he moves southward across Tennessee, narrowly winning the Battle of Shiloh, April 6–7, 1862. Meanwhile John Pope fights his way down the Mississippi almost to Memphis. Union forces thrust deep into the South, winning battles at Mill Springs, Kentucky, and Pea Ridge, Arkansas, forcing the Confederates to abandon southern Kentucky, much of middle and west Tennessee, and southwest Missouri. Early in April, General Albert Sidney Johnston's army assails Federal troops under Grant at Pittsburg Landing, Tennessee, but Johnston is killed and his Confederate army beaten in the two-day Battle of Shiloh. In Mississippi in June, Union amphibious forces converge on but fail to capture the Confederate stronghold of Vicksburg.

July brings a dramatic shift in the tide of war as Confederate armies invade Union territory from the trans-Mississippi to the Atlantic seaboard. To the east of Grant, Don Carlos Buell has occupied Nashville, and when Confederate General Braxton H. Bragg invades Kentucky, Buell stops him at Perryville on October 8, but allows him to return to Chattanooga. Buell is succeeded by William S. Rosecrans, who clashes again with Bragg at Murfreesboro (Stones River) in a bloody three-day battle, December 31, 1862–January 2, 1863, and Bragg retreats to Chattanooga. In northern Mississippi, Grant's attempts to take Vicksburg are thwarted by slashing Confederate cavalry raids on his supply lines. The blockade tightens as Union forces capture Roanoke Island and Fort Macon on the North Carolina sounds and bombard Fort Pulaski, Georgia, into surrender.

1863 — The High-Water Mark of the Confederacy

With the spring thaws in April, the 1863 campaigns open along the Rappahannock River when Ambrose Burnside's replacement, General Joseph Hooker, leads the Army of the Potomac upstream to slip around Lee's left flank. Lee responds aggressively and during the first week of May wins what has been called his greatest victory—Chancellorsville. The Army of the Potomac meets Lee and Jackson on May 2–5, 1863, and is defeated once again, but the defeat is rendered somewhat hollow by the death of Stonewall Jackson, a victim of "friendly fire." The victory, however, gives the Confederates the opportunity to march northward into Pennsylvania as Lee now undertakes a second invasion of the North.

The Army of the Potomac follows and, now under General George G. Meade's direction, confronts Lee with a stinging defeat at

Gettysburg. After three days of bloody fighting, July 1–3, Lee has failed to break the Union lines, and is forced to escort his remaining troops back to Virginia. Gettysburg is usually regarded as the decisive battle of the war, as its loss might have tipped the balance toward peace in the war-weary North. It also marks the last Confederate offensive in the East.

After Lee's retreat into Virginia, both armies spend the next three months recuperating while the military front alternates between the Rappahannock and Rapidan rivers to the west of Fredericksburg. Both armies are also reduced in strength as troops are ordered west to bolster operations around Chattanooga. Lee's attempt to turn Meade's flank in October results in defeat at Bristoe Station. A similar move by Meade south of the Rapidan culminates in a stalemate at Mine Run at the end of November.

Grant moves against Vicksburg and after brilliantly outmaneuvering his opponents in the Yazoo swamps lays siege to Vicksburg. One of the greatest campaigns in military history ends after a 47-day siege, and the Confederacy's mighty bastion succumbs to Union arms when Grant receives the Confederate surrender on, fittingly, July 4, 1863.

Five days later Port Hudson in Louisiana surrenders and the Mississippi is now opened to Union navigation. Lincoln proclaims that "The Father of Waters again goes unvexed to the sea." The South is now cut in half along the mighty river. Meanwhile, Rosecrans's brilliant Tullahoma Campaign forces Bragg to abandon most of Tennessee and concentrate his efforts around Chattanooga. In September, Rosecrans occupies Chattanooga and pursues Bragg into Georgia, where, at Chickamauga Creek, the Confederates turn on the Northerners and drive them back.

To relieve the beleaguered Federal troops, the Union government rushes reinforcements to Chattanooga, selects Grant to command in the West, and replaces Rosecrans with General George H. Thomas. In several battles around Chattanooga between October and November, Grant's armies defeat Bragg's troops, forcing them to retreat to Dalton, Georgia, where Bragg is succeeded in command by General Joseph E. Johnston. The two-week siege of Union-occupied Knoxville by General James Longstreet's Confederate troops ends December 3 with the approach of a relief column led by General William Tecumseh Sherman.

1864 — The Tide Turns

The last full year of campaigning in the East begins with Federal forces east and west making a unified effort to wear down the South's will to continue fighting. Grant is promoted to lieutenant general and transferred east to command all Union armies. He calls for a war of attrition against the Confederacy's two principal armies: Robert E. Lee's Army of Northern Virginia and Joseph E. Johnston's Army of Tennessee.

Leaving Sherman to deal with Johnston, Grant concentrates on Lee. Their first encounter, the Battle of the Wilderness, opens on May 5, and for the next forty days the armies remain locked in a deadly struggle. Grant suffers a "technical defeat" at the hands of Lee, but instead of retreating, Grant side-slips and confronts Lee again at Spotsylvania Courthouse. He proceeds then to flank the Confederate commander and moves to the North Anna River, then to the Chickahominy, on ground that McClellan had occupied two years before. An attack at Cold Harbor, Virginia, on June 3 proves to be a serious Union mistake and occasions violent criticism in the North because of the appallingly heavy losses. In truth, however, Grant is accomplishing his objective of whittling down irreplaceable Confederate armies, and he now spreads his troops southward across the James River and deploys to the east, besieging Petersburg as well as Richmond. The enemies settle into a siege that is punctuated by Grant's relentless efforts to outflank the Confederates and seize vital transportation arteries. His attempt to capture Petersburg outright fails at the ill-conceived and poorly executed Battle of the Crater. Meanwhile, General Jubal Early's Confederate troops expel Union forces from the Shenandoah Valley and march to the outskirts of Washington before being turned back at Fort Stevens, north of Washington, thwarting Early's plans to invade Maryland. Outnumbered but defiant, the Rebels return to the valley where, in a series of hard-fought engagements, General Philip Sheridan erases Early's army from the war.

Early in May, with Atlanta as his objective, Grant's successor Sherman attacks Johnston at Rocky Face Ridge west of Dalton. For the next eight weeks the two armies grapple their way south into central Georgia. On July 17, with Sherman's armies approaching Atlanta, Confederate President Jefferson Davis fires Johnston and replaces him with General John Bell Hood. Hood abandons Johnston's defensive strategy and boldly sends his troops to attack Sherman in a series of costly battles that only serve to underscore the futility of such tactics.

Hood now seeks to divert Sherman by moving against his base at Nashville, Georgia. Sherman, however, refuses to take the bait, and Hood is defeated by George H. Thomas, just south of the city. After setting Atlanta ablaze, Sherman cuts loose and heads for Savannah, in his famous "march to the sea," splitting the Confederacy and devastating the country through which he passes. A Union fleet meets Sherman at Savannah, and after refitting, he moves northward into the Carolinas, confronted once again by Johnston, who has been restored to command.

Elsewhere, the blockade continues to tighten as Union amphibious forces seize the forts guarding the entrance to Mobile Bay. In the famous "Damn the torpedoes!" action, Admiral David Farragut's oceangoing squadron crushes the Confederate fleet.

1865 — Defeat with Honor

With the war of attrition, desertions, and the breakdown of transportation during the winter, the lot of the Confederacy is a desperate one. The year begins with Union forces capturing Fort Fisher, guarding the approaches to the Cape Fear River and Wilmington, North Carolina. Both Grant's and Lee's armies are equally largely inactive and still entrenched around Petersburg, but with each passing week, the hopelessness of Lee's cause becomes more apparent. Early in February, Grant sends his cavalry and infantry south and west of Petersburg in an attempt to sever the only remaining supply lines into the city and to force Lee to extend his already strained defensive positions. Confederate attempts to halt the movement are checkmated at Hatcher's Run. As March begins, Lee realizes that he cannot hold the Petersburg-Richmond lines much longer. On the 25th he makes a desperate attempt to extricate his army by attacking the Federal Fort Stedman east of Petersburg. The attempt fails, and Lee gives President Davis the disheartening news: "I fear now it will be impossible to prevent a junction between Grant and Sherman...." Shortly thereafter, the Federals achieve the inevitable and break the thin Confederate defenses at Five Forks, southwest of Petersburg. Lee evacuates Richmond and Petersburg and moves west in the hope of uniting with Johnston. On April 9 however, Sheridan's cavalry and infantry bar his way, and that same day at Appomattox Court House, Lee surrenders to Grant. Given the horrific losses, the terms are generous. All officers and men are paroled and most arms and supplies are surrendered, but the officers are allowed to retain their sidearms. All men who claim a horse or mule are allowed to take them home to work their farms. Lee's surrender on April 9 will create a snowball effect that will lead to the total surrender of the Confederacy.

Joseph E. Johnston is restored to the command of what is left of the Army of Tennessee and given the impossible task of stopping Sherman's armies that are now sweeping northward through South Carolina, having conquered Georgia. Yankee troops occupy Columbia on February 17 and compel the evacuation of Charleston that evening. Entering North Carolina, Sherman defeats Johnston at Averasboro and at Bentonville.

At Goldsboro, Sherman is joined by General John M. Schofield's force, fresh from victory at Kinston. The outnumbered Johnston surrenders his troops to Sherman on April 26 at Durham Station. Meanwhile, in Alabama, Mobile falls to Federal forces while General James H. Wilson's Union cavalry corps sweeps through Selma and Montgomery and on to Columbus and Macon, Georgia. On May 10, near Irwinville, Georgia, his troopers capture Confederate President Jefferson Davis, who had fled Richmond when that city was evacuated on April 2. From Jonesboro, Tennessee, General George Stoneman and his 4,000 cavalrymen raid eastward across the Appalachians into southwest Virginia and North Carolina's Piedmont region. Richard Taylor surrenders Mississippi and Alabama on May 4, and Edmund Kirby Smith likewise surrenders the Trans-Mississippi Department on May 26.

Northern rejoicing at the great union victory is profoundly dampened by the tragic assassination of Lincoln by Southern sympathizer John Wilkes Booth on April 14, an act that would re-inflame Northern hatred toward the rebellious South.

1

ALABAMA

Alabama Department of Archives and History, 624 Washington Avenue, Montgomery, AL

In the late 1800s, the desire to honor those who had served the Confederacy led to the establishment of patriotic societies, the erection of monuments, and the creation of the Alabama Department of Archives and History as an institution where significant documents and artifacts could be preserved. The department was founded in 1901, and over the years its mission has broadened to ensure the preservation of the records and artifacts that tell the story of those who contributed to the formation of Alabama as a state.

The Bible upon which Jefferson Davis placed his hand while being sworn in as the first president of the Confederate States of America (courtesy Alabama Department of Archives and History, Montgomery).

Inscribed on the inside cover of the Davis inauguration Bible: "The oath of office as first President of the Provisional Government of the Confederate States of America was administered to Jefferson Davis from this Bible by Howell Cobb, President of the Provisional Congress, at the Front portico of the Capital in Montgomery on the Eighteenth day of February A.D. 1861" (courtesy Alabama Department of Archives and History, Montgomery).

The Inauguration Bible of Jefferson Davis

The Bible was initially purchased in 1853 to be used as the state Bible to swear in Alabama governors and, in fact, is still used for that ceremony. This priceless historical object today resides with the state records in the Alabama Archives.

JEFFERSON DAVIS AS PRESIDENT

Unknown to most is that in meetings of his own Mississippi legislature, Davis argued against secession, but when a majority of the delegates

---

Jefferson Davis. A constitutional convention met in Montgomery, Alabama, in early 1861. On February 9, Davis was named "provisional president of the Confederate States of America," and on February 18 he was inaugurated as provisional president (courtesy Library of Congress).

opposed him, he gave in. The Confederate government moved to Richmond, Virginia, in May, 1861, and on May 29, Davis and his family took up residence there in the so-called White House of the Confederacy. He was inaugurated as provisional president February 18, 1861, in Alabama.

Davis was elected to a six-year term as Confederate president on November 6, 1861. He had never served a full term in any elective office, and this was to be no exception. He was inaugurated to his elected term on February 22, 1862.

Davis was not an ideal selection: Prideful, stubborn, doctrinaire, and often narrow-minded, he was not willing to compromise to achieve greater goals, which prevented him from becoming a great chief executive. "He does not know the arts of the politician and would not practice if understood," wrote his wife, and she was right. But his unswerving devotion and loyalty to the South was unquestioned, and he was willing to work himself almost to death for what he saw as a noble cause. For all his faults, he was the best man available in February 1861, a time when the South was suffering from a dearth of good statesmen.

Minié Ball, 1862

Invented by French army captains in the 1840s and later adopted by the United States government, the Minié ball was one of the chief forms of ammunition in the Civil War. The Alabama Department of Archives and History holds a Minié ball that lodged in the face of a soldier, William Joeb Reynolds, during the Battle of Perry-ville on October 8, 1862. The bullet was surgically removed in 1910.

This Minié ball slammed into William Joeb Reynolds' face on October 8, 1862, during the fierce battle at Perryville, Kentucky, as Reynolds clambered over the breastworks. The ball lodged directly over Reynolds' right eye, where it remained until July 5, 1910, when surgeon Dr. Charles Thigpen of Montgomery, Alabama, removed it. Subsequently it was donated to the Archives and History Department of Alabama by L. H. Reynolds, Judge of Probate, Chilton County, on June 5, 1931 (courtesy Alabama Department of Archives and History, Montgomery).

Battle of Perryville and Stones River

Confederate General Braxton Bragg's autumn 1862 invasion of Kentucky had reached the outskirts of Louisville and Cincinnati, but he was forced to retreat and regroup. On October 7 the Federal army of Major General Don Carlos Buell converged on the small crossroads town of Perryville, Kentucky, in three columns. Union forces first skirmished with Rebel cavalry on the Springfield Pike before gray-clad infantry arrived, and the fighting became more general, on Peters Hill. At dawn of the next day, fighting resumed on Peters Hill as a Union division advanced up the pike and halted just before the Confederate line. The fighting then stopped for a time.

After noon, a Confederate division struck

the Union left flank and forced it to fall back. When more Confederate divisions joined the fray, the Union line made a stubborn stand with a brave counterattack, but finally fell back with some troops routed. Buell did not know of the events on the field, or he would have sent forward some reserves. Even so, the Union troops on the left flank, reinforced by two brigades, stabilized their line, and the Rebel attack sputtered to a halt. Later, a Rebel brigade assaulted the Union division on the Springfield Pike but was repulsed and fell back into Perryville.

The Yankees pursued, and skirmishing occurred in the streets just before dark. Union reinforcements were threatening the Rebel left flank by now. Bragg, short of men and supplies, withdrew during the night, and, after pausing at Harrodsburg, continued the Confederate retreat by way of Cumberland Gap into East Tennessee. The Confederate offensive was over, and the Union controlled Kentucky.

2

ARKANSAS

Prairie Grove Battlefield State Park, from Interstate 540 in Fayetteville, travel west on U.S. 62 just eight miles to the park, located on the eastern edge of Prairie Grove

The park was founded by the United Daughters of the Confederacy in 1908 as a place for Civil War veteran reunions. Today, the park preserves an important part of the historic battlefield and boasts a unique collection of buildings depicting life in the region before, during, and after the Civil War.

Prairie Grove Battlefield has been nationally recognized as one of the most intact Civil War sites. The ridge and fields look much as they did at the time of the battle on December 7, 1862.

Sword from the Prairie Grove Battlefield

On display at the Prairie Grove Battlefield State Park is an 1840 cavalry saber recovered from the battlefield by an Iowa soldier.

THE BATTLE OF PRAIRIE GROVE

The battle of Prairie Grove, waged on December 7, 1862, was the most decisive Union victory in the state of Arkansas during

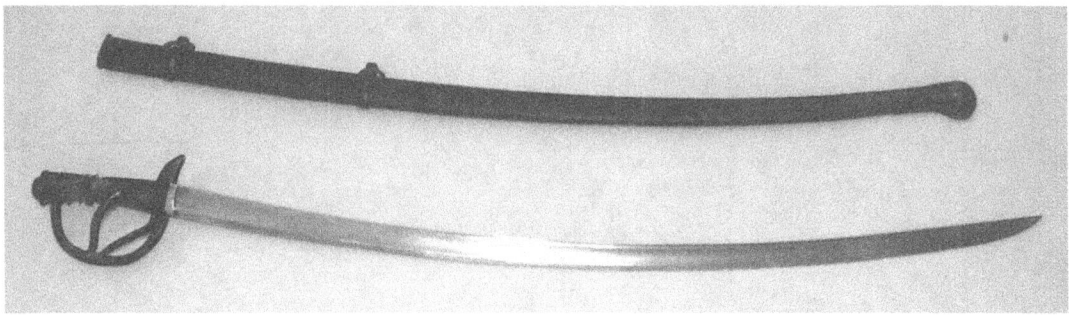

The pictured sword is a Schnitzler & Kirschbaum 1840 cavalry saber, recovered by Private Leonidas L. Wilson of Company B, 20th Iowa Infantry, from the Prairie Grove Battlefield. On the quillon are etched the words, "Picked up by L.L Wilson, Prairie Grove, ARK. Dec. 7, 1862." Wilson kept the saber as a souvenir of war. According to his obituary, he had assembled an extensive collection of historic relics, as well as stuffed animals from his father's taxidermy business. Much was destroyed by a house fire, the sword being one piece that survived, albeit damaged (courtesy Prairie Grove Battlefield State Park).

the Civil War. In the preceding November, a Union army under the command of U.S. General James Blunt invaded northwest Arkansas from southwest Missouri. Blunt was a very aggressive commander, and soon marched deep into Arkansas, right in the expanse of the Boston Mountains. Although Blunt won a small battle at Cane Hill on November 28, he had isolated himself and was almost 100 miles away from the nearest Union army, based at Springfield, Missouri, and commanded by General Francis Herron.

In early December, General Thomas Hindman, based east of the Boston Mountains, decided to strike at Blunt and his strong army while Blunt was isolated from reinforcements. But while Hindman prepared for the attack, General Herron, in Springfield, ordered one of the longest and greatest forced marches of the entire Civil War. In five days, Herron marched his army an astounding 110 miles from Springfield to just north of the Confederates' army.

Stunned by the rapid arrival of Herron's army, Hindman turned north and attacked Herron on December 7 near Prairie Grove Church. Because of the rigors of the forced march, Herron's army was severely depleted, but nonetheless, managed to hold its ground and actually push the Confederate forces back until early in the afternoon, when at last the weakened Union forces gave way to the Confederates' superior numbers. Victory seemed to favor the Rebels, but before Hindman was able to push the Union forces back across the Illinois River, he encountered General Blunt's waiting army, which managed to stop Hindman's army's advance.

As night fell over the battlefield, the fighting ended, and Hindman continued to hold the high ground, but events that occurred early that evening turned the tide of the battle. Stragglers from General Herron's forced march began to return to their army, strengthening the Federals. Hindman soon realized that the loyalty of many of his conscripts was in doubt, as desertion grew rampant during the night. Realizing that he would not be able to sustain another attack, Hindman and his forces left Prairie Grove and gave up the high ground and, ultimately, northern Arkansas, to the Union.

The Conciliation Quilt

Also on display at Prairie Grove is a quilt made of pieces from Confederate and Union

Twenty-one-year-old Benna McAvoy of West Virginia created this intricate quilt in 1917, using a briar stitch design (courtesy Prairie Grove Battlefield State Park).

uniforms. The pieces came from the uniforms of 21-year-old Benna McAvoy's two uncles— Robert McAvoy, who served in the Confederate Army, 25th Regiment, Virginia Infantry, and William McAvoy, who served in the Union Army, 10th Regiment, West Virginia Infantry. After the war the two brothers despised each other, and at family gatherings relatives had to disarm them to keep them from killing each other. After some years the brothers made peace with each other, and four quilts symbolizing the reconciliation were made, this one and three others made by Benna's sisters. The brothers' uniforms were cut up, each quilt containing pieces of the Confederate and Union garments, symbolizing the reuniting of both the family and the country. Each quilt had different stitching so the girls could identify their individual quilt. Of the four quilts, only this one is known to survive.

3

DISTRICT OF COLUMBIA

Library of Congress,
101 Independence Avenue NW,
Washington, DC

The Library of Congress is the largest library in the world, with more than 130 million items on approximately 530 miles of bookshelves. The collections include more than 29 million books and other printed materials, 2.7 million recordings, 12 million photographs, 4.8 million maps, 5 million music items and 58 million manuscripts.

Photographs of U.S. Grant and Robert E. Lee

Unique in their scope and richness, the prints and photographs in The Library of Congress collections today number more than 13.7 million images. These include photographs, fine art, popular prints and drawings, posters, and architectural and engineering drawings, many dating from the Civil War.

A WAR IN PHOTOGRAPHS

The American Civil War was the first large and prolonged conflict recorded on photographic film. During the conflict, dozens of photographers, both as private individuals and as employees of the Confederate and Union governments, photographed civilians and civilian activities, military personnel, equipment, activities, and the locations and aftermaths of battles.

The collection of Civil War photographs represents a portion of the Anthony-Taylor-Rand-Ordway-Eaton Collection of Civil War Views housed in the Prints and Photographs Division of the Library of Congress. The nucleus of that collection is the negatives taken during the war under the supervision of famed photographer Mathew Brady. After the war, these were transferred to the photographic supply firm of H. T. Anthony Company as payment for debts owed them by Brady. The negatives were purchased in the 1870s by Colonel Arnold A. Rand and General Albert Ordway, veterans of the war and collectors of war memorabilia. To Brady's negatives, they added about 2,000 negatives made by Alexander Gardner, a photographer who had worked for Brady but who left him early in the war to set up his own business. Rand and Ordway sold the entire collection to John C. Taylor, who used the negatives to make stereographic prints and lantern slides which he sold during the 1880s. In 1907 the negatives were bought by Edward B. Eaton, who used them in several books on the Civil War. The most notable of these was the ten-volume work, *The Photographic History of the Civil War*. In 1916 the collection was placed in storage, where it remained until the library purchased it in 1943. The library's acquisition included 7,500 original glass plate negatives and about 2,500 copy glass and film negatives, providing a total of about 3,750 different views and about 2,650 different portraits. After acquiring the collection, the

These two well-known photographs of Generals Ulysses S. Grant (left) and Robert E. Lee are two of the 2,000 Civil War pictures in the Library of Congress collection (courtesy Library of Congress).

library made a concerted effort to copy the original glass plates onto film, most often in an 8"×10" format.

Although many photographers covered the Civil War, the name Mathew Brady is a synonym for Civil War photography; he is, in fact, the best-known professional photographer in the history of American picture–taking. He was born around 1822 and in 1847 opened a gallery in Washington. By 1850 he was the leading photographer of his time.

In the middle 1850s, Brady brought Alexander Gardner, an expert on enlarging, from his home in Scotland to practice still another new development. As a result, "imperial photographs," huge prints as large as 17 x 20, were introduced to a delighted and amazed public.

With the outbreak of Civil War, Brady's absorbing passion determined his career as he decided to record by means of the camera the most important event in American history during the nineteenth century. After organizing a staff of photographers which at one time numbered as many as twenty, Brady equipped and sent them to the various fronts. Among those who took to the field for Brady was Alexander Gardner. Brady himself was frequently in the field and on several occasions under fire.

At the close of the war, Brady fell on difficult times. Only a few friends who collected a sum of money saved him from from burial in potter's field.

A Sharp-Shooter on Picket Duty

Painter Winslow Homer documented the war for *Harper's Weekly*. He sketched this Union Soldier in 1862. His notes about the drawing are preserved.

Famed maritime painter Winslow Homer is also remembered for this image. At age 25, he documented the Civil War for *Harper's Weekly*, creating beautiful etchings and paintings of horrific events. This etching of a Union sharpshooter soldier is dated November 15, 1862, and is titled "The Army of the Potomac—A Sharp-Shooter on Picket Duty." The shooter is perched in a pine tree and steadies his fourteen-pound James target rifle on a limb; the weapon was accurate up to 500 yards. The action is placed in a peach orchard in Yorktown in April 1862, and the soldier's face reveals intense concentration as he draws a bead on the next casualty of war (courtesy Library of Congress).

Sharpshooters at Yorktown

General George B. McClellan landed his army at Fort Monroe in March 1862, determined to conquer the Virginia peninsula immediately. In his path was only a small contingent of Confederates, commanded by General John Magruder, and occupying a line across the tip of the peninsula between Yorktown and the Warwick River. Magruder moved his men from one point to another to create the impression of having more troops than he actually did. To enhance the bluff, he even emplaced "Quaker guns"—logs painted black to resemble cannon. Magruder was less than confident, however: "I have made my arrangements to fight with my small force," he wrote to his superiors, "but without the slightest hope of success."

On the other side of the line, McClellan was seriously concerned about Magruder's position. Confederate batteries at Gloucester Point on the York River were hindering Union naval operations, preventing McClellan from transporting troops upriver beyond Yorktown, and the ironclad CSS *Virginia* sealed the James River. Probing the Yorktown line, McClellan's forces were surprised to find the Warwick River a significant stream. Units that struck Magruder's defenses nearer Yorktown later reported considerably strong enemy forces.

McClellan decided on a siege—bring up heavy artillery, and blast the Confederates out of their works. He chose this cautious course because he believed that Magruder was

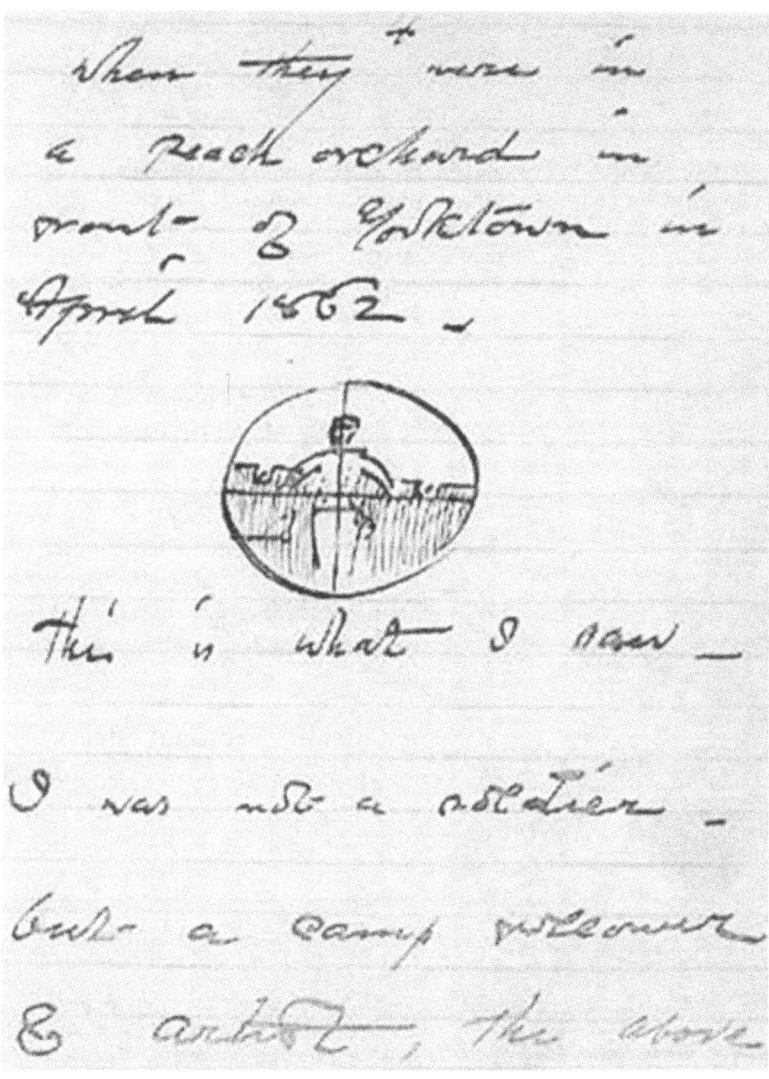

Homer's notes and haunting sketch of the intended victim of the sharpshooter (courtesy Library of Congress).

quently, the Federals surged forward in pursuit, and the Siege of Yorktown ended.

By far the most dangerous duty during the siege of Yorktown was being assigned to the advanced picket line, which called for a close watch on the enemy while avoiding becoming a sharpshooter's target. Early in the siege Union sharpshooters held a decided edge in this deadly contest. Among the units in the Army of the Potomac was a regiment recruited by Colonel Hiram Berdan that was composed of expert marksmen armed with special rifles equipped with telescopic sights.

Winslow Homer was fascinated by sharpshooters and sketched the scene in his haunting illustration while attached to the Union Army at Yorktown.

While Homer gained fame for this illustration, we find that he was disturbed by what he saw as the brutal image of the sharpshooter. In a fascinating letter Homer describes his recollections of these snipers: "I was not a soldier but a camp follower & artist. [During the battle of the Peninsular, Homer attached himself to the soldiers of the 61st New York.] The above impression

indeed as strong as he appeared. The Union general wrote, in fact, that the Confederates had "probably not less than 100,000 men, and possibly more."

The siege lasted throughout April. The Confederates assured themselves that McClellan was the primary threat to Richmond and reinforced Magruder with General Joseph E. Johnston's army, but on May 3, three days before McClellan's intended to approach Yorktown, Johnston's troops withdrew up the peninsula seeking more favorable circumstances in which to confront the Federals. Subse-

[referring to his sketch] struck me as being as near murder as anything I ever could think of in connection with the army & I always had a horror of that branch of the service."

Nevertheless, "The Sharpshooter" established Winslow Homer's reputation and made him one of the most sought-after artists of his era. This illustration brought joy to the lives of recruitment officers because "The Sharpshooter" led men to recruiting offices in droves.

This sketch and other oil paintings of the "Sharpshooter" were completed in his Manhattan studio and based on his memory and rough sketches of battlefield events. The oil paintings differ from the *Harper's Weekly* image in one extra detail—missing is a canteen hanging in the tree, indicating that the sniper is expecting a lengthy stay at his post.

Colonel Hiram C. Berdan Portrait

Berdan created a terrifying new force for the Union Army, a company of specially recruited sharpshooters. A sharpshooter himself, Berdan invented the Berdan rifle and other weapons, including a submarine gunboat.

Lincoln's Personal Effects

President Abraham Lincoln had a number of mundane items with him the night he was shot, April 14, 1865.

Sniping, or sharpshooting, served as a psychological weapon from the outset of the Civil War. Champion marksman Hiram C. Berdan of New York was authorized to raise a regiment of sharpshooters for Federal service and sponsored competitions for potential marksmen in the summer of 1861. To qualify, a recruit had to place ten shots in a ten-inch circle at 200 yards, firing any rifle he chose from any preferred position. Berdan organized sharpshooter companies in New York City and Albany, and in New Hampshire, Vermont, Michigan, and Wisconsin. Mustered in as the 1st Regiment Sharpshooter/U.S. Volunteers, November 25, 1861, the unit saw service in every eastern campaign through autumn 1864 (courtesy Library of Congress).

WHEN ABRAHAM LINCOLN WAS SHOT

The seemingly everyday items pictured were given to Lincoln's son Robert Todd Lincoln upon the president's death. Associated with the tragic assassination, the items taken from Lincoln's pockets became relics, and were kept in the Lincoln family for more than seventy years. They were donated to the library in 1937 as part of an endowment from Lincoln's granddaughter, Mary Lincoln Isham, which included several books and daguerreotypes, a silver inkstand, and Mary Todd Lincoln's seed-pearl necklace and matching bracelets.

It is unusual for the Library of Congress to keep personal artifacts among its holdings, so they were not put on display until 1976, when then-Librarian of Congress Daniel Boorstin believed that their exposure would

When President Lincoln was shot at Ford's Theatre in Washington, D.C. on April 14, 1865, he was carrying the items pictured: two pairs of spectacles, a lens polisher, a pocketknife, a watch fob, a linen handkerchief, and a brown leather wallet containing a five-dollar Confederate note and nine newspaper clippings, including several favorable to the president and his policies (courtesy Library of Congress).

humanize a man who had become "mythologically engulfed," as he put it. Humanizing or not, the availability of these artifacts has further piqued interest in Lincoln, and the contents of his pockets are among the sacred items visitors to the library most often ask to see.

A playbill, part of a collection of Lincolniana donated by Alfred Whital Stern, announces the fateful performance of "Our American Cousin."

Stern assembled the most extensive collection of Lincolniana ever owned by a private individual, including a large amount of conspiracy literature and large numbers of newspaper accounts of the assassination, including the *New York Times* account pictured here. Stern's important gift to the library in 1953 included books, broadsides, paintings, photographs, medals, manuscripts, and memorabilia.

Portrait of Confederate Secretary of War Judah P. Benjamin

Benjamin served in various cabinet posts in the Confederacy and recognized the value of blockade-running. He later became and leading lawyer in England.

CONFEDERATE DEPARTMENT OF STATE RECORDS

Nearly all the records of the Confederate Department of State were saved during the evacuation of Richmond. Preparations for moving the records were made in March 1865, and clerk William J. Bromwell moved three cartons of departmental records to a barn near Richmond; he was also ordered to transfer seven additional cartons to Danville Female College in Danville, Virginia. With the end of the Confederacy near, Secretary of State Judah Benjamin instructed Bromwell to take all of the records to Charlotte, North Carolina. Bromwell left Richmond with three containers and stopped in Danville to retrieve the seven aforementioned cartons. He arrived in Charlotte on April 1, 1865, and placed the ten containers—one of which held the great seal—in the courthouse in strongboxes and marked each container with his own initials. The surrender at Appomattox, Jeff Davis's flight and subsequent capture, and Benjamin's escape to England had the effect of making Bromwell formal custodian of the records.

Evidence indicates that Bromwell and John T. Pickett, the former Confederate envoy to Mexico, planned to sell the records. Bromwell returned to Richmond after the war and began practicing law, but he moved to Washington toward the end of 1866 to become an associate in Pickett's law office. It is possible that he recovered the department's records at this time and took them to Washington, where Pickett became the agent for their sale.

Pickett failed in his initial efforts to sell the records to the U.S. government. Secretary of State Seward was not interested in 1868, and when Secretary of War Rawlins recommended the purchase in 1869, the price was considered too high. The president's offer of a small partial payment with an appropriation to be recommended later was not accepted. Pickett also failed to interest private purchasers such as William W. Corcoran, the Washington banker to whom the records were offered for $25,000, and Jacob Thompson, an ex-Confederate Army officer and agent.

After 1871, however, when Congress provided adjudication of the claims of Southern loyalists, the government became interested in possibly using the records in that connection. Commander Thomas O. Selfridge examined the records, then deposited at Hamilton, Ontario, in Pickett's presence, and reported on April 15, 1872, that he believed them to be the entire archives of the Confederate Department of State. On June 10, 1872, Congress appropriated funds to enable the secretary of the treasury to buy records. It was agreed that $75,000 would be paid to John T. Pickett for the archives. The records were placed in the Treasury Department and used in later years by the Commissioners of Claims, U. S. Court of Claims, and attorneys for the Justice Department, in adjudicating war claims.

In 1904 the librarian of Congress obtained an order from President Roosevelt for the transfer of the Confederate State Department records to the library. Since some were still being utilized by the Treasury Department for the settlement of claims, it was agreed that only diplomatic records

Controversial Confederate Secretary of War Judah Benjamin — called "the brains of the Confederacy" — burned all of the Department of State's secret records before Richmond was evacuated. Fleeing to England, he was the only member of the Confederate government never to return to the United States. He practiced law in England until 1883 and died in Paris on May 6, 1884 (courtesy Library of Congress).

would be transferred. A schedule listing the records delivered to the library was signed on Nov. 23, 1906. The Treasury Department transferred the remainder of the records on October 26, 1910. After this arduous journey, the groups of records now rested in the Manuscript Division of the Library of Congress.

At the time he sold the Confederate records to the U. S. Government, Pickett retained some duplicates and copies of department correspondence. He offered them to the Southern Historical Society in August 1873, but the offer was declined. On April 1, 1886, Pickett sold this collection to the War Department "for the sum of $5 & other valuable considerations." At an unknown date the collection was lent to John Hay, possibly for use in writing his biography of Lincoln. After

Hay's death the records (14 volumes) remained in his Washington house, then used by his daughter, the wife of Senator James D. Wadsworth. In April 1925, Senator Wadsworth informed the Library of Congress of their existence, and in May the library acquired them.

National Museum of Health and Medicine, 6900 Georgia Avenue, NW, Washington, DC 20306

The fatal bullet removed from Abraham Lincoln's skull. It rests today in the National Museum of Health and Medicine, Armed Forces Institute of Pathology, Washington, D.C. (courtesy Medicine, Armed Forces Institute of Pathology).

The National Museum of Health and Medicine, a division of the Armed Forces Institute of Pathology, was founded in 1862 as the Army Medical Museum, the purpose of which was to study and improve medical conditions during the Civil War. The museum houses a collection of over 24 million items including archival materials, anatomical and pathological specimens, medical instruments and artifacts, and microscope slide-based medical research collections. The collections are focused on the history and practice of American medicine, military medicine, and current medical research issues.

On February 5, 1865, two months before he was assassinated, Lincoln posed for a series of portraits at Alexander Gardner's studio. While Gardner was processing this photograph, the negative broke, and he made only this single print before destroying the damaged negative. After Lincoln's death, the photograph acquired a special significance. The crack in the plate — near the spot on Lincoln's forehead where Booth's bullet struck — seems to foreshadow the assassination (courtesy Smithsonian Institution).

By the President of the United States of America:

A Proclamation.

Whereas, on the twenty-second day of September, in the year of our Lord one thousand eight hundred and sixty-two, a proclamation was issued by the President of the United States, containing, among other things, the following, to wit:

"That on the first day of January, in the "year of our Lord one thousand eight hundred "and sixty-three, all persons held as slaves within "any State or designated part of a State, the people "whereof shall then be in rebellion against the "United States, shall be then, thenceforward, and "forever free; and the Executive Government of the "United States, including the military and naval "authority thereof, will recognize and maintain "the freedom of such persons, and will do no act "or acts to repress such persons, or any of them, "in any efforts they may make for their actual "freedom.

"That the Executive will, on the first day

The Bullet that Killed Lincoln

John Wilkes Booth assassinated Abraham Lincoln on April 14, 1865. He originally planned to kidnap the president and hold him for ransom, but changed his mind when Lincoln supported voting rights for blacks.

Portrait of Lincoln by Alexander Gardner

Gardner took this photograph three months before Lincoln's death.

National Archives, 700 Pennsylvania Avenue NW, Washington, DC

The National Archives is the U.S. Government's collection of documents that are records of important events in American history. The National Archives and Records Administration (NARA) is the government agency that preserves and maintains these millions of files and materials and makes them available for research. The National Archives' Civil War photograph collection includes 6,000 photographs from the Matthew B. Brady collection, purchased for $27,840 by the War Department in 1874 and 1875; photographs from the Quartermaster's Department of the Corps of Engineers; and photographs private citizens donated to the War Department. The Archives' Cartographic Branch houses 8,000 Civil War maps. In addition, the archives has on display the Declaration of Independence and the Emancipation Proclamation.

Emancipation Proclamation

The Emancipation Proclamation, signed by President Lincoln in 1863, freed only slaves in Confederate states, not those in border states or Union held territory in the South.

FREEING SOME OF THE SLAVES

The battle of Antietam was an engagement that served as a turning point that changed the entire course of the Civil War. Antietam not only halted Lee's bold invasion of the North but thwarted his efforts to force Lincoln to sue for peace. It also provided Lincoln with the political victory he needed to silence some critics and announce the abolition of slavery in the South. And, with that Proclamation of Emancipation, Lincoln was able to broaden the base of the war.

The proclamation reads, "Whereas, on the twenty-second day of September, in the year of our Lord one thousand eight hundred and sixty-two, a proclamation was issued by the President of the United States, containing, among other things, the following, to wit:

"That on the first day of January, in the year of our Lord one thousand eight hundred and sixty-three, all persons held as slaves within any State or designated part of a State, the people whereof shall then be in rebellion against the United States, shall be then, thenceforward, and forever free; and the Executive Government of the United States, including the military and naval authority thereof, will recognize and maintain the freedom of such persons, and will do no act or acts to repress such persons, or any of them, in any efforts they may make for their actual freedom...

Smithsonian Institution, The National Mall, Between 4th and 17th Streets SW, Washington, DC

The Smithsonian Institution, the world's largest museum complex and research organization, comprising seventeen museums and the National Zoo, is located in the Washing-

---

Opposite: The original Emancipation Proclamation is in the National Archives in Washington, D.C. The five-page document was originally tied with narrow red and blue ribbons attached to the signature page by a wafered impression of the Seal of the United States. Most of the ribbon remains; some parts of the seal are still decipherable; other parts have worn off (courtesy National Archives).

Bullet-riddled oak stump

The Smithsonian enshrines what was an oak tree, until it was shattered by bullets in a battle at Spotsylvania, Virginia, in 1864. Oak trees grow on the site once again.

> ### Spotsylvania's Bloody Angle
>
> On the morning of May 12, 1864, the front line of General Robert E. Lee's Army of Northern Virginia—some 1,200 entrenched Confederates—awaited the assault of 5,000 Union troops from the 2nd Corps of the Army of the Potomac. Here, at a slight bend in the line, occurred the most savage, longest sustained hand-to-hand combat of the war. The opposing troops fired muzzle to muzzle and bayoneted and clubbed one another across the logs of the parapet.
>
> This battle is best described by eyewitness Horace Porter in his 1897 book, *Campaign with Grant*:
>
> The battle near the "angle" was probably the most desperate engagement in the history of modern warfare and presented features which were absolutely appalling. It was chiefly a savage hand-to-hand fight across the breastworks. Rank after rank was riddled by shot and shell and bayonet-thrusts, and finally sank, a mass of torn and mutilated corpses; then fresh troops rushed madly forward to replace the dead, and so the murderous work went on. Guns were run up close to the parapet, and double charges of canister played their part in the bloody work. The fence-rails and logs in the breastworks shattered into mere splinters, and trees over a foot and a half in diameter were cut completely in two by the incessant musketry

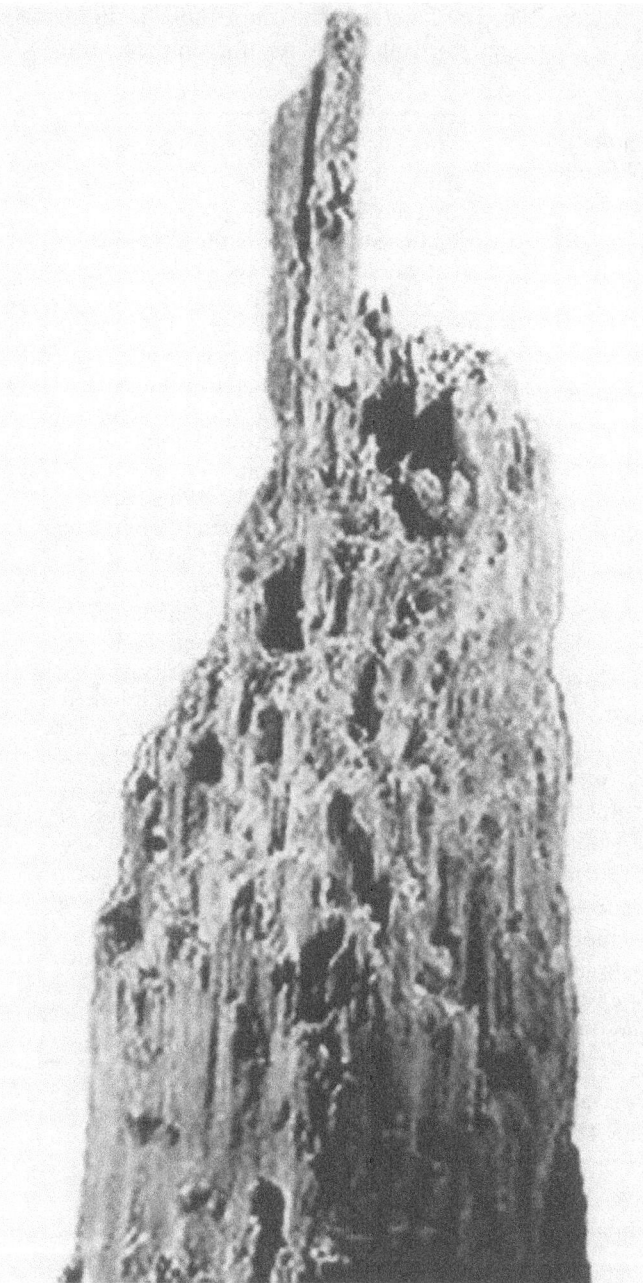

This bullet-shattered stump, displayed in the Smithsonian, was once a healthy oak tree in a rolling meadow just outside Spotsylvania Court House, Virginia (courtesy Smithsonian Institution).

ton, D.C., metropolitan area, and contains a staggering number of exhibits. This great multitude of items represents the treasured icons of our past, the vibrant art of the present, and the scientific promise of the future.

The bullet-ridden stump shown on page 28 was once a healthy tree, which stood ten yards to the right of the oak trees in the photograph.

fire. We had not only shot down an army, but also a forest. The opposing flags were placed thrust against each other; and muskets were fired with muzzle against muzzle. Skulls were crushed with clubbed muskets, and men stabbed to death with swords and bayonets thrust between the logs in the parapet which separated the combatants. Wild cheers, savage yells, and frantic shrieks rose above the sighing of the wind and the pattering of the rain, and formed a demoniacal accompaniment to the booming of the guns as they hurled their missiles of death into the contending ranks. Even the darkness of night and the pitiless storm failed to stop the fierce contest, and the deadly strife did not cease till after midnight. Our troops had been under fire for twenty hours, but they still held the position which they had so dearly purchased.

My duties carried me again to the spot the next day, and the appalling sight presented was harrowing in the extreme. Our own killed were scattered over a large space near the "angle," while in front of the captured breastworks the enemy's dead, vastly more numerous than our own, were piled upon each other in some places four layers deep, exhibiting every ghastly phase of mutilation. Below the mass of fast-decaying corpses, the convulsive twitching of limbs and the writhing of bodies showed that there were wounded men still alive and struggling to extricate themselves from their horrid entombment. Every relief possible was afforded, but in too many cases it came too late. The place was well named the "Bloody Angle."

Portrait of General George Armstrong Custer

Custer was promoted to brigadier general in the Union Army at 23, and was present when Lee Surrendered. He died in an Indian massacre in 1876.

LEE'S RETREAT AND SURRENDER

In the days just before Lee's surrender, it was George Custer's men who played a major supporting role in blocking the enemy's retreat near Appomattox.

In April 1861, when Fort Sumter was fired upon, George Armstrong Custer had still to take his final examinations at the United States Military Academy. He graduated that June, last in a class of thirty-four. Custer's ambition to fight in the war was realized immediately, and he participated in the conflict from beginning to end, from Manassas to Appomattox. Fearless and fortunate, Custer made the most of every opportunity to engage the enemy, and promotions followed. Having entered the war a second lieutenant in the 2nd Cavalry, Custer became a brigadier general of volunteers only two years later. At twenty-three, he was the youngest officer ever to wear a star. Before the war was over, he was donning a pair and was commanding the 3rd Division of Sheridan's cavalry corps.

The Civil War effectively ended on April, 9, 1865, at Appomattox Court House, Virginia, when Generals Robert E. Lee and Ulysses S. Grant signed the surrender terms. That morning, Lee concluded that victory was impossible and remarked, "There is nothing for me left to do but to go and see General Grant, and I would rather die a thousand deaths."

The nation's return to peace marked the opening of an age that would raise the United States to new and undreamed of heights in wealth, productivity, and world influence.

The chairs used by Lee and Grant, along with the table on which Grant signed the terms of surrender to end the Civil War were quickly appropriated as souvenirs by Union officers. The historic furnishings were reunited at the Smithsonian in the early twentieth century: Grant's chair was bequeathed in 1906, the table arrived in 1912, and Lee's chair was donated in 1915.

General E. W. Whitaker purchased the

Brash young General George Armstrong Custer was a cavalry commander under General Philip Sheridan. Robert E. Lee had requested an immediate cessation of hostilities and sought to learn Grant's proposed terms of surrender, so a white linen dish towel was cut in half and served as a makeshift flag of truce. It was carried by a Captain Simms, a staff officer under General James Longstreet, into Custer's federal lines. After the war, Sheridan presented the flag to Mrs. Custer in appreciation of the loyal service performed by her husband. The flag is on display in the Smithsonian (courtesy Smithsonian Institution).

caned armchair from Wilmer McLean, and it remained in Whitaker's possession until November 3, 1871. He then presented the chair to the relief fund of the Nathaniel Lyon Post, Grand Army of the Republic, to be awarded to the person selling the most tickets for a benefit performance for the military drama "Home and Country" performed at the Opera House in Washington, D.C. Captain Patrick O'Farrell sold 96 tickets and thus became the chair's new owner. That night he was offered $100 for the chair but declined to sell. In 1915 his widow, Bridget E. O'Farrell, donated the chair to the Smithsonian.

As for the chair Grant sat in, General Henry Capehart of the U.S. Volunteers acquired it from McLean for $10 in gold coins. He then handed the chair to General Wilmon W. Blackmar, who "carried it back to our lines before him on his horse." In 1893 Capehart gave the chair to Blackmar, who left it in his will to the national collections. The inscription on the chair reads: "This is the chair in which General U.S. Grant sat when he signed the Articles of Capitulation resulting in the surrender of the Confederate Army by General R. E. Lee at Appomattox Court House, Virginia, April 9th, 1865."

General Grant used a small spool-turned table to sign the document setting forth the surrender terms. After the signing, Lieutenant General Philip H. Sheridan offered two $10 gold coins to McLean, who refused the money; the table was taken anyway with McLean's consent, and the money was thrown on floor. The historical item was then presented to Elizabeth, the wife of Major General George A. Custer. The presentation reads:

Appomattox Court House, April 10, 1865, My dear Madam.

> I respectfully present to you the small writing table on which conditions of the surrender of the Confederate Army of Northern Virginia was written by Lt. General Grant, and permit me to say, Madam, that scarcely an individual in our service has contributed more to bring about this desirable result than your very gallant husband.
>
> Very respectfully, Phil. H. Sheridan, Major General (To) Mrs. Gen'l Custer, Washington D.C."

In 1912 Mrs. Custer lent the table to the National Museum. In 1936, ten years after Mrs. Custer's death and according to the terms of her will, the loan became a bequest, and the table has remained in the national collections ever since.

4

FLORIDA

Museum of Florida History, 500 South Bronough Street, Tallahassee, FL

Opened in 1977, the Museum of Florida History collects, preserves, exhibits, and interprets evidence of past and present cultures in Florida and promotes knowledge of and appreciation of this heritage. As the state history museum, it focuses on artifacts and eras unique to Florida's development and on roles that Floridians have played in national and global events.

Florida's flag of secession

Female secession supports created a flag when Florida became the third state to leave the Union, after South Carolina and Mississippi.

FLORIDA SECEDES FROM THE UNION

In early January 1861, a special convention of delegates from around the state met in Tallahassee to consider whether Florida should leave the Union. Governor Madison Starke Perry and Governor-elect John Milton were both strong supporters of secession. For days, the issues were debated inside and outside the convention. In a minority opinion, former Territorial Governor Richard Keith Call, acting as a private citizen, argued that secession would bring only ruin to the state.

On January 10, 1861, the delegates voted 62 to 7 to withdraw Florida from the Union. The next day, in a public ceremony on the east steps of the Capitol, they signed a formal Ordinance of Secession, and news of the event led to local celebrations. Later, the delegates adopted a new state constitution. Florida was the third state to leave the Union, and within a month it joined with other Southern states to form the Confederate States of America.

At the war's end, the pictured banner still hung in the Capitol; a Union Army officer reportedly took it as a trophy during the postwar occupation of the building. It is recorded, however, that the officer later felt guilty about taking the banner and gave it to a Mrs. Hasson, the wife of a military doctor, to return to the state. The Hassons moved to the western U.S. shortly after this incident, and it was not until 1911 that Mrs. Hasson sent the flag to a Florida member of the United Daughters of the Confederacy, who then returned it to the State of Florida. Because of its extremely fragile condition, the secession flag is not on display in the museum's Civil War exhibit.

National Park Service Gulf Islands National Seashore, Route 292, southwest from Pensacola; turn east on Johnson Beach Road

The forts of Gulf Islands National Seashore span a period of almost 150 years, from

Top: This flag was presented to Florida Governor Madison S. Perry and unfurled by Governor-elect John Milton on the east porch of the state capitol when delegates signed Florida's Ordinance of Secession on January 11, 1861. The flag was created by Helen Broward of Broward's Neck in Duval County and other southern women who supported the secessionist cause. The three large stars represent the first three states to leave the Union: South Carolina, Mississippi, and Florida. The flag's motto, "The Rights of the South at All Hazards!" echoes the uncompromising position of Southern supporters on the eve of the Civil War. The banner reportedly hung above the speaker's desk in the Florida House of Representatives throughout the war. Flag image and text courtesy of the Museum of Florida's web page: www.museumofflorida history.com

the Spanish colonial *Bateria De San Antonio* (1797) to the World War II-era *Battery 234*. This fact underscores the historic value of the anchorages at Pensacola Bay, Florida, and Ship Island, Mississippi. Most striking among these are the American "third system" forts: Fort Pickens, Fort Massachusetts, Fort Barrancas, and the Advanced Redoubt, all of which saw action during the Civil War.

Carte de visite Showing an Award for Bravery

The card shows a medal presented to Union Major Adam J. Slemmer and his

Right: Major Adam J. Slemmer (courtesy National Park Service Gulf Islands National Seashore).

The most unusual Civil War item at the National Park Service's Gulf Islands National Seashore collection is probably a *carte de viste* of the "Pickens Medal," awarded to Adam Slemmer and the men of Company G, 1st U.S. Artillery, by the New York Chamber of Commerce in recognition of their heroic stand at Fort Pickens during the months leading up to the war (courtesy National Park Service Gulf Islands National Sea-shore).

artillery company for holding Florida's Fort Pickens throughout the war.

PICKENS MEDAL

When Florida seceded from the Union in January 1861, state officials quickly ordered Florida troops to seize key federal forts and arsenals throughout the state. At Pensacola, federal troops relocated from the mainland to the more defendable Fort Pickens on Santa Rosa Island. Florida Confederate troops, supported by soldiers from Alabama, demanded the surrender of the fort, but Federal Lieutenant Adam J. Slemmer refused.

Were it not for a gentleman's agreement between Northern and Southern officers, the Civil War might easily have started earlier in 1861 at Fort Pickens, rather than at Fort Sumter. A truce was worked out in which the North agreed not to reinforce the fort, and the South agreed not to attack it. Immediately following the Southern bombardment of Fort Sumter, on April 12, 1861, however, Union forces landed near Pensacola to reinforce Fort Pickens. The standoff at Pensacola continued for several months. Lt. Slemmer's actions prevented Southern troops from capturing the primary fort guarding Pensacola Bay, thus severely limiting the value of the Pensacola Navy Yard to the Confederacy. Fort Pickens was one of only four forts in the South to remain in Union control throughout the war. The other three were Fort Jefferson in the Dry Tortugas, Fort Taylor in Key West, and Fort Monroe in Norfolk, Virginia.

Union forces conducted a raid in which they burned a Southern ship, and in early October the Confederates launched a large, nighttime raid on Santa Rosa Island. On October 9, Confederate forces landed approximately 1,000 troops on the island in an assault that overran the camp of a Union army regiment. The Rebel troops were forced to withdraw, however after Union reinforcements from Fort Pickens arrived on the scene.

5

GEORGIA

Three years of Civil War had laid waste to large parts of Virginia, Mississippi, and Tennessee, but Georgia remained relatively unscathed. Her farms and factories, cites and towns, and railroads and seaports remained intact and were still a vital part of the Confederate war machine. Soaring wartime prices and severe shortages made daily life more difficult on the home front, and every community mourned the loss of loved ones killed in battle, but for most Georgians, the war was something far away, a dark and distant cloud on the horizon. This was about to change.

By the spring of 1864 the Confederacy was weakening and the mighty war production capabilities of the industrial North were being employed at full capacity. Grant had been promoted to military commander-in-chief and had ordered a concerted offensive by all Union armies. His orders to Sherman at Chattanooga, Tennessee, were to attack the Confederate army in Georgia. "Break it up, and go into the interior of the enemy's country as far as you can, inflicting all the damage you can upon their war resources."

Sherman's 100,000 men and 254 pieces of artillery departed their encampments, which were located south and east of Chattanooga, during the first week in May. Ahead lay General Joseph E. Johnston's 65,000 Confederates with 187 cannon, along Rocky Face Ridge in the mountains of northwest Georgia, near Dalton. Although Confederate authorities wanted Johnston to march north into Tennessee, the campaign quickly devolved into a fight to save Atlanta, the railroad hub and war manufacturing and storage center for the Confederacy.

In August, Sherman placed Atlanta under siege. Both sides attempted cavalry raids to break the other's grip, but to no avail. Whenever Rebel forces attempted a breakout, Sherman shifted troops to cut the railroads that linked Atlanta with the rest of the South. On August 31 he seized the last one, the Macon & Western. Rebel General John Bell Hood, after losing a two-day battle near Jonesboro, ordered all public property destroyed and the city evacuated. Sherman entered on September 2 and then triumphantly telegraphed the news to Washington: "Atlanta is ours, and fairly won."

The fall of Atlanta was a crippling blow to the Confederacy's capacity and will to make war. Coupled with Union victories elsewhere, the end was now in sight. The North rejoiced, and on November 8, Abraham Lincoln was re-elected president, endorsing a "fight to the finish." Not long after, Sherman left Atlanta in ruins and began his soon-to-be-famous "march to the sea."

Southern Museum of Civil War and Locomotive History, 2829 Cherokee Street, Kennesaw, GA

The Southern Museum of Civil War and Locomotive History in Kennesaw, Georgia, is a trip back in time. With three impressive permanent collections, the museum offers a wide range of exhibits, including a glimpse into the daily lives of soldiers during the Civil War, a reproduction of a turn-of-the-century locomotive factory, and an exciting depiction of the Civil War's "great locomotive chase."

The museum contains a growing collection of Civil War-related materials. It houses a small but varied selection of U.S.A. and C.S.A. railroad quartermasters' documentation, Confederate and Georgia Railroad currency, original Civil War era sheet music, soldiers' enlistment/promotion documentation, letters written by soldiers serving in both armies, and a variety of Civil War history periodicals.

The General

A Union spy attempted to hijack this Southern locomotive and was hanged for his efforts. A hundred years later, a second hijacking occurred. The U.S. Supreme Court ultimately awarded the engine to the state of Georgia.

The Great Train Chase

Early on the morning of April 12, 1862, in Big Shanty (Kennesaw), twenty-one Federal soldiers dressed as Confederates, led by civilian spy James J. Andrews, stole the locomotive *General* and three boxcars and headed north with a plan to destroy the Western and Atlantic Railroad, a crucial supplier to Confederate armies. The crew and passengers were eating breakfast at a nearby hotel and, hearing the engine pull out of the station, conductor William A. Fuller and two others gave chase on foot for two miles. The men located a railroad crew and commandeered a platform car, propelled by pushing long poles or pushing off on railroad ties with their feet.

At the Etowah River, the pursuers picked up a steam-powered yard locomotive, *Yonah*, belonging to Cooper's Iron Works. Meanwhile, the Federal raiders had been delayed an hour in Kingston, where southbound train traffic had to be switched to the side to let the hijacked train pass. Four minutes after Andrews and company rolled north, the *Yonah* came puffing into Kingston. Also delayed in Kingston, Bill Fuller abandoned the *Yonah* and pursued on foot; he quickly commandeered yet another locomotive, the *William R. Smith*. Farther north, Andrews's raiders, in an effort to halt their Southern pursuers, were destroying tracks and gathering wood to help burn bridges. At Adairsville, the General had to wait to let the southbound *Texas* get by and continued steaming north. Behind them, Fuller had to abandon the *Smith* when he came to some destroyed track. Proceeding again on foot for three miles, Fuller and his men came upon the southbound *Texas*. When told of the situation, the engineer threw the *Texas* in reverse to pursue the *General* backwards at more than sixty miles an hour. When the *Texas* closed on the *General* near Resaca, Andrews's men released a boxcar to slow it up, but the *Texas* simply slammed into the car and then pushed it on down the tracks. Other attempts to slow the *Texas* were unsuccessful; furthermore, the *General* was running out of fuel as it roared through Tunnel Hill and Ringgold.

If the desperate raiders could get beyond Chattanooga, a few miles away, they would be safe behind Northern lines, but it was not to be, as the engine ground to a halt. Andrews then ordered his men, "Jump off and scatter! Every man for himself!" Soon all of the raiders were captured and imprisoned in Chattanooga. Eight escaped, six were exchanged for Southern prisoners, and eight, including Andrews, were hanged and buried in Atlanta. The Medal of Honor, the nation's highest award for valor, was established by the U.S. Congress and given to the raiders. Andrews himself, as a civilian and a spy, received none. The dead were later reinterred in Chattanooga National Cemetery, the daring men's ultimate goal during the raid.

The General continued to serve the

Opposite: Map of the Georgia Campaign (courtesy National Park Service).

The famed *General* with the caption "Engine *Hero*— Destroyed partially by Rebels when evacuating Atlanta, Ga. This is the Engine used by Mitchel's men in their attempt to burn the R.R. bridges. They were caught and hung in Atlanta Ga" (*The Official Atlas of the Civil War*).

Nashville, Chattanooga, & St. Louis Railway until its retirement on May 30, 1891, where it rested on a siding at Vinings, Georgia, for awhile. Within a year, though, the General was restored and was put on display at several reunions and at the World Exposition in Chicago. In 1901 the General was moved to Chattanooga for permanent display at the Union Depot. This was not the end of the story, though. The famed locomotive traveled again, from Chattanooga to Chicago; in 1939 it was shipped to Flushing Meadows, site of the New York World's Fair. After a few more exciting trips, the General finally was brought to rest once more at Chattanooga's Union Depot.

Or so it seemed. In 1961, ninety-nine years after the first great chase, the second "battle" for the General began as key railroad people cut the fence surrounding the General and ordered a crew to come in with crossties and sixty feet of rail for constructing a temporary track. After it was completed, a diesel locomotive and two flatcars came in and hooked up to the General's long outmoded pin couple; slowly the old engine began to move. It was then loaded aboard the two flatcars. It was 1 A.M., and the streets of Chattanooga were deserted, so no one witnessed the mysterious "abduction." The General left Chattanooga, was shunted around the Nashville rail yard, and then coupled to a fast freight for the trip to Louisville, Kentucky. The following morning when the famed locomotive was found to be missing, the press gave extensive coverage to the "theft."

As it turned out, the General's kidnapping was done by loyal employees of the Louisville and Nashville Railroad. They had

The *General*, colorfully refurbished at its 150th birthday celebration. After a lengthy court battle, the *General* was awarded permanent residence at the Southern Museum of Civil War and Locomotive History in Kennesaw, Georgia. The locomotive may not be unique, but its story is incomparable (courtesy Southern Museum of Civil War & Locomotive History, Kennesaw, Georgia).

recaptured their historic train and with much loving care completely overhauled the train and converted it to an oil-burning steam locomotive. In April 1962, with bell ringing and steam hissing, the General made several historical runs. It was hard for some of the passengers to believe that they were actually riding behind the engine that, 100 years before, had led to the hanging deaths of the Union spy James J. Anderson and seven others! The General reenacted the "great locomotive chase" of April 12, 1862, with more than 100,000 spectators along the line, from Kennesaw to Ringgold, Georgia. Afterward, the General was loaded onto a special flatcar that carried it thousands of miles over the eastern United States for the next few years, making a stop at the second New York World's Fair in 1964.

The General's freewheeling, lifestyle intensified on April 5, 1967, when the state of Georgia passed a resolution expressing a desire to have the celebrated locomotive returned to the Peach State. The City of Chattanooga, however, argued that it possessed ownership rights. The General remained in Chattanooga as a long legal battle ensued. A federal judge ruled that the train belonged to Louisville and Nashville Railroad, which could dispose of it as it wished. The City of Chattanooga appealed the ruling, though, and the case eventually went all the way to the U.S. Supreme Court. In 1970 the high court found in favor of the state of Georgia, assuring that the General would return. Preparations were made to welcome the General to the Kennesaw Civil War Museum. On February 17, 1972, in a light drizzling rain, several hundred people gathered as the General was formally presented to Governor Jimmy Carter and the people of Georgia. After 110 years, the little engine that could had found a new home and today can be visited at the Big Shanty Museum at Kennesaw.

Chickamauga and Chattanooga National Military Park, Chattanooga, TN

From Interstate 75: At Exit 350 take Battlefield Parkway (Georgia 2) west to Fort Oglethorpe. Turn left at the intersection of Battlefield Parkway and Lafayette Road. Go one mile on Lafayette Road to the park entrance and visitor center.

Chickamauga and Chattanooga National Military Park, the nation's first and largest, was created in 1890 to preserve and commemorate these two battlefields. The 5,200-acre Chickamauga Battlefield, scene of the last major Confederate victory of the Civil War, contains numerous monuments, historical tablets, wayside exhibits, and walking trails. Visitors can explore the major points of interest by auto, following a seven-mile park tour. The Visitor Center includes fascinating exhibits, including the Claude E. and Zenada O. Fuller Collection of American military shoulder arms.

The Chickamauga Battlefield

The Chickamauga battlefield treasure is the park itself: It was the first National Military Park. No battlefield park of this quality and magnitude could be found in any other nation of the world. The park was officially dedicated on September 20, 1895. Most of the 1,400 monuments and historical markers on the battlefields were planned and placed by General H. V. Boynton and other veterans of the battles, under the supervision of the War Department, which administered all national military parks until they were transferred to the National Park Service in 1933.

THE BATTLES OF CHICKAMAUGA AND CHATTANOOGA

On the fields and hills near Chattanooga, Union and Confederate armies clashed during the fall of 1863 in some of the toughest fighting of the Civil War. The prize was Chattanooga, key rail center and gateway to the heart of the Confederacy. The campaign that brought the armies here began late in June 1863 when General William S. Rosecrans's Army of the Cumberland, almost 70,000 strong, moved from Murfreesboro, Tennessee, against Confederate General Braxton Bragg's 43,000-man Army of Tennessee, which was dug in twenty miles to the south defending the road to Chattanooga. Six months earlier, these same armies had clashed at Stones River, where, after a fierce three-day struggle, the Confederates had retreated. Now, through a series of skillful marches, Rosecrans forced the Southerners to withdraw again, this time into Chattanooga itself. There, Bragg dug in once more, guarding the Tennessee River crossings northeast of the city, where he expected Rosecrans to attack, but late in August the Federals crossed the river well below Chattanooga, and again Bragg had to withdraw southward.

Bragg concentrated his forces at LaFayette, Georgia, twenty-six miles south of Chattanooga. Reinforcements from Mississippi, East Tennessee, and finally Virginia eventually swelled his ranks to more than 66,000 men. On September 18, after twice failing to destroy isolated segments of Rosecrans's army, Bragg tried to wedge his troops between the Federals and Chattanooga by sending elements of his army to the east bank of West Chickamauga Creek along a line from Reed's Bridge to just downstream of Lee and Cordon's Mill. This, too, failed.

Fighting began shortly after dawn on September 19, when Union infantry encountered Confederate cavalry at Jay's Mill. This brought on a general battle that spread south for nearly four miles. The armies fought desperately all day, often hand-to-hand; gradually the Rebels pushed the Federals back to LaFayette Road. On September 20, Bragg again tried to drive between the Union force and Chattanooga, but failed to dislodge Rosecrans's line. When Rosecrans shifted troops to meet the attacks, however, a gap opened briefly in the Federal line just as General James Longstreet's Confederates assaulted that very point. The Southerners smashed through the hole, routing Rosecrans and half his army. Some of the Federals rallied and formed a new battle line on Snodgrass Hill. Here, they held their ground against repeated assaults and earned for General George H. Thomas the nickname "Rock of Chickamauga."

After dark, Thomas withdrew his men

Two of the many monuments at the Chickamauga and Chattanooga National Battlefield Park.

from the field, and the defeat forced the Union troops to retreat into Chattanooga. The determined Confederates pursued, occupying Missionary Ridge, Lookout Mountain, and Chattanooga Valley. By placing artillery on the heights overlooking the river and blocking the best roads and the rail lines, the Southerners prevented most Federal supplies from entering the city. Unless something was done to break the Confederate stranglehold, Rosecrans's army would have to surrender or starve.

Aware of Rosecrans's plight, authorities in Washington sent reinforcements to his relief. General Joseph Hooker came from Virginia late in October with 20,000 men, and Sherman brought in 16,000 from Mississippi. In mid-November George Thomas replaced Rosecrans as head the Army of the Cumberland, and Ulysses S.

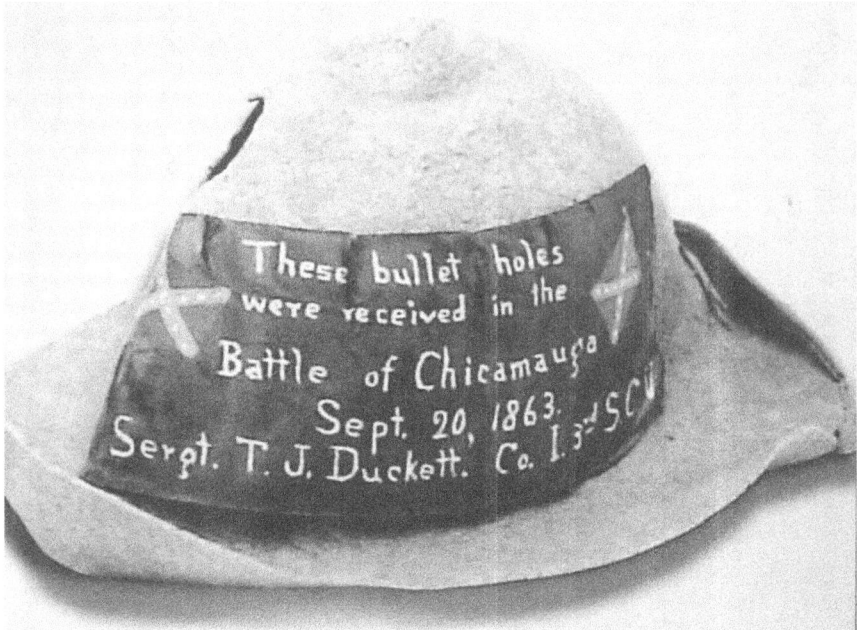

This bullet-pierced, high-crowned beehive style hat was worn by South Carolina Sergeant T.J. Duckett at Chickamauga and serves as a reminder that the difference between life and death on the battlefield was often only a matter of inches.

Grant assumed overall command. After that, the situation began to change dramatically. On October 28 Federal troops opened a shorter supply route (called the "Cracker Line") from Bridgeport, Alabama. On November 23, Thomas's men attacked and routed the Confederates from Orchard Knob. On the 24th, aided by a heavy fog that enshrouded the slopes of Lookout Mountain during most of the day, Hooker's soldiers pushed the Confederates out of their defenses around the Cravens House. On November 25, with most of Bragg's army now concentrated on Missionary Ridge, Grant launched Sherman's troops against the Confederate right flank and sent Hooker's men from Lookout Mountain to attack the Confederate left. Thomas's soldiers, in the center at Orchard Knob, were held in reserve.

Hooker was delayed crossing Chattanooga Creek, and the Confederates halted Sherman's attack. To relieve the pressure on Sherman, Grant ordered Thomas's Army of the Cumberland to assault the rifle pits at the base of Missionary Ridge. This was quickly accomplished. Then, without orders, Thomas's men scaled the heights in one of the great charges of the war. The Confederate line collapsed and Bragg's troops fled to the rear. During the night they retreated into Georgia. Union armies now controlled the city and nearly all of Tennessee. The next spring, Sherman used Chattanooga for his base as he started his march to Atlanta and the sea.

The Historic Cannonball House, 856 Mulberry Street, Macon, GA

The Cannonball House was constructed between 1853 and 1855 as a winter home for Judge Asa Holt and his wife, Mary Palmer Holt. On the morning of July 30, 1864, the house was struck by a Hotchkiss shell fired from across the Ocmulgee River by troops led by Union General George Stoneman, who was under the command of General William T. Sherman. The house remained a private residence for descendants of the Holt and Canning families until 1962 and is endowed with a few original pieces and other antebellum furnishings, many of which came from local

Macon families. The military museum displays artifacts from the Civil War, including a dress uniform that belonged to one of the youngest generals in the Confederate Army. There are also examples of swords, firearms, cannonballs, period clothing, and flags, including an authentic First National Flag and a St. Andrew's Cross Banner Flag.

The Massenburg's Battery (Jackson Artillery) Flag

Confederate Captain Thomas L. Massenburg ended up with this battle flag, which saw much action during the war. In later life, he refused to part with it, although one star was cut out and presented to Jefferson Davis.

THOMAS MASSENBURG AND HIS GEORGIA BATTERY

Before the Civil War commenced, Captain Theodore Parker and the Macon Volunteer Artillery corps known as the "Jackson Artillery" organized on January 23, 1861. The day after the corps was ordered to St. Simons Island to protect the state's property against possible Federal invasion. From August of 1861 until the end of the war, this battery saw much fighting, from Chattanooga to Mobile Bay. Later on in the war, the outfit changed its name to "Massenburg's Battery."

It was an autumn afternoon in the rolling hills of northwest Georgia near a stream called Chickamauga. Usually this was a time for the peaceful, gradual changing of the seasons, but on this twentieth day of September, 1863, a huge battle was in progress as two great armies struggled to prevail. They fought all the previous day without a discernible decision, but the men of Captain Thomas L. Massenburg's Georgia Battery had yet to be engaged. Dawn of the second day had been quiet as Confederate forces shifted in place to attack Yankee positions. Shortly before noon, as Longstreet's wing poised to strike Rosecrans, the Federals mistakenly opened a gap in their defensive line by unnecessarily withdrawing a division. Before the mistake could be corrected, Longstreet struck the gap, resulting in chaos in the Federal lines as units collapsed and withdrew.

About noon, two 10-pound parrot rifles of

Captain Thomas L. Massenburg's niece presented this torn but proud battle flag carried by Massenburg's Battery, Georgia Light Artillery (Jackson Artillery), to the Historic Cannonball House in Macon, Georgia, after it was established as a museum by the United Daughters of the Confederacy in 1962 (courtesy of Historic Cannonball House).

Captain Massenburg with fellow veterans from Macon, Georgia, at the 1877 Confederate Veterans' reunion (courtesy of Historic Cannonball House).

Massenburg's Georgia Battery were ordered up and positioned in an open area near Kelly Fields where they began to lay down fire upon the Federals, who were falling back to positions on Snodgrass Hill. The field upon which they had positioned the guns clearly showed evidence of frantic combat the day before; debris from the struggle littered the area.

Massenburg's Battery continued on to Chattanooga where it was involved in the disastrous fighting there. At Lookout Mountain, a parrot gun belonging to the battery exploded while being fired, wounding several men standing near it. The shell from the gun exploded near the depot in Chattanooga three miles away in the midst of General Thomas's staff, killing and wounding eleven men. At Missionary Ridge, Confederate Sergeant Willis Price, acting gunner, aimed at and killed with a shell a mounted officer advancing at the head of his command a mile away. During the subsequent attack on Missionary Ridge, the rapidly advancing Federals overwhelmed Massenburg's Battery, and in retreat the Confederates lost their guns and baggage. In the closing day of the entire war, Captain Massenburg and all the surviving members of the unit made their way back to Macon to try to reestablish their prewar lives. Massenburg would go on to be active in civic affairs, serving as clerk of the city council for many years and running a successful business as a druggist.

When Jefferson Davis visited Macon for the Reunion of Confederate Veterans in 1887, the flag on display at the Cannonball House was flown by the Jackson Artillery of Macon during the assembly of the troops. Artillery veterans cut out a single star from the flag and presented it to the ex–Confederate president. The flag fell into the hands of Captain Massenburg. Colonel Fred Massey of the *Cincinnati Gazette* saw it as it floated over the heads of the old veterans and finding out its owner, approached the captain in this way: "I don't want to make you mad, and what I say must not be taken with any such intention, but I want that flag, and I tell you frankly I will pay you well for it."

"It's not for sale," said the captain.
"I'll make you a very good offer for it," replied Colonel Massey.
"How much?"
"I'll give you $5,000 for it." That was a huge sum in those days.
"Well, my friend, you can call it sentimentalism or blank foolism, but money can't buy that flag unless I am actually starving."
And those who knew Captain Massenburg knew that he meant every word he said.

Kennesaw Mountain Battlefield, Kennesaw, GA

Kennesaw Mountain is a 2,888-acre National Battlefield Park that preserves an important Civil War battleground of the Atlanta Campaign, which, in fact, started here. Over 5,350 soldiers were killed in the battle from June 19, 1864, through July 2, 1864. The National Park Service has preserved historic earthworks, cannon emplacements, and monuments.

"Napoleon" Smooth-Bore Howitzer

This Napoleon is part of the Kennesaw Mountain Museum collection. It is most unusual for a battlefield museum to ascertain that it has an artillery piece actually used in its battle. The diligent archivist at Kennesaw Mountain, however, matched the serial number, weight, and date of manufacture stamped on the muzzle of a howitzer at the site against a magnified photograph. It is an exact match and a fine piece of detective work by members of the Kennesaw staff.

FAILURE OF THE
FRONTAL ATTACK

It was a sweltering hot and clear Monday, June 27, 1864, when some of the heaviest fighting of the Atlanta Campaign occurred. During Sherman's advance to Atlanta his patience was worn out by Johnston's evasive tactics, so he decided on a bold frontal attack against Confederate lines on Kennesaw Mountain. In a few hours, Sherman learned the lesson that Cold Harbor had taught Grant. The Union troops were repulsed with over 2,000 killed and wounded. Conversely Johnston suffered only 500 casualties. After this tragic affair, Sherman would resume the slower-paced flanking attacks, as opposed to frontal.

Georgia Capitol Museum, 431 State Capitol, Atlanta, GA

The Georgia Capitol Museum preserves and interprets the history of the Georgia State Capitol building as well as the events that have taken place within its walls. To carry out this purpose, the museum collects, maintains, and exhibits significant artifacts, including historic flags and works of art.

The Georgia Secession Banner

Upon learning of Abraham Lincoln's election, a large crowd gathered around the Greene Monument in Johnson Square in Savannah on November 8, 1860, and raised a banner emblazoned with a coiled rattlesnake and the words "Our Motto Southern Rights, Equality of the States, Don't Tread on Me." Six days later, Savannahians raised the "State Rights flag" of 1829 — a banner of blue silk. One side features a pine tree and a rattlesnake, with the mottos "State Rights" and "Don't Tread on Me;" the reverse displays the Georgia coat of arms. Newspapers described these banners as the "Colonial flag of Georgia." During November and December 1860, similar flags appeared in Macon, Atlanta, Newnan, and Griffin.

The rattlesnake was a popular colonial symbol of American defiance and unity before and during the Revolutionary War; likewise, in the nineteenth century, Georgians in a show of defiance called for state unity by raising the rattlesnake banner. When delegates at the Secession Convention at

The "Napoleon," or Model 1857 smoothbore howitzer, was named for French emperor Louis Napoleon. This 12–pounder artillery piece, photographed by George N. Barnard, was used by the Rebels in Georgia. In the closing days of the Civil War, this was the most common piece of artillery in both the Union and Confederate armies (courtesy Kennesaw Mountain Battlefield).

Milledgeville signed the Ordinance of Secession on January 21, 1861, John T. Stephens of Monroe County wrote home: "We have raised the Colonial flag of Georgia on top of the Capitol. It has a snake on it and the coat of arms of Georgia."

The reverse side of this banner features an elaborately painted coat of arms from the 1799 Great Seal of Georgia. The history of this particular hand-painted silk banner is unknown, but it might have served as a political banner for the State Rights Party of 1832–1840, or during the secession crisis of 1860–1861.

Flag of the 1st Georgia Infantry, "City Light Guards"

The 1st Infantry probably retired this flag following the Battle of Atlanta. General W.H.T. Walker's Division sustained heavy losses in that battle, resulting in the breakup of that organization. Subsequently, the 1st Georgia Infantry and the balance of General Hugh Mercer's Brigade were transferred to General Patrick Cleburne's division.

The state of Georgia acquired this silk flag in 2003 from Emory University in Atlanta. The accession record states that the flag belonged to "Capt. S. Yates Levy's command during the Civil War, [and was] originally the property of H.F. Willink, acting adjutant." Samuel Yates Levy was captain of the City Light Guards, a Savannah company organized on March 4, 1861. Levy's unit became Company D, 1st Georgia Infantry Regiment, under the command of Colonel Charles H. Olmstead.

This battle flag, which rests today in the Georgia Capitol Museum, was presented by Captain Samuel Y. Levy to Colonel Charles H. Olmstead in Savannah on the evening of May 26, 1864. According to Private Charles Thiot of the 1st Infantry, the flag that Levy gave the regiment had a "white ground with the Confederate Cross and stars." It was made in part from the wedding dress of a lady "now a refugee from the Yankees." Olmstead declared that he and his men "would defend that flag with our lives; though we may be overpowered and defeated, no spot of disgrace shall ever tarnish its purity." The day after the presentation, the regiment marched to the Central Railroad Depot and boarded cars to join the Army of Tennessee. By May 29, the regiment was in the trenches near Dallas, Georgia (courtesy The Capitol Museum, office of secretary of state).

Civil War "colors"

A battle flag was a flag carried into combat by Civil War regiments. Both armies used these flags, which they also referred to as "colors," to locate their troops on the battlefield, in camp, and on the march; battle flags were guides—wherever the flags went, the soldiers followed. Flags led the charge or the retreat. A regiment's flag was carried by a "color sergeant," who was the central man in the color guard, which was composed of six corporals whose job it was to protect the color sergeant and the flag of the regiment. The regiment's flag was a source of great pride, and to lose the flag in battle was a great disgrace. The capture of an opponent's flag was, in turn, a great honor. While infantry regiments had their flags, there were also special flags made for headquarters, artillery, cavalry, and even the quartermaster and engineers—almost every unit had one.

Flag of the 60th Georgia Infantry

The 60th Georgia Infantry formed in May 1862 at Camp Calhoun, near Savannah, from the merger of the 4th Georgia Infantry Battalion and several newly organized companies. The following month the 60th left for Virginia, where it saw service in summer, fall, and winter in the Seven Days,' Second Manassas, Maryland, and Fredericksburg campaigns.

In 1863, the regiment participated in the Chancellorsville and Gettysburg campaigns. Sometime after the return of Lee's army from Pennsylvania and before the opening of the 1864 Overland Campaign, the 60th received the Second National Confederate flag shown here. William F. Gilbert was the regimental ensign in April 1864. He had first volunteered

This Confederate battle flag was surrendered to the Union at Appomattox Courthouse. Carried by the consolidated 60th and 61st Georgia Infantry in the final months of the war, it was returned in 1905 to the state of Georgia by the U.S. War Department (courtesy The Capitol Museum, office of secretary of state).

to carry the flag on August 1, 1863, the regiment having lost four previous color bearers in action. Gilbert proudly bore the flag through various battles of the 1864 Overland Campaign and Early's Raid on Washington. In the Battle of Third Winchester on September 19, 1864, Gilbert was wounded and captured, but still the regimental banner did not fall into Union hands.

On January 18, 1865, the handful of survivors of the 60th and 61st Georgia Regiments were consolidated into a single regiment with one stand of colors.

The Atlanta History Center's DuBose Civil War Collection, 130 West Paces Ferry Road NW, Atlanta, GA

The 9,200-square-foot DuBose Gallery, with 1,400 displayed objects, is one of the nation's largest and most comprehensive repositories of objects from these pivotal events in our country's history. Tangible objects such as cannons, uniforms and flags make history come alive, and poignant photos and personal stories show the impact that the war had on those who experienced it. Maps explain the sequence of events. Videos interpret what happened and why. Touchscreen computer learning stations can answer your questions and deepen your under-standing. You'll find this center a powerful and fascinating experience, no matter what your level of interest in, or knowledge of, the Civil War.

THE ATLANTA CAMPAIGN AND TWISTED RAILS

"Atlanta was too important a place in the hands of the enemy to be left undisturbed, with its magazines, stores, arsenals, workshops, foundries, and more especially its railroads, which converged there from four great cardinal points."

William T. Sherman

In one sense, the Civil War was primarily a battle for ports and railroad junctions, and

Atlanta was the last remaining rail hub in the Confederate Deep South. As residents watched Sherman's steady progress towards the city during the summer of 1864, slaves hired from their owners at $25 a month — good money in those days — built an impressive twelve-mile ring of fortifications. (It is interesting to note that a Rebel private was earning nine dollars a month during this conflict.) Sherman's solution to these fortifications was to cut off the important rail lines in and out of the city, creating a "circle of desolation" that would starve the Confederates out. His strategy focused on the four railroads that intersected in Atlanta. The Western & Atlantic, Sherman's supply line to Chattanooga, was controlled by Union forces. Union demolition crews ripped up thirty miles of the Georgia and Atlanta & West Point Railroads, and after several fierce battles Sherman gained control of the Macon & Western Railroad on September 1, 1864. Atlanta's fate was sealed.

One Confederate wrote:

> From here we tore up the railroad for miles. We were experts at tearing up railroads and the enemy as equally as deserving of praise for their success in rebuilding them. Men used to say that the Yankees took hold of one end of the railroad iron as soon as we let go of the other. We did all we could to give them trouble. We would pull up the iron rails then pile the ties as high as our waists, lay irons across and set the ties afire. As the iron rails would heat in the center the weight of the ends would bend them so as to be useless until straightened. We used to take a rail by the ends, when hot in the middle, carry it to a tree and wrap it around coil like. While we were working destruction of one end the enemies were busy relaying rails upon the other. The enemy with equal industry replaced it and we scarcely got out of hearing the whistle of the engine.

The rails in the sketch were cut from the Western and Atlantic line and were heated red-hot over huge bonfires and twisted around trees to prevent railroad repairs. They were dubbed "Sherman neckties," after the advancing Union general. The DuBose Collection contains some of the rails. Theo R. Davis sketch, ***Battles and Leaders of the Civil War***, The De Vinne Press, 1887, Volume IV, page 665

As General John Bell Hood's Confederate forces abandoned Atlanta, they set fire to a 28-car ammunition train at Schofield Rolling Mill, near Atlanta, Georgia. The explosion destroyed the train and left a path of devastation half a mile wide. The undercarriage axles were all that remained of the train (courtesy Library of Congress).

The Cyclorama, 800 Cherokee Avenue, Grant Park, Atlanta, GA

Nowhere can the true drama of the Civil War Battle of Atlanta be more appreciated than at the Cyclorama. This thrilling display allows visitors to step back to July 22, 1864, and experience a "virtual" Battle of Atlanta. The heroism of soldiers fighting bravely for causes they believed in is brilliantly portrayed as the painting, foreground figures, music and narrative combine to astonish a visitor. The Atlanta Cyclorama has been on display in that city since 1893. It is the longest running show in the United States.

Painting of General John A. Logan Leading a Charge, Part of the Atlanta Cyclorama

The Battle of Atlanta was one of a series of engagements fought from May to September, 1864. Tradition says that the panorama depicting the Battle of Atlanta was commissioned in 1883 to help boost the stock of General (then Senator) John A. Logan, a candidate for the vice presidency on the ticket with James G. Blaine in 1884. Logan had replaced General James B. McPherson during the early fighting for Atlanta, setting up a defensive line. Upon hearing of his appointment to top command, Logan fired off a dispatch to Sherman, proclaiming that he was surrounded by the entire Confederate army and requested instructions. A sar-

General John A. Logan commissioned this painting of himself galloping forward to restore the broken line at the Troup Hurt House, followed by a hatless Captain Francis DeGress and a complement of staff officers. Artistic license seems probable, in that the general is depicted wearing a full dress wool frock coat, high boots, and gauntlets, belying the fact that the area had experienced a severe drought and an unusually hot July, even for Georgia (courtesy City of Atlanta).

donic Sherman replied, "Tell General Logan to fight 'em! Fight 'em like hell!"

Measuring 42 feet high and 359 feet in circumference and weighing over 9,334 pounds, the cyclorama painting was completed in 1886 by a group of German, Austrian, and Polish artists. After several years as a touring exhibit the painting was brought to Atlanta in 1892 where it was purchased by philanthropist George V. Gress and given to the city in 1898. In 1921 the painting was housed in the current Cyclorama building. In 1979 the Cyclorama was closed for a massive restoration that took three years and $11 million.

Fort Pulaski National Monument (Savannah)

From Interstate 95, take exit for I-16 about 15 miles west of Savannah. From I-16, take U.S. Highway 80 East. Follow signs for Fort Pulaski, Tybee Island, and beaches. Fort Pulaski National Monument entrance is approximately fifteen miles east of Savannah.

Fort Pulaski National Monument offers visitors the chance to experience many interesting and exciting activities and events year-round. Fort Pulaski itself is a large-scale outdoor exhibit. The main structure, together with outlying works of drawbridges, ditches, and dikes, is a fine example of historic military architecture. Indoor exhibits highlight the history of Fort Pulaski from the fort's construction to its eventual fall due to advancing military technology.

Fort Pulaski

The battle for Fort Pulaski in April 1862 marked a turning point in military history: it featured the first significant use of rifled can-

The reconstructed Fort Pulaski is of itself an exemplary treasure (courtesy Fort Pulaski National Monument).

nons in combat. These accurate, long-range weapons shattered Fort Pulaski's walls from over a mile away. After thirty-hours of bombardment, the fort surrendered. The battle surprised military strategists worldwide because it signaled the end of masonry fortifications.

THE BATTLE FOR FORT PULASKI

Fort Pulaski was built in 1847. When South Carolina seceded from the United States in 1860, it set in motion the beginning of the Civil War. The governor of Georgia ordered Fort Pulaski to be taken; a steamship carrying 110 men from Savannah traveled downriver, and the fort was signed over to the state of Georgia. Following the secession of Georgia in February 1861, Confederate troops moved into the fort and prepared for possible attack.

Fort Pulaski was considered invincible. Its seven and a half foot thick solid brick walls were backed with massive piers of masonry. The broad waters of the Savannah River and wide swampy marshes surrounded the fort on all sides.

A year later, however, on the morning of April 10, 1862, Union forces asked for the surrender of the fort to prevent needless loss of life. Colonel Charles H. Olmstead, commander of the Confederate garrison, rejected the offer. Fort Pulaski was prepared for a possible infantry attack, but it never endured a direct land assault because Union troops, with 36 guns including the new James rifled cannon, began a long, sustained bombardment of the fort. The new cannon could fire a rifled projectile farther and with greater accuracy than the larger and heavier smoothbore cannon. Within thirty hours, rifled cannon shells breached one of the fort's corner walls. Shells now passed through the fort dangerously close to the fort's main powder magazine. Reluctantly, Colonel Charles Olmstead surrendered.

The Confederate flag was lowered halfway and a final gun was fired from a casemate. Then the flag was hauled down and the white sheet of surrender took its place. An era in coastal fortifications had come to an end.

Within six weeks of the surrender, Union forces repaired the fort, and all shipping in and out of Savannah ceased. The loss of Savannah as a viable Confederate port crippled the Southern war effort.

National Infantry Museum, Building 396, Fort Benning, GA

The National Infantry Museum was established at the home of the U.S. Infantry in 1959. It now boasts 30,000 square feet of exhibit space. Visitors are exposed to an ever-changing kaleidoscope of edged weapons, uniforms, footwear, mess equipment, fine oil paintings, firearms, bronzes, helmets, a set of Civil War dominoes, playing cards, a painted eagle drum, a bugle, and military-type vehicles from a 1902 Studebaker Utility Wagon to the legendary Jeep.

Union Infantry Drum

After the battle of second Manassas ended on August 30, 1862, this drum was found by an African-American named Ezekiel Beverly who was about thirty years and lived in the vicinity. Luckily for posterity, he kept the drum safe for sixty years.

In July 1921, reserve officer Captain James D. Harrover was visiting at Manassas and found the drum still in the possession of Mr. Beverly, who was now ninety years old. Captain Harrover obtained the drum by promising Beverly that it would be returned to the 14th Infantry Regiment. Harrover then sent it to the First Chief of Infantry, Major General Charles S. Farnsworth, who forwarded it to the regiment, where it was received on December 9, 1921.

While Mr. Beverly desired no reimbursement for the drum, the officers of the regi-

The drummer boy who used this drum to communicate commands to his fellow infantrymen during the Battle of Second Manassas lost it during the unrelenting onslaught of musketry and artillery fire. He had carved his last name "Williams" inside the drum. His unit was the 14th Infantry Regiment, 2nd Division, V Corps, commanded by Major General Fritz-John Porter (courtesy National Infantry Museum).

ment gave him $30 for saving a valuable piece of their unit's history. Thus, the drum is on display at the National Infantry Museum.

THE ROLE OF DRUMS

For the infantry, drums were used to announce daily activities, from sunrise to sunset. Reveille was sounded to begin the day at 5 A.M., followed by an assembly for morning roll call and then a breakfast call. Sick call was sounded soon after breakfast, followed by assemblies for guard duty, drills, or to begin the march. Drummers were also important on the march to keep soldiers in step during parades and to call them to attention. In battle, drums were sometimes used to signal maneuvers and give signals for the ranks to load and fire their weapons. The artillery and cavalry relied solely on buglers, who were as important in their roles as the drummers were to the infantry. When not playing for their respective regiments, musicians often joined with regimental or brigade bands to play marching tunes or to provide field music for parades, inspections, and reviews.

The Mary Willis Library, Liberty Street, Washington, GA

The Mary Willis Library was founded in 1888 by Dr. Francis T. Willis in memory of his daughter and as a gift to the people of his hometown and county. An 1894 catalog of the library states that the cost of building was $15,000; the furniture and the first collection of books, $2,000; and that a fund of $10,000 was provided as an endowment.

In addition to the collection of current library materials, Mary Willis Library has an invaluable core collection of rare books on Georgia history, books by local authors, family memorabilia, and Washington newspapers of the time.

Architect Edmund Lind of Atlanta designed the library in the warm brick tones and picturesque profile of the fashionable high-Victorian style. Tall stained-glass windows light the high-beamed interior where the original furnishings are still in use. The central window commemorating Mary Willis was made at the Tiffany factory in New Haven.

In 1972 the library was included in the National Register of Historic Sites.

Chest That Housed Confederate Gold

The Confederate treasury was hastily evacuated just before the fall of Richmond in 1865. Chests full of gold and silver passed through Washington, Georgia, thought to be a safe haven.

THE CONFEDERATE GOLD TRAIN

The tale of Confederate gold begins in Richmond, Virginia, on April 2, 1865. That is the day Jefferson Davis was interrupted during worship in St. Paul's church with an urgent dispatch saying that Grant and his men in blue had finally smashed through the lines at Petersburg.

Walking straight to the War Office to confer with John C. Breckinridge, Davis sent messengers to summon his cabinet members. Before they arrived, he got off a dispatch to General Robert E. Lee, urging him to hold out for one more day because a Sunday-night evacuation would threaten "the loss of many valuables, both for want of time to pack and of transportation."

Lee replied that the government should leave Richmond by 8 P.M. Then he added a long message in which he spelled out his plans for raising black recruits for his decimated regiments.

Since one railroad linking the capital with Danville was still in operation, the president had two special trains assembled. One was designed to transport key officials and members of their families to "a convenient point of safety." The other, assigned to Captain William H. Parker of the C.S.A. Navy, was designated as a special cargo train.

Parker, who knew that his freight would consist of double-eagle gold pieces, silver coins, gold ingots, silver bricks, and kegs of Mexican silver dollars from the Confederate treasury and the banks of Richmond, hastily assembled a special body of guards. Having no one else on whom he could call, he used midshipmen from a training vessel on the James River; some were as young as twelve.

Around midnight the two special trains left Richmond, unable to accommodate the scores of frightened civilians who begged to go along. The train packed with American golden double eagles, ingots, silver bars, and oak chests of jewels had been loaded on Sunday, April 2, 1865, by officials of the Confederate treasury. That night, as the train crept across the James River Bridge, its military passengers watched the city of Richmond being destroyed by fire. Quartermaster officials had torched the many warehouses that stored liquor, food, and clothing for the Confederate forces. No doubt to bolster their courage, member of the local populace retrieved much of the liquor. The fire spread to other buildings and quickly grew out of control. Under the influence of alcohol and against a background of burning buildings, men, women, and children became a howling, uncontrollable mob intent on pillaging the city. They broke into local stores searching for liquor as fires and explosions were breaking out near the railroad station. The treasure train was only an hour or so behind a train that was carrying President Davis and his entourage.

Davis, his cabinet members, and his wife had started on what they at first expected would be a short journey that would take them safely behind Confederate lines. Instead, they were forced to extend their withdrawal, eventually splitting up and taking to horseback when the rail lines ended.

Following orders, Parker headed for Charlotte, North Carolina, and the old United States Mint building, which had been selected

This valued relic, now housed at the Mary Willis Library, is one of three chests brought to Washington, Georgia, in May, 1865. It contained gold coins from the Confederate treasury.

as a safe place to store millions in hard money. News that Union cavalry were on the march made Parker abandon the mint, first packing gold and silver into boxes and kegs and bags that once held flour, coffee, sugar, and shot.

In a seesaw attempt to stay ahead of Federal forces, the guardians of the treasure moved through South Carolina and into Georgia, and then re-crossed the state line several times. Parker had turned the gold and silver over to John H. Reagan, C.S.A., acting secretary of the treasury. Reagan passed responsibility to Secretary of War Breckinridge, and he immediately put Brigadier General Basil Duke in charge. Heading a body of fewer than one thousand men, who constituted the only remaining Confederate force east of the Mississippi River, Duke put the treasure into six wagons and assigned eight veterans to guard each wagon.

Filing out of Abbeville, South Carolina, Davis and members of his cabinet, all on horseback, moved well ahead of the treasure-filled wagons. Their destination was Washington, Georgia, across the Savannah River, considered to be still safely under Confederate control.

As the treasure wagons continued south towards Washington, hungry, unpaid Confederate troops demanded back pay from the treas-

An artist's depiction of the fall of Richmond on the night of April 2, 1865. Exploding shells in the city's arsenal created an inferno in the center of the city. Richmond's role as the capital of the Confederacy was at an end (courtesy Library of Congress).

ure. The veteran guards unloaded several boxes and kegs, and each man was paid twenty-six dollars, for a total of $108,322.90. The remaining treasure—now valued at $143,000—continued in the wagons heading towards Washington, Georgia.

The last payment in Washington was $88,006 in gold coins. It was entrusted to Paymaster James A. Semple and his chief clerk, Mr. Edward M. Tidball. Semple was ordered to conceal the gold in the false bottom of a carriage and take it to Charleston or Savannah and then ship it to financial agents Fraser, Trenholm & Company in London for safekeeping.

In Washington, Georgia, President Davis had asked Micajah Clark to assume responsibility for the $35,000 in gold that had been given to him in Greensboro and was now packed in his personal baggage. Except for this $35,000, the Confederate treasury was depleted.

Cut off from the west, the presidential caravan continued south towards the Florida line with hopes of escaping to England via Cuba or Nassau. On May 8, out of desperation, everything on wheels was abandoned. Some of the money from heavy chests with $35,000 in gold coins was distributed, Postmaster General John Reagan receiving $3,500, which he placed in his saddlebags. The postmaster was already carrying $2,400 worth of the coins in a money belt that weighed ten pounds. After the distribution, the chests contained about $25,000 in coins.

Captain Micajah Clark, along with several officers and the remaining $25,000 turned over to them by Jefferson Davis, made their way to the plantation of Senator David Yulee near Gainesville, Florida. After a heated debate it was decided to divide the gold among the party. Quartermaster Watson Van Benthuysen, President Davis's cousin, took one-quarter of the treasure, or $6,250, for Mrs. Davis and her children. Nine men, including Captain Clark, took $1,940 each, plus an additional $955 each for travel expenses. A scout and guard were paid $250 each and five black servants were paid $520 each.

As this follow-the-money saga continued, General John Breckinridge was not captured, and with his $10,000 in gold coins he made his way to Havana, Cuba. He then sailed to England, but after President Andrew Johnson issued an amnesty proclamation, he returned to Kentucky in 1869; thereafter he devoted himself to the practice of law.

Judah Benjamin, the Confederate secretary of state who had obtained "some gold for travel expenses," with some difficulty escaped to Great Britain, where he had $12,500 credited to Mrs. Jefferson Davis's account in London.

The $86,000 in gold bullion and gold coins given to Paymaster James Allen Semple and Chief Clerk Edward M. Tidball for safekeeping in London simply "disappeared." That was a great deal of money in 1885; today this gold that vanished in the closing days of the Confederacy would be of immense value.

Although Semple himself disappeared, this much is known about his estranged wife: in February 1839, eighteen-year-old Letty Tyler, daughter of the tenth president of the United States, John Tyler, married Captain James Semple, U.S.N., of Virginia. From the start their marriage was stormy and President Tyler sent Semple on a three-year assignment at sea as a means of postponing any potential divorce between Semple and his daughter. Later, in about 1844, when Letty's stepmother, the widowed Julia Tyler, helped James Semple during a difficult financial period in his life, Letty Semple wrote her estranged husband that while they would not divorce, she no longer considered him her spouse

In the early days of the Civil War, Letty Semple lived in Williamsburg, Virginia. During the Peninsular Campaign she moved to the safety of the town of Chatham, Virginia, and stayed in the log kitchen dependency of Colonel Coleman D. Bennett. The cabin was located behind the Bennett home on North Main Street. Destitute, she moved to Baltimore after the war and managed to find enough financing to open a school, the "Eclectic Institute for Young Women." Letitia "Letty" Tyler Semple died on December 28, 1907.

6

ILLINOIS

*Rock Island Arsenal Museum,
Building 60, North Avenue,
Rock Island, IL
61299–5000*

The Rock Island Arsenal Museum was established on Independence Day, 1905, and is the second oldest U.S. Army museum. Arsenal Island was home to a Confederate prison camp, the Rock Island Prison Barracks. The arsenal's diverse products included leather horse equipment, meat cans and canteens, paper targets, artillery recoil mechanisms and carriages, and the Model 1903 rifle, serial number 1.

Watercolor of Rock Island Prison by a Confederate Prisoner

Rock Island Prison was built by the Union to confine captured Confederates and was located in the Mississippi River between the cities of Rock Island and Davenport, Iowa. The island, about three miles long and a half-mile wide, had the disadvantage of poor drainage and was partly swampy. The Federals approved construction of the prison July 1863, and in mid-August the quartermaster general instructed the builder that barracks for prisoners on Rock Island should be put up in the roughest and cheapest manner, creating mere shanties. The eighty-four barracks were all enclosed by fencing. A cookhouse was attached at the end of each barrack. All barracks were poorly ventilated and inadequately heated, with small stoves in each. An artesian well on the island supplied some of the water for the prison but most was drawn from the river with a steam pump. Inside the prison, water was always scarce and, when the pump failed, nonexistent.

After the war ended in 1865, Rock Island Prison barracks were emptied of prisoners, and the buildings were turned over to the U.S. Army Ordnance Department to be used as storehouses, barracks, and officers' quarters. Nothing is left of the prison buildings today, however.

General John Buford's Sword

On display at the museum is a sword belonging to Rick Island native John Buford.

PRISONERS OF WAR

During the Civil War the Union forces captured between 215,000 and 220,000 prisoners, not including the Confederate armies that surrendered at war's end. The Confederate forces captured a similar number, some 200,000 to 211,000 men. Close to 26,500 Southerners and 22,600 Northerners died in prison camps. Their suffering became legendary.

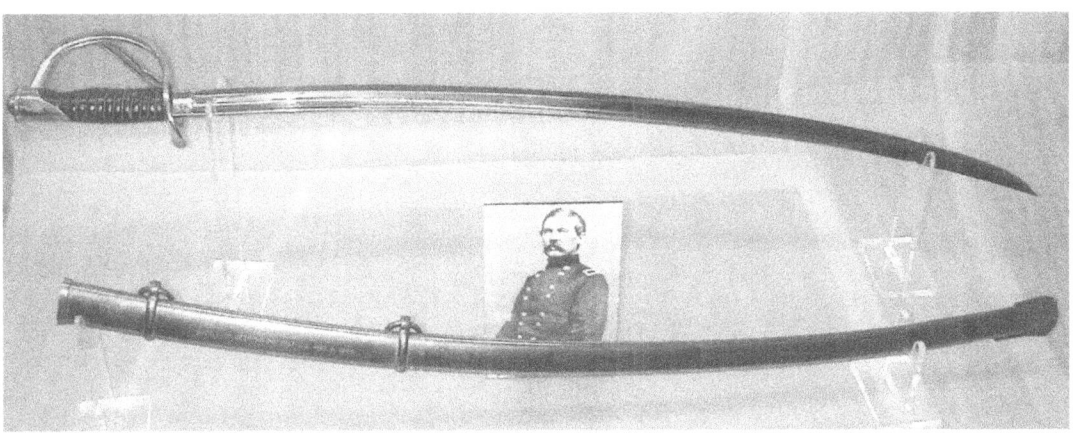

Top: John Gisch, a Confederate prisoner in the Rock Island Arsenal Prison Barracks, created this watercolor of the facility (courtesy Department of the Army, Rock Island Arsenal Museum). *Bottom:* General John Buford's sword is on display at the Rock Island Arsenal Museum. Buford was a native of Rock Island who graduated from West Point. A cavalry officer, he fought with valor at Second Manassas and later at Gettysburg. After surviving the latter, he died of typhoid fever (courtesy Department of the Army, Rock Island Arsenal Museum).

At the very beginning of the war, because there were no places to detain prisoners, both sides released them on parole, on an oath to take up arms no more. Many prisoner exchanges took place in the field without much appropriate military negotiation. The first Federals retained by the Confederates were confined in converted tobacco warehouses in Virginia. Soon, both North and South were turning training camps, state penitentiaries, college buildings, and various public facilities into military prisons; even an old slave market in St. Louis served as a prison.

The public demanded that prisoners be exchanged, but it took more than a year to agree on a system of exchange. A cartel signed an agreement on July 22, 1862, which stated that captives were to be paroled and exchanged, one general for one general, one private for one private, and so on (with sixty privates equal to one general). The commissioners of exchange failed to agree on procedure in executing the cartel provision, however, and violations and arguments were frequent, with major problems arising over the exchange of former slaves captured while serving as Union soldiers. This reflected one of the underlying causes that led to the Civil War; the South considered the blacks runaways who should be returned to their owners, whereas the North demanded that they be treated the same as other prisoners of war.

General Grant strongly believed that the exchange of prisoners was of great disadvantage to the North, which did not suffer the manpower shortage characteristic of the South. Acrimoniously, he wrote: "Every man we hold, when released on parole or otherwise, becomes an active soldier against us.... If a system of exchange liberates all prisoners taken, we will have to fight on until the whole South is exterminated."

On April 17, 1863, Grant ordered that all prisoner exchanges cease. They were not resumed until the exchange of sick prisoners in February 1865.

7

IOWA

State Historical Society of Iowa,
State of Iowa Historical
Building, 600 East Locust,
Des Moines, IA
50319–0290

This museum ensures that the essential evidence of government is created, maintained for as long as it is needed, and is available to the citizens of the state and to the public in general. Artifacts include antique cars, an 1860s stagecoach, a governor's executive desk, place settings nearly 250 years old, and an 1899 "Locomobile," powered by a Stanley Steamer engine, which was a gasoline-fueled burner that boiled water to create steam power, thus allowing the vehicle to move virtually silently over the road.

Section of fence from a Confederate prison in Columbia, S.C.

Iowa's Samuel H.M. Byers escaped Confederate custody by cutting a hole through a wooden stockade wall.

THE "HOLE STORY" OF BYERS'S ESCAPE(S)

On November 25, 1863, Lieutenant Samuel H.M. Byers of the 5th Iowa Infantry was captured by Confederate troops at the Battle of Chattanooga, Tennessee, and taken to Libby Prison, Richmond, Virginia.

Prison life did not agree with Lieutenant Byers, and he escaped several times, only to be recaptured. He was eventually transferred to Charleston and finally to Columbia, South Carolina. Here, he heard of the successful march of General Sherman and wrote a poem "When Sherman Marched Down to the Sea." The poem was set to music and sung by the prisoners' glee club. A copy of the song was secreted out of prison in the hollow leg of an exchanged prisoner and presented to General Sherman.

The resourceful Byers escaped once again and joined Sherman's advancing forces. General Sherman took a fancy to the young lieutenant and assigned him dispatch duties between his headquarters and General Grant and President Lincoln. Samuel Byers rose to the brevet rank of major, and by war's end, the song had been published and was popular throughout the North. Byers died in 1933 at age 95.

Sherman Will March to the Sea—First and Last verse
by S.H.M. Byers

Our camp fires shone bright on the mountains
That frowned on the river below,
While we stood by our guns in the morning
And eagerly watched for the foe—
When a rider came out from the darkness
That hung over mountain and tree;
And shouted, "Boys, up and be ready,
For Sherman will march to the sea."
O, proud was our army that morning
That stood where the pine darkly towers,

Top: On February 15, 1865, Lieutenant Samuel H. M. Byers, cut this hole though the stockade wall to escape from the prison at Columbia, South Carolina. After the war he returned and retrieved this section as a personal souvenir. It is on display at the State Historical Society of Iowa (courtesy The State Historical Society of Iowa). *Bottom:* Samuel H.M. Byers (courtesy of the State Historical Society of Iowa).

> When Sherman said: "Boys, you are weary,
> This day fair Savannah is ours."
> Then sang we a song for our chieftain
> That echoed o'er river and lea,
> And the stars in our banner shown brighter
> When Sherman marched down to the sea.

8

KENTUCKY

Simpson County Archives and Museum, 206 N College Street, Franklin, KY, 42134

Simpson County Archives and Museum is located in the old jail and jailer's residence and is the repository of old circuit court and county court documents, tax records, marriage records, wills, and deeds. The organization also maintains extensive family history files and genealogical collections for Simpson, Allen, Logan, and Warren counties in Kentucky, and Robertson and Sumner counties in Tennessee. Available are many old scrapbooks, collections, family Bibles, assorted manuscripts, census records, funeral home records, local papers on microfilm, maps, picture files, obituary files, local history files and memorabilia, as well as an extensive genealogical library.

Drawings of Civil War Officers, Walls of Simpson County Jail

These drawings depict a number of Civil War period officers in uniform and could date from any time during and immediately after the war. Of the thirty or more years these buildings served as a jail, no period saw as much activity as the years during and after the Civil War.

THE SIMPSON COUNTY JAIL

According to a court order of June 10, 1865, the "Jail of Simpson County was taken possession of by military authorities of the United States, the key taken from the jailer, and possession thereof retained by said military."

Simpson County was divided between Northern and Southern sentiments. Many of the pro-Southern people lived in west Simpson County and the pro-Northern or anti-secessionist people lived in the eastern part of the county.

The jail housed some of its most notable prisoners in period following the Civil War. One group was the infamous Captain Ellis Harper and his gang of Confederate guerrillas, among whom were listed several men with Simpson County ties. The following is an April 27, 1863, report from Union Major A. J. Cropsey, 129th, Commanding Regiment:

Sir: I have to report to the general commanding that a band of thirteen guerrillas, on the evening of the 23rd instant, attacked a Union man named Thomas Nowil, at his residence, some four miles from our camp. After severely wounding him, they succeeded in capturing; took him his family without hat or coat; took him off some fifteen miles and there murdered him, literally hewing him to pieces. With them were some at least of what Captain Peddicord used to call his "command"—Ellis Harper—Berryman, and,

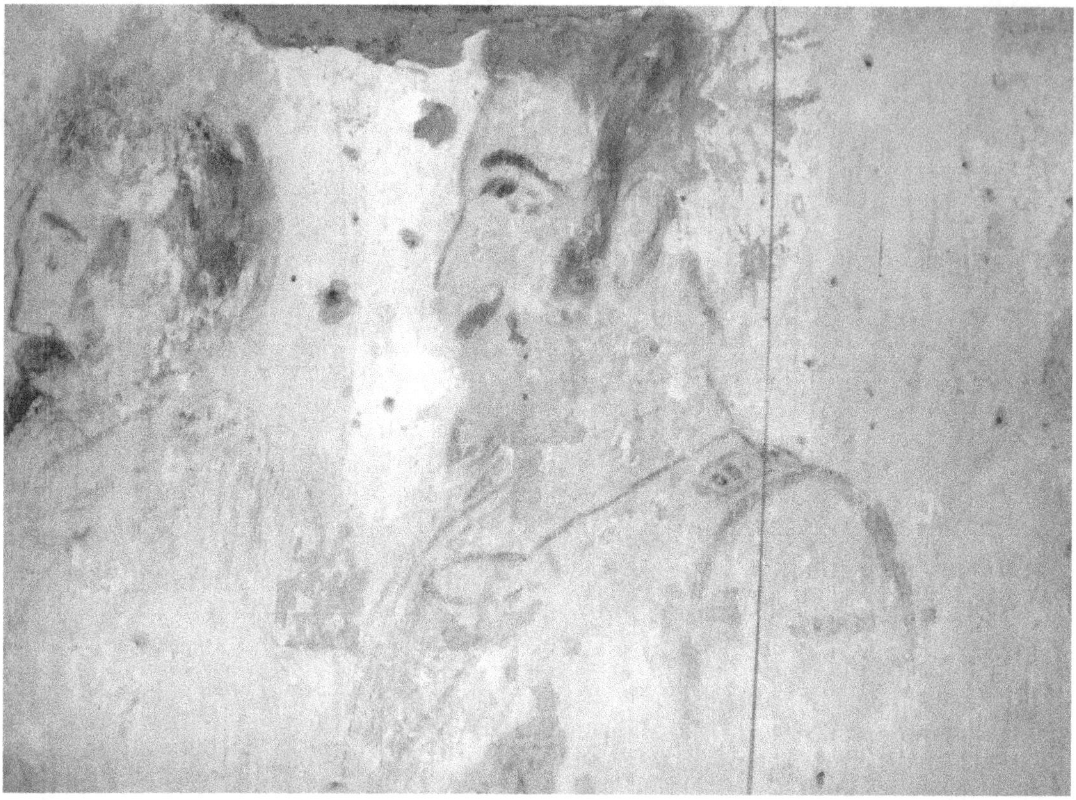

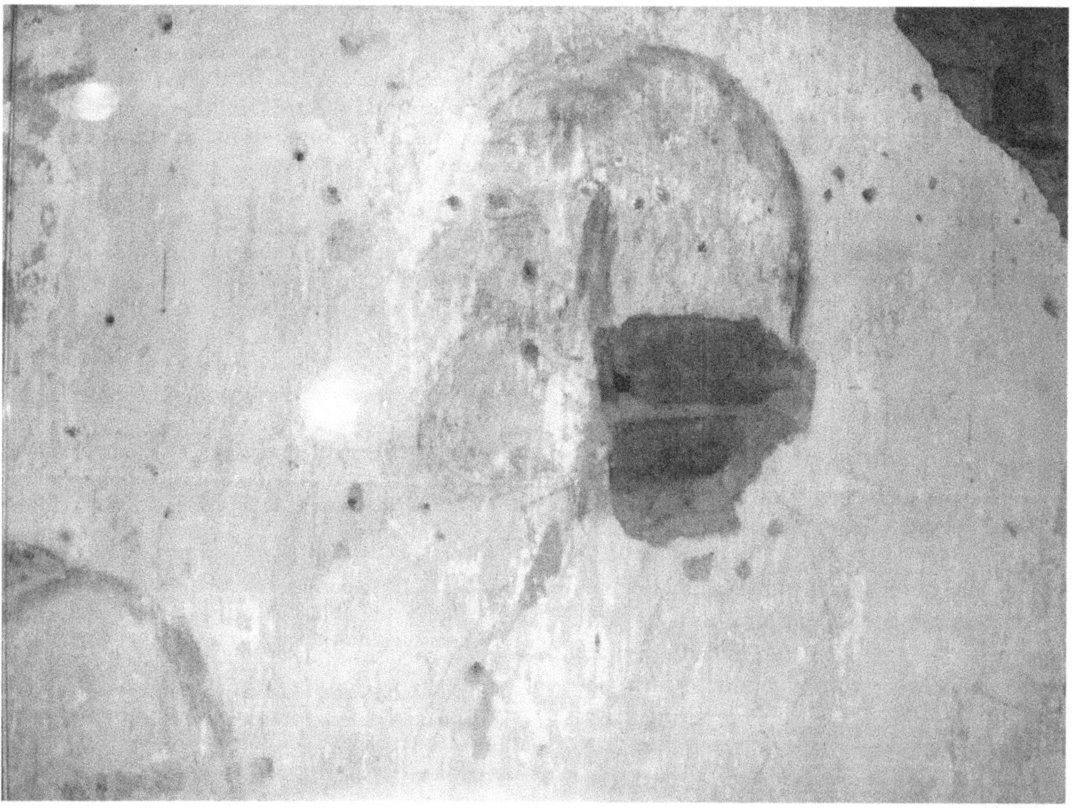

some say, Peter Blane. As we could not take the murderers, I sent down yesterday the fathers of Harper and Berryman.

Shortly after the end of hostilities, eleven grand jury indictments were returned against Harper and his men including murder, robbery, and malicious shooting. The few of Harper's men who were apprehended were lodged in the Simpson County Jail, including Seaton Moye of this county. When Moye was being transferred to the Warren County Jail for his own protection, Harper and his men ambushed the group and freed Moye. He was later recaptured and moved to Louisville in hopes that Harper and his men would not seek revenge in Simpson County.

Harper then learned that fellow partisan Captain Champ Ferguson had been seized at his home only three days after receiving his own parole and had been imprisoned at Nashville, awaiting trial on charges of treason. A few weeks after hearing of Ferguson's arrest, he also learned that the Kentucky partisan "Sue" Mundy had been hanged before a crowd of 12,000 onlookers in Louisville. No fool, Harper shortly thereafter disappeared, making himself scarce for the next five years. Only after obtaining special pardons from the governors of both Tennessee and Kentucky did he return home.

Ellis Harper then moved to Lebanon, in Wilson County, Tennessee, where he married into a prominent family and resided until his untimely death. On June 25, 1908, he was shot and killed by a much younger man after a heated political argument related to the Carmack-Patterson election.

Opposite: Workers restoring the Simpson County Jail in 1990 uncovered four large and many smaller drawings from underneath paneling and wallpaper. The Simpson County administrator had no idea when the drawings were made. There are no dates on the walls, nothing written about the drawings, and no county court records survived a courthouse fire in 1882. The four fairly competent large drawings appear to have been made by the same person; the many smaller drawings are quite amateurish (courtesy Simpson County Archives and Museum).

9

LOUISIANA

Louisiana State Museum Presbytere, 751 Chartres Street, Jackson Square, New Orleans, LA

New Orleans' most prominent heritage attraction is the Louisiana State Museum, a complex of national landmarks housing thousands of artifacts and works of art reflecting Louisiana's legacy of historic events and cultural diversity. The museum operates five properties in the famous French Quarter: the Cabildo, Presbytere, 1850 House, the Old U.S. Mint, and Madame John's Legacy. It also runs the Louisiana State Museum branch in Patterson, one in Baton Rouge, the Old Courthouse in Natchitoches, and the E.D. White Historic Site in Thibodaux.

The Mysterious Submarine

The incomplete history of this Civil War submarine, in the collection of the Louisiana State Museum, can be traced to 1878, when a

young boy swimming near the mouth of the Bayou St. John pointed out the sunken submarine to a dredge crew working nearby. The crew removed the vessel from Lake Ponchartrain and placed it on a nearby levee. For years after its recovery the boat lay in neglect on the lakeshore.

In 1942 it was acquired by the Louisiana State Museum, and museum officials believed it to be the *Pioneer*, the first Confederate submarine. In April 1862, as New Orleans fell to Union Navy Commander David Glasgow Farragut, the *Pioneer* was scuttled in the New Basin Canal. It was quickly discovered in its watery grave and brought ashore by a Federal team of experts who examined the machine. In 1868, the *Pioneer* was reportedly auctioned as scrap by federal authorities for $43. Ten years later the sub reemerged in the general area; surely it had to be the *Pioneer*.

The problem of authenticating the vessel's identity vexed researchers for years. Then, in 1997, naval historian Mark K. Ragan found detailed drawings of the *Pioneer* in the National Archives. The *Pioneer* drawings did not match the iron vessel in the Louisiana State Museum, with its ¼-inch-thick hull, thirty feet in length and four foot diameter. Later, a private collection, discovered in 1999, of *Louisiana Sketches 1864* contained a drawing of the *Pioneer* with a little conning tower, a manhole in the top, and small circular glass windows in its side. This surely did not match the mysterious machine in the Louisiana State Museum Collection.

The boat's actual identity may never truly be known, but it is certain that the enigmatic icon of iron is an extremely rare example of maritime ingenuity.

Opposite: In 1895 this mysterious submarine was put on display at the Spanish Fort where it became a prominent landmark. Two young boys sit on supporting beams while a third youth rests his elbow on the starboard diving plane. Note the single propeller blade (courtesy Louisiana State Museum).

10

MARYLAND

*Antietam National Battlefield,
5831 Dunker Church Road,
Sharpsburg, MD 21782*

The National Park Service operates a visitor center and museum store at the site of the bloodiest one-day battle in U.S. history.

Six generals were killed or mortally wounded at the Battle of Antietam — three Union and three Confederate. Today, the place where they were killed is marked by a mortuary cannon comprised of a cannon barrel muzzle-down in a block of stone. About 23,000 soldiers were killed, wounded, or missing after twelve hours of savage combat on September 17, 1862. The Battle of Antietam ended the Confederate Army of Northern Virginia's first invasion into the North and led to Abraham Lincoln's issuance of the preliminary Emancipation Proclamation.

THE BATTLE OF ANTIETAM

"I began to feel wretchedly faint of heart, for it seemed timely that the coming of battle meant my certain death...."

"The third shell struck and killed my horse and bursting, blew him to pieces, knocked me down, of course, and tore off my right arm..."

Pvt. Ezra E. Stickley, Company A,
5th Virginia Infantry

The Battle of Antietam (or Sharpsburg) on September 17, 1862, climaxed the first of Confederate General Robert E. Lee's two attempts to carry the war into the North. About 40,000 Southerners were pitted against the 87,000-man Federal Army of the Potomac under General George B. McClellan.

After his successful summer campaign, Lee marched his Army of Northern Virginia into Maryland, hoping to find vitally needed men and supplies. McClellan followed, first to Frederick (where through rare good fortune a copy of the Confederate battle plan, Lee's Special Order No. 191, fell into his hands), and then westward twelve miles to the passes of South Mountain. There, on September 14, at Turners, Fox, and Crampton Gaps, Lee tried to block the Federals. But because he had split his army to send troops under Stonewall Jackson to capture Harpers Ferry, Lee could hope at best only to delay the Northerners. McClellan forced his way through, and by the afternoon of September 15 both armies had established new battle lines west and east of Antietam Creek near the town of Sharpsburg. When Jackson's troops reached Sharpsburg on the 16th, Harpers Ferry having surrendered the day before, Lee consolidated his position along the low ridge that runs north and south of the town.

The battle opened at dawn on the 17th when Union General Joseph Hooker's artillery unleashed a murderous fire on Jackson's men in the Miller cornfield north of town. "In the time I am writing," Hooker reported, "every stalk of corn in the northern and greater part of the field was cut as closely as could have been done with a knife and the slain lay in rows precisely as they had stood in their ranks a few moments before." Hooker's troops advanced, driving the Confederates before them, and Jackson reported that his men were "exposed for near an hour to a terrific storm of shell, canister, and musketry."

About 7 A.M., Jackson was reinforced and succeeded in driving the Federals back. An hour later, Union troops under General Joseph Mansfield counterattacked, and by 9 o'clock had regained some of the lost ground. Then, in an effort to extricate some of Mansfield's men from their isolated position near the Dunker Church, General John Sedgwick's division of Edwin V. Sumner's corps advanced into the West Woods. There, Confederate troops struck Sedgwick's men on both flanks, inflicting appalling casualties.

Meanwhile, General William H. French's division of Sumner's corps moved up to support Sedgwick but veered south into Confederates under General D.H. Hill, posted along an old sunken road separating the Roulette and Piper farms. For nearly four hours, from 9:30 A.M. to 1:00 P.M., bitter fighting raged along this road (afterwards known as Bloody Lane) as French, supported by General Israel B. Richardson's division, also of Sumner's corps, sought to drive the Southerners back. Confusion and sheer exhaustion finally ended the battle here and in the northern part of the field generally.

Southeast of town, Union General Ambrose E. Burnside's troops had been trying to cross a bridge over Antietam Creek since 9:30 A.M. Some 400 Georgians had driven them back each time. At 1:00 P.M., the Federals finally crossed the bridge (now known as Burnside Bridge) and after a two-hour delay to reform their lines, advanced up the slope beyond. By late afternoon they had driven the Georgians back almost to Sharpsburg, threatening to cut off the line of retreat from Lee's decimated Confederates. Then, at around 4:00 P.M., General A. P. Hill's division, left behind by Jackson at Harpers Ferry to salvage the captured Federal property, arrived in the field and immediately entered the fight. Burnside's troops were driven back to the heights near the bridge they had earlier taken. The Battle of Antietam was over. The next day Lee began withdrawing his army across the Potomac River.

Although neither side gained a decisive victory, Lee's failure to carry the war effort effectively into the North caused Great Britain to postpone recognition of the Confederate government. The battle also gave President Lincoln the opportunity to issue the Emancipation Proclamation, which, on January 1, 1863, declared free all slaves in states still in rebellion against the United States. Now the war had a dual purpose: to preserve the Union and to end slavery.

Stonewall Jackson's Note of Thanks for Breakfast

On the morning of September 16, 1862, Stonewall Jackson had been invited to the spacious West Main Street brick home of Dr. Jacob Grove for breakfast. Because Jackson was preparing for the forthcoming battle, he declined the invitation. The doctor's daughter Julia, bestowing particular attention upon the Confederate general, sent a breakfast to his camp. Jackson wanted to send a written note of thanks, but the carrier, not knowing her name, identified the girl simply as the "the fair one." With a rare flash of humor, Jackson replied, "Well, she has sent my breakfast to the field; I will call her Miss Fairfield."

This letter was written a day before the battle of Antietam, the bloodiest single day of fighting in American history. One terrible clash in a small cornfield resulted in 12,000 causalities in just four hours. Reading this note of appreciation for breakfast, one cannot help but feel the chilling contrast between so cordial a letter written just hours before such brutal butchery.

Portraits of Phillip and Elizabeth Pry

Phillip Pry's prosperous farm and home were taken over by Union commander George McClellan to use as his headquarters during the battle.

Major General Israel B. Richardson, a Vermonter, was forty-six years old when he led his troops at Antietam. He commanded a division of the II Corps that attacked the Sunken Road. Richardson was wounded in the

Top: This peaceful early morning photograph of Main Street, Sharpsburg, Maryland, can only hint at the colossal tragic event that happened in the village. The Battle of Antietam resulted in 23,000 casualties (courtesy Library of Congress). *Bottom:* This letter was written to the youthful Julia Grove by Stonewall Jackson on the day of the bloodiest in American history, Antietam.

action at Bloody Lane and was taken to the Pry house, where he died in an upstairs bedroom on November 3. President Lincoln visited the Pry house to see the wounded Richardson during his four-day visit in early October, when he gave his Proclamation of Emancipation speech.

Sampler sewn by Elizabeth Pry

A young girl's training work in the "womanly arts" was destined to end up in the files of a national battlefield park.

These photos of Phillip Pry and his wife rest in the files of the Antietam Battlefield Park.

Bookmarks and Needlepoint Belonging to Private Jared Wheeler

Wheeler was wounded at Antietam and discharged. Some of his belongings were given to the Antietam National Battlefield in 1982. They are not on public display.

List of bare-footed soldiers

This document (see page 74) was sent to Col. R.F. Hoke and is now at Antietam.

AN ARMY WITHOUT SHOES

After Antietam, the Army of Northern Virginia retreated back across the Potomac River and returned to Virginia to begin its winter encampment. Almost half of the men were without shoes even though it was common practice to rummage the battlefield and remove the shoes from men killed in battle.

General Isaac Trimble had distinguished himself in various campaigns but suffered a wound from an exploding bullet prior to the Battle of Antietam, which kept him out of the war for almost a year. His brigade was subsequently placed under the command of Colonel Robert F. Hoke. Both men survived the war, but Trimble was again wounded and then captured during the Battle of Gettysburg. Federal surgeons subsequently amputated Trimble's leg.

Shoes would continue to be a major problem during the four-year conflict. The following is a letter written by Robert E. Lee:

To General Alexander R. Lawton
Quartermaster General,
   Richmond, Virginia

                  Headquarters, Army of
                      Northern Virginia
                      January 19, 1864
  General:

I desire to state more fully to you my views with reference to procuring a supply of shoes for the army, as I fear that unless great efforts are made, the return of the season of active

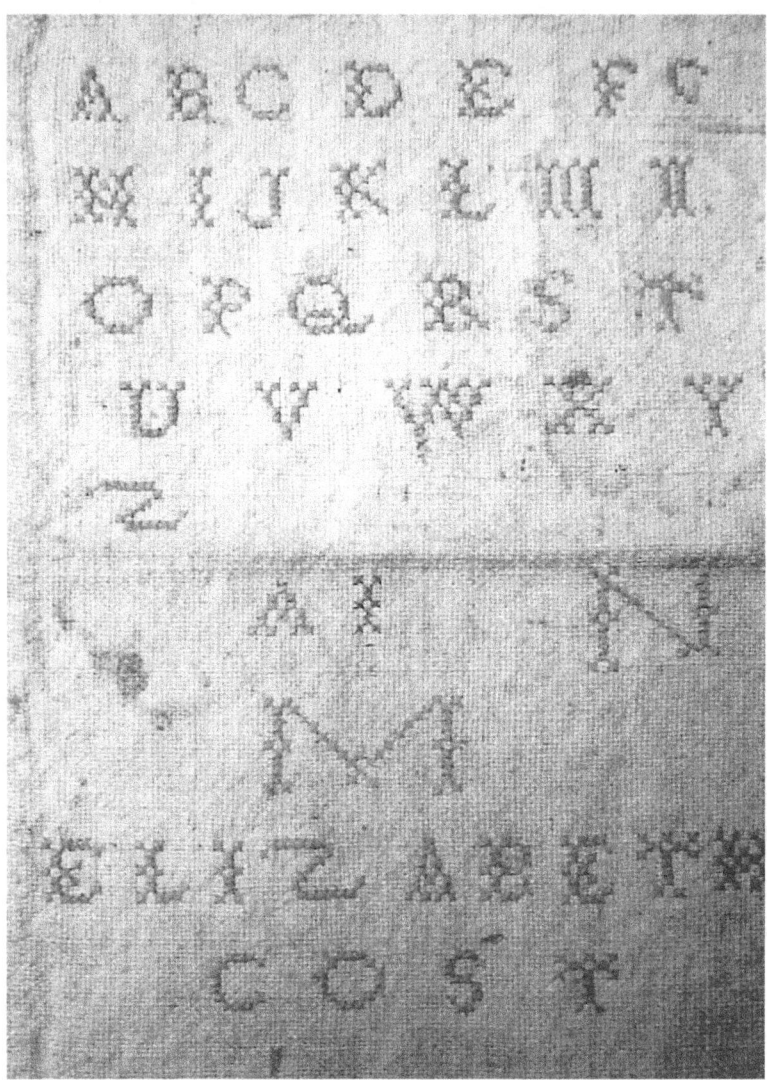

Mrs. Pry, née Elizabeth Cost, worked a sampler as part of her education, a practice that became common for young girls beginning in the mid–eighteenth century. These creations were normally patterned A–Z and 0–9 along with a birthday or a significant message. One can only guess at what the A, symbol, N, and M represent in Mrs. Pry's sampler, one that may remain forever in the dark files of the National Park Service.

may be devised to procure leather in sufficient quantities. I caused a requisition for the least amount that we could get along with, viz, 37,500 pounds to be made, of which we have only received 8,000 or 9,000 pounds. I hope that the rest will be forthcoming. I think there is leather, and enough, in the country concealed by speculators, of which we never hear until the enemy captures and destroys it. Such was the case at Salem, where General Averell reports that he destroyed cords of it. Such was also the case at Luray and Sperryville. That at Luray was in the hands of a speculator named [Peter B.] Borst, I am informed, who had concealed it there. If this leather cannot be had in any other way it should be impressed. [Confiscated]

In researching letters and documents it is most interesting to note the continuing shortages of shoes, clothing, and food, but ammunition seems to have been plentiful for both the Confederacy and Union.

operations will find a large number of the men barefooted.

It is the opinion of the Quartermaster of this army that if we were supplied with tools and materials, from one-third to one-half of the army could be shod by the system of brigade shoemakers, already brought to your attention. I am satisfied that this system can be made an important auxiliary of the department, and am anxious that some measure

The Maryland Historical Society, 210 West Monument Street, Baltimore, MD

The Maryland Historical Society's Museum houses an astonishing collection of treasures; from eighteenth- and nineteenth-century paintings and silver, to twentieth-

century objects of everyday life, the museum collection celebrates Maryland's rich and diverse history. Among its more than 300,000 objects, the most significant collection in the world of both Maryland cultural artifacts and Americana, are over 2,000 paintings, Baltimore-painted furniture, and one of the world's largest collections of nineteenth-century American silver, quilts, costumes, ceramics, glass, dolls, toys, and sports objects.

Antietam Shadowbox

Made by John Philemon Smith in 1886, the box uses items from the battlefield.

Smith inscribed the inside panel of this shadowbox, "The material from which this board is composed was found on the Battle Field of Antietam." The text inside the box records the dedication of the Antietam National Cemetery in 1867, a list of the Union soldiers who died at or shortly after Antietam, and the installation of the Private Soldier Monument. The centerpiece is a miniature replica of the Private Soldier Monument added to Antietam National Cemetery in 1880. Black bunting and forty-eight-star flags were added to the top of the box in 1912 to commemorate the fiftieth anniversary of the battle.

The exterior frame is labeled "Antietam National Cemetery Memorial Tablet Board. Cemetery Dedicated September 17, 1867"; it is signed in the lower right, "Designed and constructed by J. P. Smith, Sharpsburg, MD August 6, 1886."

Private Jared Wheeler, Company A, 80th Regiment, Connecticut Volunteer Infantry, was wounded at Antietam and discharged on disability. His military file and a few belongings were deeded to the Antietam National Battlefield in August of 1982, and include his *carte de visite* and (*see above*) two cloth book markers — "Richmond 1865" and "Abraham Lincoln."

Page 74, top: A needlepoint in the Jared Wheeler collection with the haunting plea "Remember Me." Sadly, these mementos now reside in a dark filing cabinet in a dark room and may never see the light of day again.

ANTIETAM NATIONAL CEMETERY

In 1865, the State of Maryland purchased eleven-and-one-quarter acres for a national cemetery near the Antietam battlefield. By fall 1867, all the known Union dead from Maryland battlefields had been reinterred. Confederate remains were later moved to nearby Maryland and West Virginia cemeteries. The Antietam National Cemetery was dedicated on September 17, 1867, the fifth anniversary of the battle.

Immediately above: This distressing document in the archives of the Antietam National Battlefield is addressed to Colonel R.F. Hoke, Commanding Trimble Brigade, near Bunker Hill, Virginia, October 4, 1862. It is titled "Report of number of barefooted men in Brigade," and lists the number of Confederate soldiers lacking shoes.

John Philemon Smith was a seventeen-year-old student when his hometown of Sharpsburg witnessed the Battle of Antietam. The terrible day overwhelmed the small town and left a lasting impression on Smith. He spent the rest of his life as a teacher and historian, preserving Antietam's memory.

Fort Foote Park (Fort Washington)

Fort Foote is located on the Potomac River in Prince George County. From the Beltway (I-95), take exit 3, Indian Head Highway south (MD210) and drive for approxi-

John Philemon Smith designed and made this shadowbox in 1886. Shadowboxes and relic show boards were common methods of displaying battlefield collections after the Civil War. His "tablet board," as Smith referred to it, is unique for its focus on Antietam National Cemetery, its replica of the Private Soldier Monument, and for the extensive use of text throughout (courtesy Maryland Historical Society).

mately 3.5 miles to Old Fort Road. Turn right for one mile to Fort Foote Road S, and turn left. Follow the winding road through the residential area to the entrance site on the left.

Fort Foote Park is part of the National Park Service's National Capital Parks system. It became a park after World War II.

Fort Foote

Eight miles downriver from the nation's capital, Fort Foote was considered "a powerful enclosed work" by its chief engineer, "and the most elaborate...of all the defenses of Washington." The long oval earthwork was constructed on Rozier's Bluff from 1863 to 1865 to strengthen the ring of fortifications that encircled Washington, D.C., during the Civil War. Fort Foote was designed to protect the river entrance to the ports of Alexandria, Georgetown, and Washington.

Today, the National Park Service has cleared paths around the ruins of what is considered the best preserved Civil War fort in the region. Remounted on carriages, two Rodman guns loom in shadows under the trees, the river still in their sights.

THE DEFENSE OF WASHINGTON

In 1862 the now-famed battle between the *Monitor* and *Merrimac* at Hampton Roads created panic in Washington, which suddenly felt

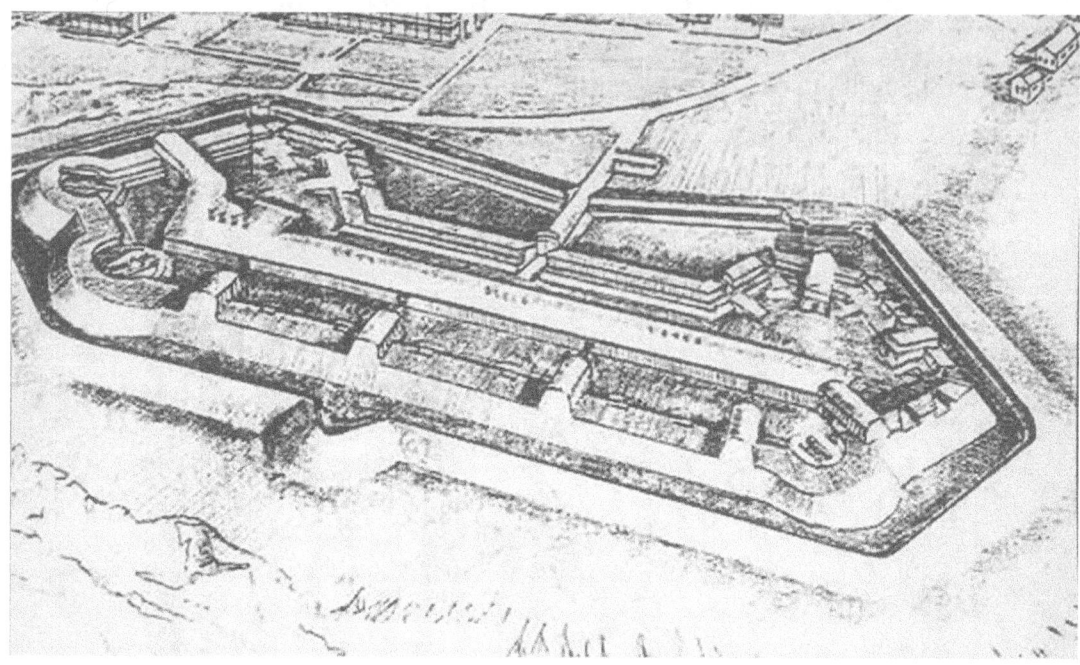

The Union built 68 strongholds like Fort Foote around the nation's capital. These thick earth-and-log structures were designed to be temporary field fortifications and could only resist moderate attacks by infantry, cavalry, and artillery (courtesy Fort Foote National Park).

The first 15-inch gun arrived at Fort Foote in the fall of 1863. By April 1865 the fort boasted two 15-inch Rodman cannons, four 200-pounder Parrott rifles, and six 30-pounder Parrott rifles. A large crowd of civilian and military observers gathered to watch the guns fire on February 27 and again on April 1, 1864. The 8-inch Parrott rifles weighed over eight tons and used sixteen pounds of powder to fire a 200-pound projectile 2,000 yards down river. But the fort's main attractions were the 15-inch Columbiads. They weighed in at twenty-five tons and required 300 to 400 soldiers to move them up the bluff from the river. Forty pounds of powder could propel a 440-pound round-shot over 5,000 yards (courtesy Fort Foote National Park).

threatened from the sea as well as on land. Furthermore, as the war unfolded, several European countries seemed eager to join the fight on the side of the Confederacy. Fort Washington, on the Potomac River sixteen miles below Washington, was considered too far away to be adequately supportive, so the protection of the city from naval attack became a critical issue, and army engineers began building earthworks to resist naval bombardment.

Fort Foote was constructed for the purpose of defending, with Battery Rogers, the water approach to the city. It was situated six miles below Washington, elevated 100 feet above the river on a commanding bluff on the Maryland shore. The essential components of the fort were completed in the fall of 1863; it had been designed as a water battery of eight 200-pounder Parrott rifles and two fifteen-inch guns. The fort was named in honor of Rear Admiral Andrew H. Foote, who distinguished himself in the actions against the Confederate forts on the Mississippi River and who had died of battle wounds on June 26, 1863.

Since Fort Foote was a seacoast fortification, care was taken to insure that it could resist moisture and naval shells. General Barnard described the work in his 1881 report: "The revetments of breast-height and slopes, and all the vertical walls of the interior structure, as magazines, bomb-proofs, galleries, &c., were made almost wholly of cedar posts, while the roofing of these structures were mainly of chestnut logs." The front of the fort was over 500 feet long and the earth walls were 20 feet thick. A central traverse ran the length of the fort and contained bombproof magazines and storage areas.

During the Civil War the fifteen-inch guns cost the government $9,000 each, but were well worth the high price; they could inflict great damage to a wooden sailing ship-of-war. Even the ironclads were not safe from the massive weapons at close range. The two guns on display at Fort Foote were cast at the Cyrus Alger Company in 1863 and 1864.

The first unit to garrison Fort Foote was composed of four companies of the 9th New York Heavy Artillery, which arrived on August 12, 1863. The post was commanded by Lieutenant Colonel William H. Seward, Jr., the son of the secretary of state. The secretary visited the post often while his son was in command, and President Lincoln visited the fort on August 20, 1863, with the secretary of war and a number of high-ranking army officers.

11

MINNESOTA

*Minnesota Historical Society,
345 W. Kellogg Blvd., St. Paul,
MN 55102–1906*

The Minnesota Historical Society has been collecting and relating Minnesota history for 150 years. The society today passes down to each generation the stories of the generations that have come before. Its collections include nearly 550,000 books; 37,000 maps; 250,000 photographs; 165,000 historical artifacts; nearly 800,000 archaeological items; 38,000 cubic feet of manuscripts; 45,000 cubic feet of government records; and 5,500 paintings, prints and drawings.

Army of Northern Virginia Battle Flag

This battle flag belonged to the 28th Virginia Volunteer Infantry, but was captured and taken to Minnesota. As recently as 2000–2001, the two states exchanged verbal volleys over its return. It remains in Minnesota.

AN EMBATTLED FLAG

A flag of the 28th Virginia Volunteers was captured from a unit of soldiers from the Roanoke Valley in 1863, during Pickett's Charge at the Battle of Gettysburg. Now, 140 years after the Civil War, neither Virginia nor Minnesota shows any sign of relinquishing its interest in the flag. Their respective governors, Congressional representatives, and Senate committees have challenged each other many times for the return of the flag to the Commonwealth of Virginia.

Minnesota has returned fire several times when Senate committees voted to ignore a request from Virginia and keep the controversial Civil War battle flag in the Northern state. Interested Virginians claim that Minnesota is obligated to return the flag under a 1905 Congressional resolution that says flags captured in battles should be returned to their originating states.

The Virginians even approached the U.S. Army and demanded that it sequester the flag and place it in the U.S. Army museum collection. The Army wisely declined, responding that it really did not possess legal standing in the fight and that Virginia would have to skirmish with Minnesota concerning any attempt to secure the battle flag.

The flag currently is in a very secure underground storage area in a steel cabinet kept at 70 degrees and 50 percent humidity year-round at Minnesota's History Center Museum in St. Paul.

The flag came to Minnesota through the heroism of a lowly private. Marshall Sherman was born in Burlington, Vermont, in 1823. He settled in St Paul in 1849 and was working as a painter when the war began. He was mustered into the First Minnesota Volunteer Infantry on April 29, 1861. We know that he was thirty-seven years old and stood 5' 6" tall,

This flag has been fought over for more than 140 years. It is the Army of Northern Virginia battle flag of the 28th Virginia Volunteer Infantry and features a blue wool bunting St. Andrew's cross with white cotton fillet sewn over a red wool bunting field. The red field has minor stains and small tears. The flag has a two-inch white wool bunting border. Thirteen white cotton stars representing the Confederate states are sewn onto the cross. Stenciled in white paint on the obverse is "28th Va Inf'y." The hoist has a white canvas lead with three whipped eyelets. The number "58," a Union "capture" number applied by the War Department, is stenciled in black paint on the lead (courtesy Minnesota Historical Society).

with a fair complexion, blue eyes, and light-colored hair.

He captured the Virginia flag at the Battle of Gettysburg on July 3, 1863, and received the Medal of Honor for the act.

After his three year enlistment was up, he was one of only a few veterans of the "Old First" to re-enlist and form the nucleus of the First Minnesota Battalion. On August 14, 1864, at the battle of Deep Bottom, Virginia, he was shot in the left foot. The wound was severe, and he had to have his leg amputated. Marshall was determined to be unfit for service in the Veteran Reserve Corps and was discharged for disability on July 25, 1865. He died in St Paul on April 19, 1896, at the age of 73.

12

MISSISSIPPI

Vicksburg National Military Park, 3201 Clay Street, Vicksburg, MS 39183

Vicksburg National Military Park commemorates the campaign, siege and defense of Vicksburg. The city had become a fortress located on high ground guarding the Mississippi River. Its surrender on July 4, 1863, coupled with the fall of Port Hudson, Louisiana, divided the South, and gave the North undisputed control of the Mississippi waterway. The Vicksburg battlefield includes 1,330 monuments and markers, a sixteen-mile tour road, a restored Union gunboat, and a national cemetery.

Vicksburg National Military Park was the final of the first five national military parks established by the Congress of the United States during the last quarter of the nineteenth century.

Map of the Vicksburg Campaign

The Vicksburg National Military Park provides visitors a diagram of the action that took place over several months in 1863.

THE IMPORTANCE OF VICKSBURG

Vicksburg was considered a purely defensive position, and Confederate strategic doctrine was tied closely to this mindset. With the strengthening squeeze of the Federal blockade, the city's location on the Mississippi River was becoming increasingly more important to the Confederate supply line running from Matamoras, Mexico. Here, materiel from the western states was ferried from Louisiana to Mississippi, to be shipped by railroad to points east. The Confederacy soon came to realize that its survival was absolutely dependent on control of the river at Vicksburg.

The land defenses for Vicksburg were anchored by nine major fortifications and support structures, six roads, and a single railroad that led into Vicksburg. The works were composed of exterior ditches six to ten feet deep. These nine strong points were connected by a line of rifle pits with parapets approximately six feet thick but with no fronting ditch, and artillery positions located at intervals along the entire front. The constructors removed the cane and trees in the ravine bottoms in front of the works as an added protective measure, providing uninterrupted fields of fire. The timber was lashed together with telegraph wire to form a broad band of impassable *abatis*, one of which was 200 yards deep.

To capture this vital Confederate distribution center, Ulysses S. Grant made several attempts to take Vicksburg in mid–October 1862 to gain undisputed control of the mighty Mississippi River. Following his repeated failures, he prepared to cross his troops in the spring of 1863 from the west bank of the Mississippi River to Bruinsburg, a point south of Vicksburg, and drive against the city from the south and east. Naval support for his campaign

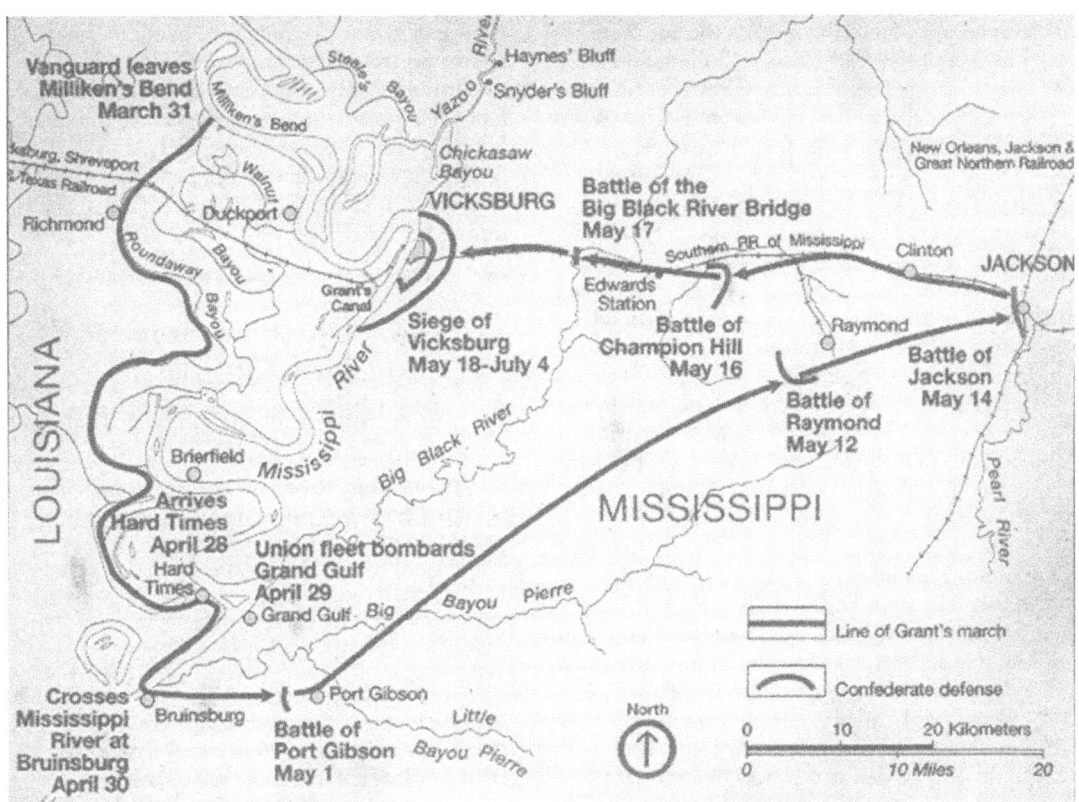

This Vicksburg Campaign Map documents those tragic events of 1863 (courtesy Vicksburg National Military Park).

would have to come from Rear Admiral David D. Porter's fleet north of Vicksburg. Running past the powerful Vicksburg batteries, Porter's vessels, once south of the city, could ferry Union soldiers to the east bank. Once there infantry would face two Confederate forces, one under General John C. Pemberton at Vicksburg and another around Jackson, Mississippi, soon to be commanded by General Joseph E. Johnston.

On the night of April 16, at Grant's request, Porter took twelve vessels including seven ironclads south past the Vicksburg batteries, losing one to Confederate fire. Porter, encouraged by light losses on his first try, ran a large supply flotilla past the batteries the night of April 22. On April 29, as John A. McClernand's and McPherson's troops gathered near Hard Times, Porter's fleet assailed Confederate batteries at Grand Gulf, thirty-three miles southwest of Vicksburg, testing the Grand Gulf area as a landing site for Union troops. Though Porter found the guns there too strong, he had succeeded in further diverting Pemberton in Vicksburg.

On May 1, the Federal invasion force engaged the Confederates in the Battle of Port Gibson. Pemberton had just over 40,000 men assigned to the Vicksburg region. Defeated at Port Gibson, Pemberton's Confederate troops moved north. The more energetic commander Grant, to Pemberton's confusion, pushed northeast. Sherman's corps joined him on May 8 and May 12, when the engagement at Raymond was fought. Johnston took personal command of the Confederates at Jackson, fifteen miles northeast of Raymond. On May 14, the Federals quickly won an engagement at Jackson, cut off Johnston from Pemberton, and ensured the latter's isolation for the rest of the campaign. In two weeks Grant's force had done what was considered impossible; they had come well over 130 miles northeast from their Bruinsburg landing site.

Ordering Sherman to destroy the heavy industry and rail facilities at Jackson, Grant turned west, following roughly the Southern Mississippi Railroad tracks to Bolton, and on May 16 fought the climactic combat of his field campaign, the Battle of Champion's Hill. With the largest Confederate force he had yet gathered to oppose Grant, General Pemberton nevertheless took a beating there and pulled his army into the defenses of Vicksburg. In a delaying battle at Big Black River Bridge, Confederates crossed the Big Black, destroying their river crossings behind them. Undeterred, Federals threw up their own bridges and continued to pursue the very next day.

Approaching from the east and northeast, the corps of Generals John A. McClernand, James B. McPherson, and William T. Sherman neared the Vicksburg defenses, Sherman veering north to take the hills overlooking the Yazoo River. Possession of these heights assured Grant's reinforcement and supply from the north. The next day, Federals made the failed first assault on Vicksburg. The second assault, on May 22, was a disaster for Union forces, and underscored the strength of the miles of Confederate works arching east around the city. Grant was now convinced that Pemberton could only be defeated by way of a protracted siege.

In the beginning, Pemberton had a dual responsibility: garrison Vicksburg and keep his army intact. He split his effort, and did neither task well. He didn't send enough troops to defeat Grant, and then withdrew the battered forces into Vicksburg. Pemberton had retreated to Vicksburg expecting in vain for Johnston to reinforce him.

The blockade of Vicksburg began with the repulse of the May 22 assault and lasted until July 4, 1863. As the siege progressed, Pemberton's 20,000-man garrison was reduced by disease and starvation, and the city's residents were forced to seek the refuge of caves and bombproofs in the surrounding hillsides. Hunger and daily bombardments by Grant's forces and Porter's gunboats compelled Pemberton to ask for surrender terms July 3. Grant offered none, but on the garrison's capitulation immediately paroled the bulk of the force. Many of these same men would later oppose him at Chattanooga. Pemberton's surrender ended the Vicksburg Campaign.

The Union eventually exchanged prisoner-of-war Pemberton in May 1864, and Jefferson Davis had to figure out what to do with a competent but unpopular officer. There was no chance of giving him high command: too many people mistrusted him and wouldn't serve under him. Pemberton then offered to serve as a private, a way of regaining respect. Eventually, he was placed back into the artillery, as only a lieutenant colonel, down from lieutenant general, and put in charge of Richmond's artillery during the long siege.

U.S.S. Cairo (Union Ironclad Gunboat, City Class)

Preserved by mud and silt, Cairo sat on the bottom of the Yazoo River for 102 years. It was raised in 1964 and later restored. The ironclad is now on display within Vicksburg National Military Park.

Torpedoed

The *U.S.S. Cairo* was one of seven ironclad gunboats named in honor of towns along the upper Mississippi and Ohio rivers. These powerful boats were formidable vessels, each mounting thirteen big guns (cannon). On them rested in large part Northern hopes to regain control of the lower Mississippi River and split the Confederacy in two.

These "city class" gunboats were designed by Samuel M. Pook and built by river engineer James B. Eads. *Cairo* was constructed at Mound City, Illinois, and commissioned in January 1862. It was destined to see only limited action in the engagement at Plum Point in May and in the battle of Memphis in June. Her most significant action came six months later when she kept a rendezvous with destiny.

The *Cairo*'s skipper, Lt. Commander Thomas O. Selfridge, Jr., was rash and ambitious, a stern disciplinarian, but an aggressive and promising young officer. On the cold morning of December 12, 1862, Selfridge led a small flotilla up the Yazoo River, north of Vicksburg, to destroy Confederate batteries and clear the channel of torpedoes (underwater mines). As the *Cairo* reached a point seven miles north of Vicksburg, the flotilla came under fire, and Selfridge ordered the guns to ready. As the gunboat turned towards shore, disaster struck. The gunboat was rocked by two explosions in quick succession, which tore gaping holes in the ship's hull. Within twelve min-

This busy-looking photograph from February 1864 underscores the importance of Vicksburg, as the steamships unload Union supplies at its wharfs (courtesy Library of Congress).

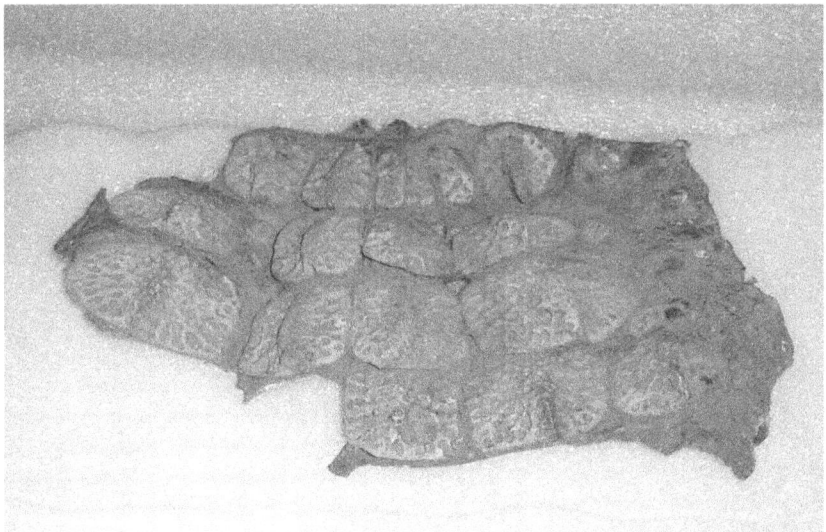

An alligator hide is witness to a Civil War event, and spurs much curiosity at the Vicksburg National Military Park. It was donated in 1959, accompanied by a card stored with the hide which reads, "Hide of an alligator which bit a soldier during the war and caused loss of leg" (courtesy Vicksburg National Military Park).

utes the doomed ironclad sank into six fathoms (36 feet) of water without any loss of life. *Cairo* became the first ship in history to be sunk by an electrically detonated torpedo.

Alligator Hide

One of the more provocative items on display at Vicksburg is the hide of an alligator that bit a soldier's leg during the Civil War. In 2005 a park ranger came upon an American alligator while on patrol. The alligator had come up a service road and was headed for the *Cairo* gunboat and the museum. He was returned to the Mississippi River.

13

NEW MEXICO

Pecos National Historical, Park Pecos, NM 87552

The visitor center at the Pecos National Historical Park contains exhibits and a ten-minute introductory film. There is a quarter-mile self-guided trail through Pecos pueblo and mission ruins, and the winter program includes tours of the nearby Arrowhead Ruin on Fridays at 1:30 P.M., Glorietta Pass Battlefield on Saturdays at 1:30 P.M., and the Historic Ranch House on Sundays at 1:30 P.M.

Pecos National Historical Park preserves 12,000 years of history, including the ancient pueblo of Pecos, colonial missions, Santa Fe Trail sites, the twentieth century Forked Lightning Ranch, and the site of the Civil War Battle of Glorieta Pass.

Saber of John E. Briney

Union soldiers like Briney helped stop the Confederate play for reinforcements in the West. He used this saber at the Battle of Glorieta Pass.

A CIVIL WAR SABER RETURNS TO GLORIETA PASS

In 1861, Confederate President Jefferson Davis approved Brigadier General Henry Hopkins Sibley's plan to raise a force of Texans to invade New Mexico territory. Although New Mexico seemed far out of range of what was basically an Eastern and Southern war, Sibley's objectives were to capture military supplies from Union forts in New Mexico and to recruit New Mexicans, Utah Mormons, and Colorado miners to the Confederate cause.

In early 1862, Sibley marched 3,400 coarse Texas farm boys, cowhands, and frontiersmen from San Antonio across Texas to El Paso. From there they followed the Rio Grande into New Mexico territory. From here the Confederates planned to invade California with aspirations of accessing the Colorado gold fields and Pacific Ocean ports.

Although seriously bloodied, after immobilizing the bulk of Union forces in New Mexico at Valverde, the Confederates had spread out across the Rio Grande valley and gobbled up small Union garrisons and occupied Santa Fe in March 1862. Fort Union, northeast of Santa Fe, was last on their list. They knew it was lightly garrisoned, and a modest contingent headed for it.

On March 28, 1862, as Confederate troops followed the Santa Fe Trail east, Union Volunteers from Colorado left Fort Union and intercepted and defeated Silbey's Confederates at the strategic Glorieta Pass. Subsequently, Union forces quickly circled through the mountains, behind the Rebels. Lowering themselves over a cliff by ropes they overran and burned the entire supply train, consisting of eighty wagons with reserve ammunition, stores, and food, and then used bayonets to savagely cut the throats of all the cavalry horses and work mules. Both sides had a scant 1,000 men

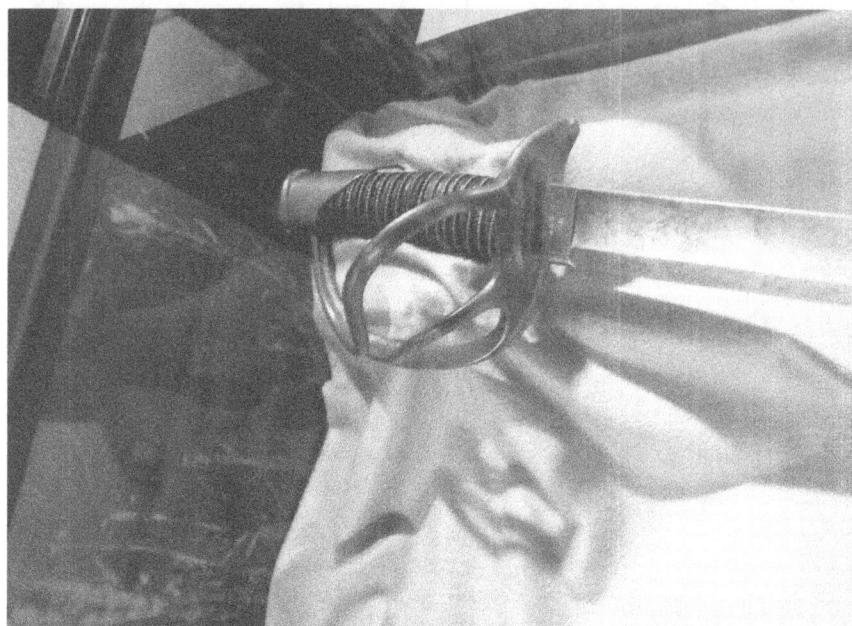

each. Casualty reports conflict, but the Confederates probably lost about 400, the Union, 200.

At a stroke Sibley's whole expedition was crippled. Short of supplies when he began, he captured few fresh materials, and now virtually nothing was left. The starving Texans retreated back down the Rio Grande to El Paso.

Top: After 140 years, this near-perfect sword was returned to the site of the battle associated with it. James W. Carroll, Jr.'s unselfish gift will help the park preserve history for researchers and the public. *Bottom:* Union soldier John E. Briney fought in the Battle of Glorieta Pass, helping to turn back the invading Confederate forces (courtesy Pecos National Historical Park).

The paternal great-grandfather of James W Carroll, Jr. was John E. Briney. When he was a child, Carroll would pull a long saber out of his grandmother's closet in Maryland and play soldier with his brother. The saber was assumed by the family to be closet clutter. For years after his grandmother passed away, the solid-steel sword, made in 1846 with a 35-inch blade and carved bronze grip, hung over a den bookcase in his parents' home. All the family knew about the sword was that it had belonged to one John Briney who had served for five years in the Union Army during the Civil War.

No stories came with the saber. Briney, the only man who knew its history, did not talk about his Civil War experiences and the story was buried with him in 1920. The questions were answered, however, in 1998 when the father of James Carroll, Jr. died. In his father's safe-deposit box, the younger Carroll found a fragile piece of folded parchment that turned out to be Briney's discharge papers. The front described the 29-year-old soldier as a man of excellent character. On the back, Briney's commanding officer had scrawled out this note:

"This soldier was in an engagement against the Confederate troops from the state of Texas at Apache cãnon New Mex. On the 26th day of March 1862. Also he was engaged against the Confederate troops at the Battle of Glorietta New Mex. On the 28th day of March 1862. Also he was engaged against the Confederate troops from the state of Texas at Per Alto New Mex. On the 15th day of April.
s//
Capt 3rd Cavalry
Com/? ?? Co,"

As Carroll read the note it "made my hair stand on end." This was a surprising discovery and Carroll was stunned. After much deliberation, Carroll donated the saber once wielded in battle and then relegated to a closet to the Pecos National Historical Park, along with a portrait and the aforementioned discharge papers.

14

NORTH CAROLINA

*North Carolina State Archives,
109 E. Jones St., Raleigh,
NC 27601*

The North Carolina State Archives collects, preserves, and makes available for public use historical and evidential materials relating to North Carolina. Its holdings consist of the official records of state, county, and local governmental units and copies of federal and foreign government materials. Also preserved are private collections, organization records, maps, pamphlets, sound recordings, photographs, motion picture film, and a small reference library. In all, the archives houses over 50,000 linear feet of permanently valuable materials containing millions of individual items. Materials in the archives' collections constitute by far the most valuable assembly of North Carolinian manuscript records in existence.

General Robert E. Lee's Special Order 191

This copy of the controversial "lost dispatch" was donated to the state archives with the papers of General D.H. Hill, who was said to have let the information fall into Union hands.

A STRATEGIC LOSS

In early September of 1862, following the Confederate victory at Second Manassas, the Army of Northern Virginia under General Robert E. Lee moved into Maryland at Frederick. There, Lee wrote out his strategic plans in great detail. On September 9, he issued Special Order 191 giving strategic information on the division of units at the beginning of his Maryland campaign. A copy was sent to General Thomas "Stonewall" Jackson, who in his own hand made a copy that he sent to General D.H. Hill. Hill kept the order with his papers, which were later deposited in the North Carolina State Archives by his family.

On the morning of September 13, 1862, George McClellan's Army of the Potomac, in pursuit of the Confederates who had invaded Maryland, drew close to Frederick. Shortly before noon, the infantry of the XII Corps bivouacked on ground recently occupied by the Confederate division of D.H. Hill. Lolling in a field south of the city, Pvt. Barton W. Mitchell of the 27th Indiana spied in the grass a package wrapped in paper. The package held three cigars, which Mitchell shared with comrades while he inspected their covering. He sat bolt upright when he realized he was holding a copy of Special Order No. 191, dated 9 September 1862 and signed by the adjutant general of the Army of Northern Virginia, Colonel Robert H. Chilton. At once he showed the order to Sergeant John M. Bless, who hastened it to their commander, Colonel Silas Colgrove. The colonel then saw to it that it was presented to McClellan himself.

The document handed to "Little Mac" was one of seven copies of the strategic order Lee had sent to his ranking subordinates. This particular copy had been intended for General

Hill; apparently a careless staff officer had lost it, though the information had reached its intended recipient through another source. The order revealed to McClellan that Lee had divided his army, sending three of its four parts southwestward from Frederick to capture the Union garrison at Harpers Ferry. With such information the Union commander could interpose among the detachments, defeating each. McClellan could not repress his glee, despite the presence of a group of local citizens whose audience with him the letter's arrival had interrupted. Later he exclaimed to a subordinate: "Here is a paper with which if I cannot whip Bobbie Lee I will be willing to go home!"

General Robert E. Lee's Special Order 191 of September 9, 1862 — the "lost dispatch" — was copied in General Thomas "Stonewall" Jackson's own hand and is a treasured document at the Cultural Resources Department of North Carolina. Pictured is page one of two of this controversial document (courtesy North Carolina Office of Archives and History, Raleigh, North Carolina).

Yet in his typical hesitant fashion, McClellan failed to exploit fully this remarkable stroke of luck. His army did not start for Harpers Ferry until the next morning, and in the interim, he painstakingly confirmed the authenticity of the order and scrutinized reports of large enemy forces in his front. Meanwhile, one of the citizens who had been at McClellan's side, a Southern sympathizer, hastened to Lee's army with the news that the order had been intercepted, enabling Lee to block McClellan's path on the 14th long enough to capture Harpers Ferry and reunite his army.

Controversy and mystery surround the story of how the orders came to be there. However, the dispatch was passed through the Union chain of command and gave McClellan advance notice of Lee's army's movements. Subsequently, Lee was defeated and driven back by McClellan's army at Sharpsburg (Antietam), Maryland on September 17, 1862.

Later, stories of the "lost dispatch" appeared in newspapers, and D.H. Hill was deemed largely to blame. In the aftermath of the Civil War, Hill carried on an extensive correspondence in an attempt to discover the circumstances surrounding the misplaced order.

Lieutenant Colonel W. W. Blackford in his book *War Years with Jeb Stuart* writes: "Each Division Commander was furnished with a copy of this paper for his information and guidance. General D.H. Hill, in leaving his camp dropped this order and it fell into the hands of McClellan, giving him full information of our position and movements as we had ourselves."

Finally, in 1885, Hill conceded that "an order from Lee directed to me was lost, I do not now doubt," but he denied that he had received it. To this day, students of the Civil War argue the question of who lost Special Order 191, how it happened, and what the long-term implications were.

The Letter of Isaac Avery

This poignant message in the archives was penned by a dying Confederate colonel, using his left hand after a bullet paralyzed him on the right side at Gettysburg.

DYING ALONE, FAR FROM HOME

Consider the circumstances of 35-year-old Colonel Isaac Erwin Avery of Burke County in the late afternoon of July 2, 1863. He and his fellow North Carolina soldiers found themselves pinned down in a wheat field under a flaming sun near the base of Cemetery Hill in a place called Gettysburg, Pennsylvania.

Avery was the grandson of Waightstill Avery, the fiery Revolutionary War hero who served as the first attorney general of North Carolina. As General Robert F. Hoke's senior colonel, Isaac Avery was thrust into command of Hoke's brigade at Gettysburg because Hoke had been badly injured and had narrowly missed losing his left arm in the fight near Chancellorsville two months earlier.

As the afternoon of July 2 wore on at Gettysburg, Union artillery placements atop Cemetery Hill and nearby Culps Hill began to roar and belch deadly fire. Then came the command from Major General Jubal Early. The small brigades of Hoke and General Harry Hays of Louisiana were to attack the heavily fortified enemy positions on East Cemetery Hill—then considered the most strategic position for Union General George Meade. From the hill, the Union soldiers could observe the Confederate assault columns in the twilight as they formed. Avery's three regiments moved to the right of Hays's Louisiana Tigers, a hard-fighting bunch of French-speaking Creoles.

Without yielding or retreating, the two brigades moved forward in the face of terrible fire from the twenty-two heavy field guns raining down a fiery curtain of shot and shell from the two hills. Well-protected Union sharpshooters sniped at the men as they made their relentless advance. The Southern soldiers hurdled fences and rock walls, and it took nearly an hour to move across the 700 yards of Pennsylvania landscape to reach the base of Cemetery Hill.

As the Confederates approached the hill, Colonel Avery was out in front, the only mounted soldier in the attack, leading his men on General Hoke's big black warhorse. As the two brigades began their ascent of the hill, they quickly smashed through the first Federal line. With darkness rapidly approaching and with thick smoke from the heavy gunfire now enveloping the hill, most of the Confederates were unaware that Avery had fallen at the base of the hill when a gunshot struck the colonel at the base of his neck on his right side.

The ball plowed its way through the blood vessels and nerves that supplied the upper extremities and resulted in an immediate paralysis to his right side. Avery was knocked from his horse, and as he lay bleeding to death so far away from home, he gathered enough strength to take from his coat a lead pencil and a scrap of paper. With his writing hand paralyzed, he used his left to scrawl a note which was addressed to his business partner and aide, Major Samuel McDow-

Top: This extraordinary letter from Colonel Isaac Avery (*bottom*) to his father was written on a piece of dingy brown Confederate notepaper and is a cherished document at the Cultural Resources Department of North Carolina (courtesy of the North Carolina Office of Archives and History, Raleigh, North Carolina).

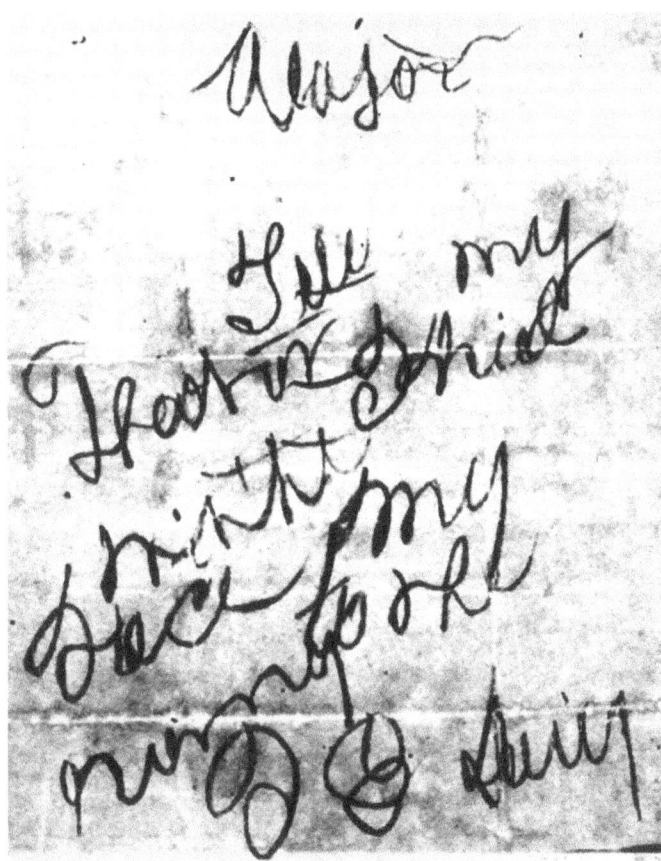

ell Tate. Colonel Isaac Erwin Avery's dying message read:

"Major: Tell my Father I died with my face to the enemy. I. E. Avery"

When the litter-bearers reached the dying officer, they found the blood-stained note near Avery's hand. His death came hours later at a field hospital.

His body was borne to the rear and later buried at or near Ball's Bluff National Cemetery near Leesburg, but was later removed to Hagerstown, Maryland.

Bennett Place, 4409 Bennett Memorial Rd., Durham, NC 27705

Bennett Place is a North Carolina Historic Site with a visitor center, trails, monuments and outdoor exhibits, with guided tours on the half-hour.

Site of Negotiations

Bennett Place was the site of negotiation for the Civil War's largest troop surrender. Today, this reconstructed farmhouse, kitchen, and smokehouse recall the lifestyle of an ordinary Southern farmer during the Civil War. This simple rural dwelling was located between Confederate General Johnston's headquarters in Greensboro and Union General Sherman's headquarters in Raleigh, North Carolina. In 1865, the two officers met at the Bennett place, where they signed surrender papers for Southern armies in the Carolinas, Georgia, and Florida. The surrender spared North Carolina the destruction experienced by her neighboring states.

The Surrender

In April 1865 two battle-weary adversaries, generals Johnston and Sherman, met under a flag of truce to discuss a peaceful solution to a tragic Civil War. The generals and their escorts met midway between their lines on the Hillsborough road, seven miles west of Durham. Seeking a proper site for a conference, Johnston suggested a simple farmhouse a short distance away. On three separate occasions the generals struggled to achieve equitable terms for surrender at the home of James and Nancy Bennett. Finally, on April 26, the Bennetts' home became the site of the largest troop surrender of the Civil War.

A controversial bottle of whiskey is prominently displayed on a table. Sherman furnished the whiskey and poured John C. Breckenridge a glass, but did not offer a refill. This prompted Breckenridge to later declare to Johnston: "General Sherman is a hog. Yes sir, a hog..." Breckenridge was the secretary of war for the Confederacy. He later escaped to Cuba and spent three years in exile before returning to his native state of Kentucky

Two days after the surrender, Captain William H. Day and other members of the Union Army arrived and offered Bennett $10 and a horse for the pictured drop-leaf table and cover. They said they had orders to take the table even if Bennett refused. With no choice but to comply, Bennett accepted Day's offer as the men left with the table and cover. Bennett was then told to walk to Durham's railroad station for the horse and payment. He waited all day but the horse and payment never came. The fate of the drop-leaf table and other items stolen from Bennetts' home is unknown.

After completing his notorious march from Atlanta to Savannah, Sherman turned his army of sixty thousand north. In March

Theodore Davis, an artist for *Harper's Weekly* and a favorite of General Sherman, made this sketch of the interior of James Bennett's house during Johnston's surrender (courtesy of the North Carolina Office of Archives and History, Raleigh, North Carolina).

The interior of the reconstructed Bennett home as it appears today.

1865 he entered North Carolina. Living off the land and destroying public buildings and factories, the Union commander brought his "total war" policy to a state that had been slow to secede. Johnston, recently placed in command of the Confederate Army of Tennessee, failed to stop Sherman at the Battle of Bentonville.

The days of the Confederacy were indeed numbered. Striving to avoid capture in Virginia, President Jefferson Davis arrived in Greensboro on April 11 and summoned Johnston to assess the strength of his army. Although Davis felt the South could continue the war, the confirmation of Lee's surrender prompted him to allow Johnston to confer with Sherman.

Accordingly, on April 17 the generals met at the Bennett farm. Before negotiations began, Sherman showed Johnston a telegram announcing the assassination of President Lincoln. Unaware of the difficulties that that tragedy would create, the generals began their conference. Sherman was prepared to offer terms similar to those that Grant gave Lee, military terms only. Johnston wanted "to arrange the terms of a permanent peace," including political terms.

At the second meeting, on April 18, Sherman submitted a "basis of agreement," which Johnston accepted. This liberal document provided for an armistice terminable at forty-eight hours' notice, the disbanding of armies following the deposit of arms in state arsenals, the recognition of state governments, the establishment of federal courts, the restoration of political and civil rights, and a general amnesty. Jefferson Davis approved those terms, but the Union rejected them in light of the hostility in Washington following the assassination of Lincoln. Grant therefore instructed Sherman to renegotiate terms similar to those given Lee at Appomattox.

Davis, who opposed the more stringent terms, ordered Johnston to disband the infantry and escape with his mounted troops. Realizing the tragedy of a prolonged war, Johnston disobeyed orders and met Sherman again on April 26. The final agreement was simply a military surrender that ended the war in the Carolinas, Georgia, and Florida, and affected 89,270 soldiers. The mustering-out of the troops and the issuing of paroles for those who surrendered took place in Greensboro. Three more Confederate surrenders followed— Richard Taylor in Alabama on May 4, E. Kirby Smith at New Orleans on May 26, and Stand Watie in the Indian Territory on June 23. Together with Lee's surrender, the Confederate forces were completely disbanded. The surren-

A 1921 fire destroyed the Bennett farmhouse and kitchen (*above*); only the stone chimney survived (courtesy North Carolina Office of Archives and History, Raleigh, NC). The farmhouse (*bottom*), one of the present buildings at the Bennett Place, was carefully reconstructed in the 1960s using Civil War sketches and early photographs as a guide. The simple farm dwelling and log kitchen convey a sense of what life was like for common citizens during a tragic period in our nation's history.

der spared North Carolina the destruction experienced by neighboring states.

In 1846, at age 40, James Bennett, his wife Nancy, and their three children had settled on the 325-acre farm in Orange County near the rail line that sparked the growth of Durham. The family cultivated corn, wheat, oats, and potatoes, and raised hogs. The versatile Bennett was also a tailor, a cobbler, and a seller of horse feed, tobacco plugs, and distilled liquor. His sons and son-in-law died during the war years. Advancing age and the loss of available labor prompted Bennett to enter into a sharecropping agreement with his in-laws. He ceased farming in 1875 and died in 1878; his wife died six years later.

15

OKLAHOMA

45th Infantry Division Museum, 2145 NE 36th Street, Oklahoma City, OK 73111

The 45th Infantry Division Museum is Oklahoma's only state operated museum dedicated to military history. The museum collects, preserves and exhibits objects relevant to the history of Oklahoma's military heritage from Spanish exploration to present day. Within the museum's collection are over 200 original Bill Mauldin World War II cartoons. Mauldin served on the staff of the 45th Division News and his "Willie and Joe" cartoons told the story of two typical World War II GI's.

The Whitworth Sharpshooter Rifle

This rifle was used throughout the Civil War by Confederate soldier Charles Thomas Ingram.

The Whitworth rifle remained in the Ingram family and was donated to the 45th Infantry Museum in the spring of 1988 by David Ingram of Shawnee, Oklahoma, and A.H. Spears of Beaufort, South Carolina, both descendants of Charles T. Ingram.

SURVIVAL OF THE "SHARPEST"

On November 16, 1838, Charles T. Ingram was born in Virginia, a state that had depleted its soil through tobacco farming and mismanagement. At this time as a result of poor agricultural crops, Virginians migrated into western territories looking for new farmland and opportunities. They moved to all parts of the republic. The largest number of emigrants, 57,000, settled in Kentucky, as another 40,700, including the Ingram family, settled in Missouri. John was still a young boy. In 1857 at the age of 19, Ingram struck out on his own to Bonham, a town in northeast Texas.

When the war broke out in 1861, the 24-year-old Ingram returned to Springfield to enlist with his friends in Company F, 3rd Regiment, Missouri Infantry. The 3rd Regiment was organized near Springfield, Missouri, in January 1862. Many of the men were from St. Louis and Jefferson and Franklin counties.

Ingram's first shoulder arm was an obsolete smooth-bore musket, but after Confederate victories at Carthage, Lexington, and Wilson's Creek, he was issued a captured Union Springfield rifle, the very best available at that time. After the Confederate defeat at Pea Ridge in 1862, Ingram and the 3rd Regiment were transferred east of the Mississippi River and assigned to the Army of West Tennessee. In October 1862, he fought in the losing, bloody battle of Corinth.

In the spring of 1863, Ingram's unit was again reassigned, this time to the Grand Gulf, Army of the Mississippi. When General Ulysses Grant's Union Army of 25,000 men crossed the Mississippi River below Grand Gulf to outflank Vicksburg, only the 1,500-man 3rd Regiment was there to oppose the invaders. The 3rd Regiment fought a delaying battle at

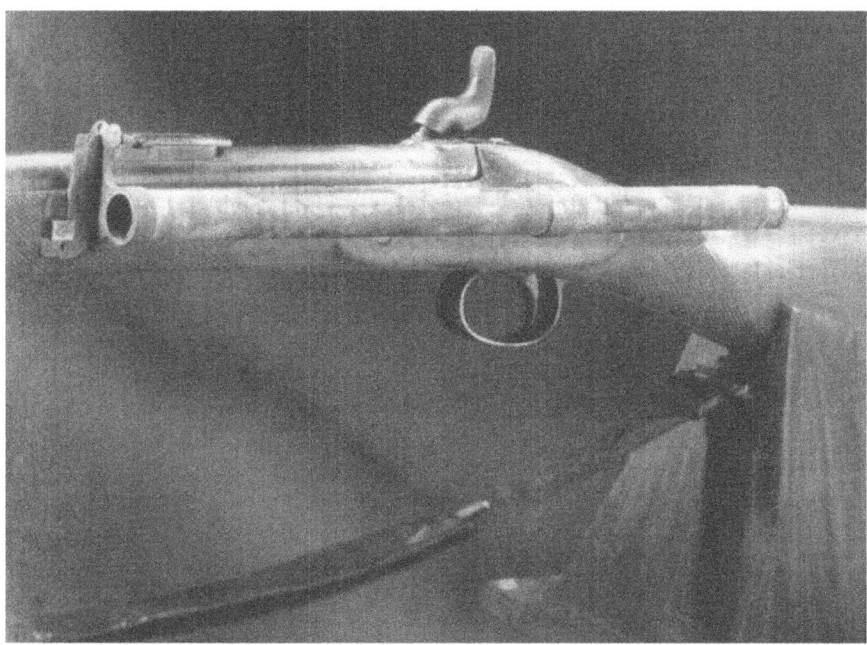

This British made Whitworth rifle on display in the 45th Infantry Division Museum was issued to Charles Thomas Ingram, who fought in 17 major skirmishes and in every campaign of the Western armies, yet he was never wounded. He refused many offers of promotion because he treasured his assignment as a Confederate sharpshooter with his deadly rifle that was accurate up to 1,500 yards. The rifle is .451 caliber and weighs 9.5 pounds, with a hexagonal bore with one twist in 20 inches. There is a Whitworth sharpshooter rifle in the State Museum at Nashville, Tennessee, and another at the Virginia Historical Society in Richmond, Virginia, but this is the only known Confederate Whitworth sharpshooter rifle with an authenticated record of combat which survives today (courtesy of the National Rifle Association).

Champion Hill and Big Black River Bridge before retreating into the fortifications of Vicksburg. The 3rd fought in various conflicts during the Vicksburg siege and surrendered on July 4, 1863. Charles Ingram along with his regiment and its commander, Colonel Francis M. Cockrell, were paroled by the grace of General Ulysses S. Grant.

After being repatriated back into the Confederate Army, Cockrell was promoted to brigadier general on July 18, 1863, and under his tutelage the Missouri Regiment became one of the best-drilled and most effective commands in the Army of Tennessee. It was at this time that 12 Whitworth sharpshooter rifles with Davidson telescopic sights and other critical Confederate supplies survived the dangerous trip through the Union blockade from England. Six of the rifles landed in Charleston, South Carolina, and six at Mobile, Alabama. These exceptional rifles, at a high cost of $500 in gold for each, were issued to the sharpshooters of the Confederate Army of Tennessee. Thus Charles Ingram acquired this remarkable rifle with a range nearly twice that of the Union Army Springfield rifle. Among the Civil War's most highly regarded weapons was this Whitworth sharpshooter rifle, which is generally rated as the most accurate small arm used. In the hands of skilled Confederate snipers, these rifles recorded hits at ranges in excess of 1,000 yards. Weighing less than 10 pounds, the Whitworth was far more portable than the heavy-barreled, bench-rested civilian target rifles.

In late 1863, Ingram joined the distinctive ranks of sharpshooters and fought a losing fight against General William T. Sherman's army in the battles of New Hope Church, Kennesaw Mountain, and Allatoona Pass. The Army of Tennessee under the command General John B. Hood further decimated this Confederate army at Franklin, Tennessee. The bitter finale came on April 9, 1865, when General Cockrell's few hundred men were overwhelmed by attacking Union forces and forced to surrender. Sharpshooter Ingram, not being assigned to a company, easily slipped away with his trusty rifle and, after stealing a horse, made his way west with the idea of joining up with General Kirby Smith in Trans-Mississippi. But when he reached the west bank of the Mississippi River he found that Smith had surrendered.

With the defeat of the South, Ingram left Mobile, Alabama, took his rifle and rode his horse to his home in Bonham, Texas. Years later, unfortunately, Mr. Ingram loaned the original Davidson scope to a friend for a Wyoming deer hunt. The scope was never returned.

Charles T. Ingram prospered in the mercantile business and in 1870 married and had four children. In 1897, the 59-year-old Ingram and his family moved to Durant in the Choctaw nation, where he engaged in the banking business. In 1908 at the age of 70, Ingram died in Durant, Oklahoma.

16

PENNSYLVANIA

Gettysburg National Military Park, 97 Taneytown Road, Gettysburg, PA 17325

Visitors to Gettysburg National Military Park should begin at the National Park Visitor Center and Museum, which offers several ways to tour the battlefield park. Plan to spend a minimum of four hours, though an entire day is more desirable if you wish to take advantage of the museum's electric map program, have a leisurely tour of the park, and visit nearby attractions. Self-guided auto tour route maps are available at the Visitor Center and Cyclorama Center information desks.

The McPherson Barn

Restored by the National Park Service in 1978, this barn and farm were the scene of the earliest fighting at Gettysburg.

THE BATTLE OF GETTYSBURG

The turning point of the American Civil War was Gettysburg, on July 1–3, 1863. In the end, the Federal Army of the Potomac under General Meade defeated the Confederate Army of Northern Virginia under General Lee. The Confederate leader escaped by a masterly retreat across the Potomac.

In the preceding December, Lee had repulsed an attack by Burnside at Fredericksburg, inflicting losses of over 10,000 men and forcing the Federals to retire behind the line of the Rappahannock River. Joe Hooker resumed the Federal offensive at Chancellorsville at the end of April, but Lee attacked him frontally and on his flanks, and Hooker was forced once more behind the Rappahannock after four days of heavy fighting. Both sides suffered heavy losses.

In June, Lee's army crossed the Potomac at two points not far from the battlefield of Antietam and perceiving that Meade, who succeeded Hooker on June 28, could isolate him in enemy country, Lee determined to turn toward Gettysburg and force the issue there in an all-out confrontation. One of Meade's primary objectives was the defense of Washington, and he took up a strong position south of Gettysburg, on Cemetery Ridge.

The great struggle began on July 1, when Union cavalry resisted the advance of Confederate troops. During the afternoon Richard Ewell's corps from the north threatened the Federal infantry which had come to Buford's help, and the Federals were driven back to Cemetery Ridge and Culp's Hill. Both armies were assembled by the afternoon of July 2, when the Union troops occupied a curve from Culp's Hill to the Devil's Den. The Confederates threatened them with a longer line, Longstreet's corps having taken up the position opposite the Round Top hills. Longstreet attacked about 4 P.M., and drove the Yankee troops back to the main ridge, but failed to carry the Round Tops, which were occupied by

The McPherson farm was located near where the first shot was fired on the first day of the Battle of Gettysburg. The fighting that swirled around the property was heavy and bloody for both sides, and it was here that Union cavalry held off Confederate infantry. Afterwards the McPherson buildings were used by Confederate surgeons as a temporary hospital. By 1978 only the barn remained, and time and the elements had exacted a heavy toll on the structure. Fortunately, it was restored by the National Park Service in that year (courtesy Gettysburg National Military Park).

Federal reinforcements. Later in the afternoon, Ewell's troops occupied Culp's Hill, and at nightfall, at Spangler's Springs, friend and foe knelt together to quench their thirst.

Meade decided to defend his positions, and early on July 3 regained Culp's Hill. After fierce artillery bombardment, Lee's center, under the command of General George Pickett, attacked strongly during the afternoon. The guns of the Federals swept the advancing troops, making great gaps in their ranks, but the ranks closed, and the advance continued; the Federal line was broken and the ridge gained, but it could not be held. Only a shattered remnant of Pickett's forces made its way back. With Meade's victory, Lee withdrew his broken army into Virginia.

When Lee's army retreated from Gettysburg, it left behind a community in shambles and more than 51,000 killed, wounded, and missing soldiers. Wounded and dying were crowded into nearly every building. Most of the dead lay in inadequate graves, hastily dug; some had not been buried at all.

This situation so distressed Pennsylvania's Governor Andrew Curtin that he commissioned a local attorney, David Wills, to purchase land for a proper burial ground for Union dead. Within four months of the battle, reinterment began on the seventeen acres that became Gettysburg National Cemetery.

The cemetery was dedicated on November 19, 1863, and the principal speaker, Edward Everett of Massachusetts, delivered a well-received two-hour oration rich in historical detail and classical allusion. He was followed by President Lincoln, who had been asked to make "a few appropriate remarks."

Lincoln's speech, the Gettysburg Address, contains 272 words and took about two minutes to deliver, and is considered a masterpiece of the English language, carved in stone at the Lincoln Memorial. The speech transformed Gettysburg from a scene of carnage into a hallowed symbol, giving meaning to the sacrifice of the dead and bestowing inspiration upon the living.

Fewer than half the Union battle dead finally interred in the national cemetery had been removed from their field graves by the day of the dedication. Within a few years, however, the bodies of more than 3,500 Union soldiers killed in the battle had been reinterred in the cemetery and the landscaping was completed. Following the war, the remains of 3,320 Confederate soldiers were removed from the battlefield to cemeteries in the South.

Cyclorama Painting of Picket's Charge

French artist Paul Philippoteaux and his team of twenty artists were hired in 1884 to complete four identical Gettysburg cycloramas; one has disappeared, one became tent material, one is in storage at Wake Forest University, and the other wound up at Gettysburg in 1913.

It had a rough journey. In its early years, the cyclorama traveled from Boston to Philadelphia, then back to Boston, and was unrolled and then packed up again and again. It was stashed in a crate, stored in a parking lot, subjected to moisture and rot, and sliced into panels for display in a Newark department store, with pieces lost along the way. Even when this slice of American heritage came under the National Park Service's stewardship in the 1940s, the neglect continued. For decades it hung improperly in a museum with poor ventilation and a leaky roof.

The painting, as ragged as an old army tent, is currently undergoing a $9 million restoration. The restorative work will recreate a foreground with props that once added

At 375 feet long and 27 feet tall, this priceless, colossal, 360-degree canvas by French artist Paul Philippoteaux is located in the Gettysburg National Military Park Museum. It brilliantly captures what was to be the beginning of the end for the Confederacy (courtesy Gettysburg National Military Park).

depth and prospective. The original three-dimensional elements—wagon wheels, canvas stretchers, fence rails, guns, canteens, grass, rocks, soil and the like—have been missing for years. Old photographs will provide the details necessary for the restoration.

PICKETT'S CHARGE

On July 3, 1863, Pickett's division lined up on Seminary Ridge to participate in the grand assault on the Union center. His 5,000 Virginians charged the Federal line on Cemetery Ridge and briefly broke through, but were thrown back after desperate fighting. Pickett lost nearly one-half of his division, including all three of his brigadier generals—Garnett, Kemper, and Armistead. His command in shambles, the general's spirit was nearly crushed. It was a terrible defeat for him and his men, but a special event that would ever after be known as "Pickett's Charge" and the high water mark of the Southern rebellion.

Frock coat of General James J. Pettigrew

A "frock" coat was so-called because of the "start" that extended down near the knee, the design was first mandated by U.S. Army regulations in 1851 and remained in use until 1872.

VALOR UNDER FIRE

The gifted General James Johnston Pettigrew fought valiantly in this famous infantry assault, where he was severely wounded in the left hand by a canister ball. Despite the great pain, Pettigrew remained with his soldiers until it was obvious that the attack had failed. Holding his bloody hand, the despondent officer walked toward Seminary Ridge and encountered General Lee. Pettigrew attempted to speak, but Lee, seeing the horrible wound, spoke first: "General, I am sorry to see you are wounded; go to the rear." With a painful salute, the handsome officer said nothing but continued to the rear.

Civilians Portrait of Virginia "Jennie" Wade

Wade was 20 and was the first and only civilian killed during the Battle of Gettysburg. She was baking bread for the Union army in the McClellan home when a bullet passed through two wooden doors and killed her. The home is now known as the Jennie Wade House and is open for tours.

A Confederate Soldier's Bible

This is one of many artifacts found on and around the Gettysburg battlefield that are on display at the park. After the departure of the armies from Gettysburg on July 5, the landscape was covered with the carcasses of horses and mounds of earth that covered the fallen combatants, many in graves so shallow that rain washed away the soil to reveal the grisly sight of hands, arms, and heads protruding from the ground. Personal effects were scattered all over the battlefield.

Photograph of a Bride

A soldier lost this photograph, most likely of his wife, on the battlefield at Gettysburg. Godey's Lady's Book in 1949 declared while the emblem of bridal purity, but during the Civil War some brides wore purple, representing honor and courage, as a tribute to the dead.

The Civil War and Underground Railroad Museum of Philadelphia, 1805 Pine Street, Philadelphia, PA 19103

Firearms, edged weapons, uniforms, accouterments, and flags are among the objects exhibited in the library and museum's three floors. Here one can view the uniform General George Meade wore while commanding the Union army at Gettysburg, the saddle upon which General John Reynolds was riding when killed at Gettysburg, and the words written by President Abraham Lincoln. The

Top: General James J. Pettigrew's frock coat is on display at Gettysburg (courtesy Gettysburg National Military Park). *Bottom:* Virginia "Jennie" Wade died instantly when struck by a sniper's bullet while baking bread in her sister's home. As the only civilian killed during the battle she has earned her place among the heroes at the Gettysburg National Military Park. An engraving of Jennie, including the brooch she wore in this picture, is on display. Her hair is parted in the middle with a braid regally crowning the top. Her kind brown eyes reflect a life too soon lost, and her youth and modesty still speak to today's generation about civilian causalities during wartime. Gold script on the bottom of the picture declares that the image was taken at "Tipton Photo, Gettysburg, Pa." A stain of dark ink tattoos the back of the photograph with the poignant words "Jennie Wade, killed at Gettysburg" (courtesy Gettysburg National Military Park).

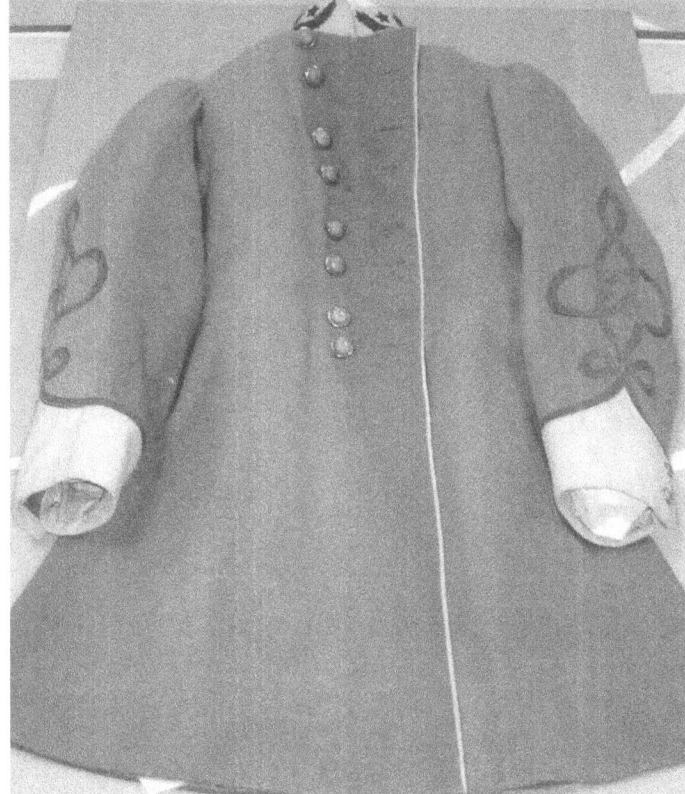

library and museum also examines such subjects as women in the war, the black soldier, military railroads, English contributions, and prisoners of war.

The Philadelphia institution is noted for its superb research facilities, which are being continually upgraded. With more than 12,000 volumes, 100 linear feet of archival/manuscript material, over 100 reels of microfilm, and nearly 5,000 photographs, the facility is one of the most comprehensive Civil War libraries in the country.

Old Baldy

Major General George G. Meade's horse, wounded at Gettysburg and in other battles, survived his master by 10 years. His head was preserved and is an artifact at the Civil War Underground Railroad Museum.

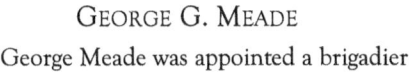

George G. Meade

George Meade was appointed a brigadier

A Confederate soldier at Gettysburg carried this originally leather-bound Bible into battle. It is embossed with acanthus leaves and the cover and back are missing; the cover page reads "Holy Bible, containing Old and New Testaments; translated out of original tongues; and with former translations diligently compared and revised by his Majesty's special command. Appointed to be read in churches" (courtesy Gettysburg National Military Park).

general of volunteers a few months after the start of the Civil War. He was assigned command of a brigade of Pennsylvania Reserves, which he led competently. During the Seven Days' Battles, Meade was severely wounded at the Battle of Glendale. He recovered in time for the Second Battle of Bull Run, after which he received a divisional command. Meade also distinguished himself during the Battle of South Mountain, and at Antietam, he replaced the wounded Joseph Hooker as commander of I Corps, again performing well.

After Hooker resigned command of the Army of the Potomac, Meade replaced him on June 28, 1863, three days before the Battle of Gettysburg, where he was victorious in the titanic confrontation that is considered the turning point of the war. Meade skillfully deployed his forces in a defensive battle, reacting swiftly to fierce assaults on his line's left, right, and center. Following severe losses during Pickett's Charge, Robert E. Lee's army retreated back into Virginia, but Meade was criticized by Lincoln and others for not aggressively pursuing the Confederates during their retreat.

When Lieutenant General Ulysses S. Grant was appointed commander of all Union armies in 1864, Meade and the Army of the Potomac became subordinate to him. Grant made his headquarters with Meade for the remainder of the war. Meade fought effectively during the Overland Campaign (including the Battle of the Wilderness) and the Battle of Petersburg, after which Grant requested that he be promoted to major general of the regular army. Although he fought gallantly during the Appomattox Campaign, Meade felt slighted that Grant and cavalry commander Major General Philip Sheridan received most of the credit. He continued to command the Army of the Potomac until the Union victory in 1865.

When the news of Lee's surrender at Appomattox arrived, Meade was uncharacteristically elated. Despite on illness, Meade rode his favorite horse "Old Baldy" up to the front to announce the surrender to his troops. Wounded at least fourteen times during the Civil War, including once at Gettysburg, "Old Baldy" survived his master by ten years, dying on Dec. 16, 1882, at the age of thirty. The brave steed spent his final years in comfortable retirement on a farm near Philadelphia. He was the riderless horse in General Meade's funeral procession in Philadelphia in 1872.

Historical Society of Pennsylvania, 1300 Locust Street, Philadelphia, PA 19107

"Found on the Gettysburg Battlefield during the war 1863" is the inked message scrawled across this photograph of an unidentified woman in her wedding dress. The purity of the white fashionable wedding gown stands in stark contrast to the death and decay of the bloody battlefield. Her right arm rests on her breast, and a crown of ivory flowers encircles her head, a symbol of new life and young love. On the back of the picture is stamped "Charles D. Federicks & Co./Specialite/587 Broadway, New York" (courtesy Gettysburg National Military Park).

The Historical Society of Pennsylvania is one of the largest family history libraries in the nation, has excellent collections on local and regional history, and offers a manuscript collection renowned for its seventeenth-, eighteenth-, and nineteenth-century holdings. The society houses nearly 600,000 books, pamphlets, serials, and microfilm reels, twenty million manuscripts; and over 300,000 graphics items, making it one of the nation's largest non-governmental repositories of documentary materials. It also holds many great national treasures, such as the first draft of the United States Constitution, an original printer's proof of the Declaration of Independence, and the earliest surviving American photograph. But the true strength of the collection is the overall breadth

Somewhat gruesome by today's standards is this example of the taxidermist's art, the head and neck of Meade's favorite horse, "Old Baldy" (courtesy Gettysburg National Military Park).

and depth of materials that together offer a rich, complex portrait of U.S. history and society from the seventeenth century to the present.

The Lotus-Eating diary

LIFE IN CONFEDERATE PRISONS

Frank T. Bennett enlisted in the 55th Pennsylvania Volunteers and was given a commission as a lieutenant colonel. In March 1862, he was captured on Tybee Island, off the coast of Georgia. He was subsequently imprisoned in jails in Charleston and Columbia, South Carolina, but was paroled in October 1862. Bennett was captured again later in the war and held in Libby Prison in Richmond, Virginia. His diary, kept during his imprisonment in South Carolina, describes the dreariness and hopelessness of prison life and includes Bennett's thoughts on slavery, Southerners, and the war. The diary was written on the pages of a softbound novel entitled *Lotus Eating: A Summer Book*. This book was probably the only paper to which Bennett had access during his imprisonment. Entries, occasionally written in pencil and sometimes scribbled in between the lines of the novel, were usually well written and at times rather eloquent. Lines of poetry can be found throughout Bennett's writings. The front of the volume has a Bureau of Pensions sticker on it, perhaps indicating that a descendant had submitted the diary in order to claim benefits.

Bennett began his diary on March 18 with a description of how and why he was captured on Tybee Island. He places the blame squarely on the shoulders of his unit's pickets, who had not kept a proper watch. He and his men were therefore caught "like mice in a trap." Bennett also comments on the kindness of his captors, one of whom shared food from his haversack with the prisoners. Bennett and the other prisoners were escorted to Charleston Jail, where they arrived on March 18.

Bennett wrote each day until March 23, and then stopped writing until May 1. He describes his first few days in Charleston Jail as not unpleasant. He was in better spirits than some of his comrades, although he acknowledged that "a glass of whiskey kindly given us by Captain Sage may have had much to do with this." Although he was aghast at "this narrow cell, the nail-studded door doubly locked and padlocked upon us and the strangely barred windows," he was hopeful that the situation would be temporary and was generally impressed with the kind treatment he received upon arrival.

When Bennett again picks up his diary on May 1, he reveals that the five weeks since his last entry had not been as pleasant as the first few days. The brutal monotony of prison life has dampened his spirits, but he finds that the visits of Sheriff Dingle, "a gentlemanly man" who visits on Sundays, were a unique pleasure. Bennett reflected that the half-hour spent with Sheriff Dingle passes more quickly than a minute on other days. Prison life was a never-ending cycle: "eat, sleep and smoke, then sleep, smoke and eat."

Bennett got a change in scenery when he was transported to a Columbia jail on May 2. Although he had found Charleston Jail unpleasant due to the "Negroes and scum of the white population" that had inhabited it, he found the Columbia jail even less pleasant. The guards in Columbia were not as accommodating, and no one smuggled newspapers to him as they had sometimes done before. Bennett continued writing regularly in his diary, usually remarking upon his ceaseless boredom: "How long would it take to make a mere animal of me! There can be naught of the godlike inside the iron bars of a prison." Bennett felt increasingly disconsolate about his situation and his hopes of being released dwindled with each passing day.

Bennett seems to have tried to escape the monotony of prison life through his diary. He describes and comments upon the conscription act, how presses on both sides grossly misrepresent the war, and speaks of the handsomeness of the Southern ladies. He also ponders the

General George C. Meade (courtesy Library of Congress).

alleged evils of slavery, stating that many white workers were in worse situations than the slaves, and that from what he had seen thus far in the South, slaves were not ill-treated or abused the way Northerners commonly thought them to be. In some passages Bennett even expresses some sympathy for the Southern cause, declaring, "If we win this war and ever succeed in subjugating the South—their farewell to democracy and liberty—we will have sold our birthright for a mess of pottage." State-

General Meade carried this model 1860 officer's sword throughout the Civil War (courtesy Gettysburg National Military Park).

LOTUS-EATING.

A SUMMER BOOK.

BY G. W. CURTIS,

AUTHOR OF "NILE NOTES OF A HOWADJI," "THE HOWADJI IN SYRIA," &c.

Beautifully Illustrated,
FROM DESIGNS BY KENSETT.

NEW YORK:
HARPER & BROTHERS, PUBLISHERS.
329 & 331 PEARL STREET,
FRANKLIN SQUARE.
1852.

Frank T. Bennett's wartime diary was written on the pages of a softbound novel entitled *Lotus Eating: A Summer Book* (courtesy of the Historical Society of Pennsylvania).

ments like this may have reflected Bennett's diminishing faith in his own government, which did not seem to make efforts toward obtaining his release. Other passages condemn the South, and Bennett often complains about the poor conditions in the jail and the nastiness of several of the guards who watch them. At one point he states, "The much-boasted chivalry of the South does not certainly show itself in the treatment of these unfortunates who, by the fate of war became inmates of its prisons."

After writing sporadically throughout the summer of 1862, Bennett wrote a handful of entries in September, then picked up his pen in early October and described his delight at learning that he was to be released. On October 7 he and several other prisoners left for Richmond, Virginia. He arrived at Libby Prison on October 10 and was paroled that afternoon. He left early the next morning, and his last entries end with the words "Home again!"

Pennsylvania Capitol Preservation Committee, Room 630 Main Capitol Building, Harrisburg, PA 17120

After the Civil War, Pennsylvania's military department was responsible for collecting the state-issued flags. Many of the colors were collected as the regiments mustered out of service. On July 4, 1866, the battle flags were officially returned to the custody of the Commonwealth. The following day the flags were moved to Harrisburg, where they were stored in special cases in the State Arsenal building. In 1872, the legislature appropriated money to furnish a flag room on the second floor of the Hills Capitol. This flag room was completed in 1873, where these treasured relics remained until 1894. Twenty years later, on June 14, 1914, after architect Joseph M. Huston had finished the new capitol building, Pennsylvania veterans came together once again to transfer their flags back to the new edifice. The flags remained virtually untouched until 1982 when the Capitol Preservation Committee initiated its "Save the Flags" project. Textile conservators carefully removed the flags from the rotunda and transported them to a state facility near the capitol. Over a period of five years, 390 Civil War and 22 Spanish-American flags were conserved. Each flag is now kept on an acid-free panel stored in custom-designed, stainless steel storage units. The flags are protected from light, dust, fluctuating temperatures, humidity, and excessive handling.

The 97th's Infantry Flag

This flag is one of 390 Civil War flags preserved at the Pennsylvania state capitol. It was carried during an attack on Fort Fisher in the regiment led by Galusha Pennypacker, who, at 20, became the youngest person ever to reach the rank of general in the U.S. Army.

> ATTACKS ON FORT FISHER
>
> Major General Benjamin Butler was relieved of command of the Army of the James and assigned to lead an amphibious expedition against Fort Fisher, which protected Wilmington, N.C., the South's last open seaport on the Atlantic coast. Learning that large numbers of Union troops had embarked from Hampton Roads on December 13, 1864, Lee dispatched Hoke's Division to meet the expected attack on Fort Fisher. On December 24, the Union fleet under Rear Admiral David D. Porter arrived to begin shelling the fort. An infantry division disembarked from transports to test the fort's defenses. The Federal assault had already begun when Hoke approached, discouraging further Union attempts. Butler called off the expedition on December 27 and returned to Fort Monroe.
>
> After the failure of his December expedition against Fort Fisher, Butler was relieved of command. Major General Alfred Terry was placed in command of a "provisional corps," including Paine's Division of U.S. Colored Troops, and was supported by a naval force of nearly sixty vessels, designed to renew operations against the fort.
>
> After a preliminary bombardment directed by Admiral Porter on January 13, Union forces landed and prepared for an attack on Major General Robert Hoke's infantry line. On the

15th, a select force moved on the fort from the rear. A valiant attack late in the afternoon, following the bloody repulse of a naval landing party, carried the parapet. The Confederate garrison surrendered, opening the way for a Federal thrust against Wilmington.

Soldiers and Sailors National Military Museum and Memorial, 4141 Fifth Street, Pittsburgh, PA 15213

The Grand Army of the Republic (GAR) conceived the Soldiers and Sailors National Military Museum and Memorial during the 1890s. It was originally built to recognize the sacrifice, valor, and patriotism of the Civil War veterans of Allegheny County, Pennsylvania. Today, it honors all of the men and women of Pennsylvania who have served the United States in its military endeavors during our country's entire history. The museum and memorial is the largest memorial building in the United States dedicated solely to America's fighting personnel, representing all branches of service while honoring both the career and citizen soldier.

Portrait of Dog Jack

This mascot of a Pittsburgh fire company saw plenty of action throughout the Civil War, when the firefighters enlisted, so did he.

A CANINE WARRIOR
AND COMPANION

Many Civil War units adopted animal mascots to cheer the troops and add a little

At the battle of Fort Fisher this second state color — the 97th Regiment Pennsylvania Infantry Flag — was hit by an astonishing 107 bullets and one canister shot. Every hole that appears in the flag is a bullet hole! The regiment's colonel, Galusha Pennypacker, was wounded twice but refused to be carried from the field until the flag was planted on the fort. Subsequently, he gallantly led the charge over a traverse and planted these colors. He won the Congressional Medal of Honor for his bravery (courtesy of Brian Hunt and the Pennsylvania Capitol Preservation Committee).

16. Pennsylvania

The parapet at Fort Fisher after the Federal Navy and seaborne expeditions against the Atlantic coast stronghold of the Confederacy (courtesy Library of Congress).

color to a life of short rations, inclement weather, and the interminable waiting that is part of every military person's life. Dog Jack, a mixed-breed canine warrior, began his illustrious career as mascot of the Niagara Volunteer Fire Company on Penn Avenue, which was headquartered close to the present-day Engine Company 3 in the Strip District of Pittsburgh. After war broke out in 1861, Jack accompanied the firefighters when they enlisted in the 102nd Regiment, Pennsylvania Infantry. "Dog Jack," as he was commonly called, first heard the hostile roar of cannon fire in the ill-fated Battle of First Manassas. In the spring of 1862 he sailed with his troops down the Appomattox River and became a participant in the Battle of the Peninsula. His commanding general was the noted General George Meade, but Dog Jack was most impressed with Thaddeus Lowe's observation balloon, equipment that caused much excitement with the Niagara Volunteer Company, under Dog Jack's command. He had to resort to barking at his men in order to enforce discipline during these moments of animation. He was said to understand bugle calls and would obey orders only from his own regiment.

At the battle of Salvage Station, Virginia, Dog Jack was captured for a couple of days but managed to escape in time to rejoin his company for the Battle of Malvern Hill, fought on July 1, 1862. During this battle, Dog Jack was badly wounded but returned to the regiment after recovering in a field hospital.

When the 102nd moved north to the area around Fredericksburg, Dog Jack continued his heroic accomplishments. He roamed freely over the battlefield, seeking out wounded and dead comrades. It was during this period of the conflict, in May 1863 at Salem Church, that Dog Jack let his guard down for a moment and the dastardly Rebels captured him. Imprisoned, the brave little fellow missed his comrades as they fought in the big battle of Gettysburg. After six months of captivity, however, the

"Dog Jack" conducted himself with such valor during his service with the 102nd Regiment, Pennsylvania Infantry, that his fellow soldiers commissioned this portrait of him at war's end. The painting hangs in the Soldiers and Sailors National Military Museum and Memorial in the Pittsburgh suburb of Oakland. The brown-and-white dog with the brown patch over his left eye reposes on the floor, his head turned to gaze straight at the viewer (courtesy of Soldiers and Sailors National Military Museum and Memorial, Pittsburgh, Pennsylvania).

102nd caught up with the courageous canine and managed to exchange a Confederate prisoner for him.

Dog Jack returned in time to experience the killing grounds of the Battle of the Wilderness, followed a day later by the Battle of Spotsylvania and the siege of Petersburg, all in Virginia. In the summer of 1864, Dog Jack and the 102nd were sent from Petersburg to the Shenandoah Valley where Jack, with the help of General Philip H. Sheridan, reinvigorated the Union forces, leading to the complete defeat of the Confederates and the destruction by fire of the Shenandoah Valley.

In the final stages of the Valley Campaign, as the Shenandoah battles were called, Jack's detachment was ordered back to Petersburg. He was serving garrison duty in Frederick, Maryland, when on December 23, 1864, the plucky mascot was listed as missing in action. Like so many of his comrades-in-arms, Dog Jack disappeared and was never found. Some guessed that the silver collar the men had purchased for him attracted the attention of the locals, who might have sold it. And the citizens of Frederick certainly would have needed the money: after all, six months earlier Confederate General Jubal Early had demanded $200,000 in greenbacks from the Frederick's citizenry or, he threatened, he would torch their town. They paid what was an exorbitant sum in those days. Whatever the truth, poor Dog Jack sacrificed himself for his country, loyal to the end to the men of the Pennsylvania 102nd.

17

SOUTH CAROLINA

Fort Sumter National Monument, 340 Concord Street Charleston, SC

The Fort Sumter Visitor Education Center at Liberty Square offers a spot by the Cooper River where visitors may sit, rest, read, and watch the harbor traffic in a very pleasant setting. Fort Sumter reached by boat in the Charleston harbor, is designated historic, so recreational activities are limited to passive pursuits such as scenic viewing and bird watching. Ranger talks are offered to each group of visitors who arrive by ferry. Wayside exhibits explain the historic resources found throughout the site and the vistas visible from the observation level.

Garrison Flags

These flags preserved at Fort Sumter were the last Union standards to fly over the fort before its surrender to Confederate forces 34 hours after the start of the war. Confederates did not evacuate the fort until Feb. 17, 1865, in the face of an advancing General William T. Sherman. The "storm flag" was used at rallies throughout the North to stir patriotism, and was "auctioned" repeatedly to raise funds for the war effort.

THE WAR IS BEGINNING

For thirty-four hours in 1861, Confederate forces constantly bombarded Fort Sumter, forcing the Federal garrison to surrender.

During the artillery duel, Confederates had launched more than 4,000 shells. Federal guns had fired infrequently but had managed to take off part of the roof of the Moultrie Hotel. Several soldiers had been wounded, as had a few civilians, but not a single person had died.

While Charlestonians staged a glorious celebration, Confederate soldiers prepared to hoist South Carolina's Palmetto flag over the captured installation. Union Major Robert Anderson, who had been promised the privilege of a final salute to his own flag, insisted upon giving it. At first he planned to fire 100 guns, but was forced to settle for just 50 because wind carried a burning ember to a stack of cartridges during the 50th salute to the U.S. flag and a great explosion injured five men and killed gunner Daniel Hough, the first casualty of the war that was now three days old.

Jubilant Southerners danced in the streets of cities. In eight states where sentiment was divided, leaders begged for action "appropriate to events that have taken place at Fort Sumter."

The Palmetto flag symbolized the start of a dreaded Civil War, or what the South would insist was a War Between the States. For the next four years Fort Sumter remained a Confederate stronghold despite frequent Union attempts to capture it. Between 1863 and 1865 determined Confederate soldiers kept Federal land and naval forces at bay. It was virtually demolished and finally evacuated

Major Robert Anderson raised this large garrison flag over unfinished Fort Sumter in Charleston harbor on December 26, 1860. It was flying in the early dawn of April 12, 1861, when Confederate forces began firing mortar shells from Charleston harbor; the missiles burst over the fort, inaugurating the Civil War. On April 13th, the garrison flag was ripped from below the fourth red stripe down (courtesy Fort Sumter National Monument).

After Fort Sumter's garrison flag was damaged, Union soldiers raised this smaller "storm flag" in its place (courtesy Fort Sumter National Monument).

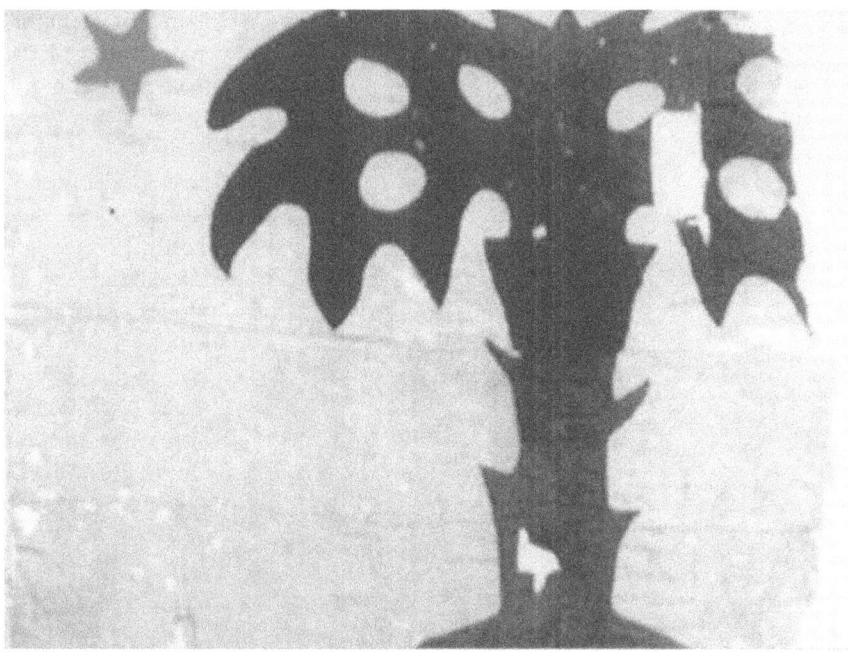

Top: On April 14, 1861, men of the 18th South Carolina Regiment raised their state's Palmetto flag over the captured fort (courtesy Fort Sumter National Monument). *Bottom:* On April 27, 1863, General Pierre Gustave Toutant ("P.G.T.") Beauregard presented the Citadel with a fifteen-inch hollow shot that had been fired at Fort Sumter by Union Navy ironclads. On April 7, the South Atlantic Squadron under Rear Admiral S.F. Du Pont had bombarded Fort Sumter but made little impact on the Confederate defenses of Charleston Harbor. Although several of Hunter's units had embarked on transports, the infantry had not landed, so the joint operation was abandoned. Hollow Shot (courtesy of the Citadel Archives and Museum, Charleston, South Carolina)

on February 17, 1865, as Sherman's troops approached Charleston.

Although Fort Sumter was not captured in the early days of the war, Charleston became a city of ruins, as later in the war 13,000 shells bombarded the port. Fired at a great elevation, the shells blew churches, hotels, stores, homes, public buildings, and stables into millions of fragments.

The Citadel Archives and Museum, 171 Moultrie St., Charleston, SC 29409

The Citadel Archives and Museum is the repository for historic material pertaining to The Military College of South Carolina. The

Major General William B. Hazen removed the shell (courtesy Library of Congress).

collection includes personal papers, photographs, diaries, engravings, uniforms, and other artifacts from 1842 to the present.

The Fifteen Inch Hollow Shot

In 1863, General P.G.T. Beauregard presented to the Citadel a shot fired by a Union navy vessel at For Sumter. Two years later, in an act of sweet revenge, Union Major General William B. Hazen, serving under the command of General Sherman, removed the shell from Columbia, South Carolina, and presented it to the United States Military Academy. Inscribed on the base are these words: "Presented to the U.S. Military Academy by Major General Wm. B. Hazen, April 1, 1865." In 1913, Secretary of War Henry L. Stimson returned the shell to the Citadel at the request of Colonel Oliver J. Bond, president of the Citadel.

SOUTH CAROLINA'S MILITARY SCHOOLS

The Citadel Academy in Charleston and the Arsenal Academy in Columbia, S.C., were known officially as the South Carolina Military Academy. The cadets spent their freshman year in Columbia and then transferred to the Citadel for the remaining three years.

After his march to the sea, Sherman set out from Savannah in two columns into South Carolina. Charlestonians and Citadel officials believed that Sherman was going to invade Charleston. Perhaps they had gotten wind of the letter of General Henry Halleck, chief of staff at Washington, addressed to General Sherman, suggesting that "should you capture Charleston, I hope that by some accident the place may be destroyed and a little salt should be sown upon the site, it may prevent the growth of future crops of nullification and secession." To which General Sherman had replied in a similar vein: "I will bear in mind your hint as to Charleston and I do not think salt will be necessary."

The college's valuable possessions were

sent to the Arsenal in Columbia for safekeeping. Ironically, Sherman's horde left Charleston unharmed but sacked the capital city, Columbia, destroying or carrying off all of the valuables that had been sent there from Charleston for safekeeping. Likewise, all of the records and valuables sent from the Citadel were destroyed with the one exception, this fifteen-inch hollow shot that had been fired by the Federal fleet at Fort Sumter in April 1863.

18

TENNESSEE

Stones River National Battlefield (Nashville)

The park is approximately thirty miles from Nashville (Interstate 24). Take Exit 76 and turn left onto Medical Center Parkway. Turn left onto Thompson Lane. Turn right, just before the Thompson Lane Bridge, onto the access road to Old Nashville Highway. Turn left at the stop sign onto Old Nashville Highway. The park entrance is about ¼ mile away, on the left.

Stones River National Battlefield manages a wealth of objects and information in its museum, archives, and library collections. Park rangers and volunteers use these collections to prepare exhibits and interpretive programs. Today, more than 6,100 Union soldiers are buried in Stones River National Cemetery. Of these, 2,562 are unknown. Nearly 1,000 veterans and some family members who served in the century since the Civil War are also interred there.

Grave marker of Lieutenant Christian Nix

Many Civil War-era grave markers were made of wood, but the high cost of maintaining them led Congress to appropriate $1 million in 1873 to erect a headstone for each grave in the national cemeteries of stone.

> ### BATTLE OF PERRYVILLE AND STONES RIVER
>
> After General Braxton Bragg's defeat at Perryville, Kentucky, October 8, 1862, he and his Confederate Army of the Mississippi retreated, reorganized, and were designated the Army of Tennessee. They then advanced to Murfreesboro, Tennessee, and prepared to go into winter quarters.
>
> Major General William S. Rosecrans's Union Army of the Cumberland followed Bragg from Kentucky to Nashville. Rosecrans left Nashville on December 26 with about 45,000 men, aiming to defeat Bragg's army. He found the Rebel army on December 29 and went into camp that night, within hearing distance of the Rebels.
>
> At dawn on the 31st, Bragg's men attacked the Union right flank. The Confederates drove the Union line back to the Nashville Pike by 10 A.M., but there it held. Union reinforcements arrived from Rosecrans's left in the late forenoon to bolster the stand and before fighting stopped that day, the Federals had established a new, strong line. On New Year's Day, both armies marked time. Bragg surmised that Rosecrans would now withdraw, but the next morning he was still in position.
>
> In late afternoon, Bragg hurled one of his divisions at a Union division that, on January 1, had crossed Stones River and had taken up a strong position on the bluff east of the river. The Confederates drove most of the Federals back across McFadden's Ford, but with the assistance of artillery, the Federals repulsed the

attack, compelling the Rebels to retire to their original position. Bragg left the field on January 4 and 5, retreating to Shelbyville and Tullahoma, Tennessee. Rosecrans did not pursue, but when the Confederates retired, he claimed the victory. Stones River boosted Union morale. The Confederates had been thrown back in the east, west, and in the Trans-Mississippi.

Although the battle was tactically indecisive, it provided a much-needed boost to the North. Lincoln later wrote to General Rosecrans, "I can never forget you gave us a hard-earned victory, which had there been a defeat instead, the nation could scarcely have lived over."

Lookout Mountain Battlefield (Chattanooga)

From Interstate 24, at Exit 178 follow signs to Lookout Mountain. At the top of Lookout Mountain follow signs to Point Park where the Lookout Mountain Battlefield Visitor Center is located.

The 3,000 acre Lookout Mountain Battlefield contains monuments, historical markers, trails, and scenic vistas. Point Park, located on the top of the mountain, is the most prominent feature. The Visitor Center, located across the street from Point Park, displays James Walker's 13'×33' painting *Battle of Lookout Mountain*.

The Battle of Lookout Mountain

Artist James Walker painted this work at the behest of General Joseph Hooker. He also painted the *Battle of Gettysburg* and, in 1862, *The Battle of Chapultepec*, which hangs in the U.S. Senate.

This grim reminder of combat, the wooden grave marker of Lieutenant Christian Nix, also resides in the museum collection at Stone River National Battlefield. It is inscribed: "Lieut Nix, 24 Wis, Buried, Jan 5." There are traces of gold leaf lettering in the inscription (courtesy Stones River National Battlefield).

THE BATTLE ABOVE THE CLOUDS

Confederate troops were posted high upon Lookout Mountain in 1863, almost 2,000 feet above the Tennessee River Valley, and rained cannon fire down upon the Union troops encamped at Chattanooga. Looking down on what was then a village, they aimed for the river and rail traffic entering with supplies from Union-controlled western Tennessee. Surrounded, and with no supply lines, the Union troops seemed destined to fall.

Their fate changed in mid–October, though, with the fresh leadership of Major General George Thomas. Shortly thereafter,

On November 23, Thomas's troops overtook Confederates occupying Orchard Knob, between Chattanooga and the mountains. The next day, in what became known as the "Battle Above the Clouds," Hooker drove his men on to victory at Lookout Mountain. Some of the bloodiest fighting took place there at Cravens House. On November 25, the last day of the battle, the Union Army crushed the Rebel line, forcing the Rebs to retreat farther south into Georgia, a retreat that would lead ultimately to the South's defeat in the Civil War. The three-day Battle of Chattanooga was one of the most dramatic turnabouts in American military history. When the fighting ceased, the hitherto underdog Union forces had driven Confederate troops away from Chattanooga and into Georgia, setting the stage for Sherman's triumphant "march to the sea" a year later.

Andrew Johnson National Historic Site, 121 Monument Avenue Greeneville, TN 37743

The Andrew Johnson National Historic Site honors the life of the seventeenth president of the United States. Andrew Johnson's presidency, 1865–1869, symbolized the United States Constitution at work in the national turmoil following Lincoln's assassination, a period in which a nation torn by civil war strived to heal itself and become unified once again. His tenure of office shaped the future of the United States and his influence continues today.

The visitor center houses a museum collection, Andrew Johnson's Tailor Shop, and a 13½-minute orientation film. The house contains a family photo album, exhibits explaining Andrew Johnson's humble origins and rise in the political world, and a timeline relating the events in Johnson's life to the current events of his time. Johnson owned this home twenty-four years, both before and after his presidency. His descendants continued to live here until 1956. Today, the house is decorated extensively with the original furnishings and belongings.

During the battle, Private Joseph R. Prentice, Company E, 19th U.S. Infantry, voluntarily retrieved the body of his commanding officer. Under direct unceasing rifle fire, he brought his mortally wounded leader off the field. For his bravery he was awarded this Medal of Honor (courtesy Stones River National Battlefield).

Major General Joseph Hooker moved into the area with 20,000 Union soldiers. Ulysses S. Grant followed. This was shaping up to be a massive battle, and Grant ordered Union engineers to construct a pontoon bridge west of town, giving the army access to shipments of food and ammunition once again. When Sherman arrived with 16,000 more men in mid–November, the Union Army was ready to fight.

This spectacular example of military art was painted by artist James Walker, who had been given a commission of $20,000 by General Joseph Hooker to paint an accurate, detailed representation of the fighting on Lookout Mountain. The painting took Walker four years to complete. This is the center of the 13-by-30-foot work; it depicts Hooker mounted on a white charger horse, facing Major John Reynolds, commander of artillery. Many years later, the 700-pound painting was stored in a barn by Hooker's relatives, the Tredwell family. In 1957, the Tredwells donated this painting to the Chickamauga and Chattanooga Military Park, and with the help of generous donations the painting was restored at a cost of $101,000 (courtesy Lookout Mountain Battlefield).

Silver Pitcher and Goblets

Among the artifacts from Andrew Johnson's Life and his family house is a silver service he was given during the Civil War.

ANDREW JOHNSON

Andrew Johnson was born December 29, 1808, in Raleigh, North Carolina, but at age sixteen he and his brother relocated to Greeneville, Tennessee, where he found work as a tailor.

After a remarkable self-education, Johnson was elected governor of Tennessee, serving from 1853 to 1857, and was elected as a Democrat to the United States Senate, serving from October 8, 1857, to March 4, 1862. When the South seceded from the Union, Johnson was the only senator from the seceding states to continue serving in Congress. He was appointed military governor of Tennessee by President Lincoln in 1862.

In 1864 he was elected vice president on the Republican Party—now renamed the "Union Party"—ticket with Lincoln. Later, succeeding the slain president, he took charge of Presidential Reconstruction—that is, the first phase of Reconstruction—which lasted until the Radical Republicans gained control of Congress in the 1866 elections. His conciliatory policies towards the South, his hurry to reincorporate the former Confederate states back into the union, and his vetoes of civil rights bills inflamed the Radical Republicans. The Radicals in the House of Representatives impeached him in 1868; he was the first president to be so treated, but he was acquitted by a single vote in the Senate.

Johnson returned to Greeneville, where he remained active in politics. He returned to public office once more in 1875, winning election to the U.S. Senate, but later that same year he suffered a stroke and died soon thereafter. The seventeenth president of the United States was laid to rest on his land in his beloved Tennessee.

The President Andrew Johnson Collection, Tusculum College, 60 Shiloh Road, Greeneville, TN 37743

The collection is housed at the President Andrew Johnson Museum and Library and is operated by the Department of Museum Programs and Studies at Tusculum College.

The collection contains approximately 100 three-dimensional artifacts, ranging from the former president's top hat and political memorabilia to a copy of Lincoln's life-mask. The museum contains over 350 linear feet of records that reflect the history of this oldest college in Tennessee. The selections include books, drawings, and prints from the eighteenth through the turn of the twentieth centuries

President Jefferson Davis's Tea-or-Coffee Train

Auctioned by Varina Davis, purchased and repurchased, sent to Abraham Lincoln, a unique porcelain tea trolley ended up in the hands of Andrew Johnson's descendants in Tennessee.

A WELL-TRAVELED TRAIN

An exquisite and novel "tea and coffee warmer" serving set had been part of the Jefferson Davis household. It was sold by auction and consignment by Varina Davis on March 28, 1885, by the Richmond firm of Ellett, Bell and Fox. Among the other items offered were a suite of rosewood and satin

This silver service was presented by the citizens of Nashville to Andrew Johnson, military governor of the state of Tennessee during the Civil War (courtesy Andrew Johnson National Historic Site).

Andrew Johnson used this military desk, also referred to as a "campaign desk," while military governor of Tennessee, 1862–1865. The desk, which is portable and could be set up easily anywhere, proved very useful during wartime. It was on exhibit for many years, but is not at present. The front folds up creating a box with lock inset and handles on each end for carrying. The interior contains many pigeonholes and two drawers. "GOV. A. JOHNSON" is painted on each side above the handles (courtesy Andrew Johnson National Historic Site).

damask parlor furniture, French glassware, vases, Japanese cabinets and boxes, a music box, dinnerware, and many other handsome articles. Mrs. Davis collected more than $8,000 in gold coins in proceeds from the sales. Three days prior to the auction this notice appeared: "A few ladies of South Fairham Parish, Essex County, Virginia, had donated to the Confederate Treasury, 1 gold bracelet, 3 gold rings, 3 gold breastpins and many other gold and silver items." It was a common practice for patriotic citizens to contribute money, gold, jewels, and silver to the relief of the treasury, but there is confirmation that the Davis's objects d'art and tea pot were not offered up for the general welfare of the citizenry.

The tongue-in-cheek story of the little tea-or-coffee train was best told on April 17, 1865, by the Richmond Whig, a Unionist newspaper published by William Ira Smith, who must certainly have gotten a kick out of publishing the article.

From Jefferson to Abraham— a Keepsake

We examined on Saturday the mechanism of one of those curious souvenirs of the war that, like their recipients "cannot escape history." We allude to a fancy coffee or tea sett [sic], we don't know which, which formerly graced the mansion of President Jefferson Davis, but which was disposed of at auction with silver, &c., by Messrs. Bell, Ellett & Co., Pearl Street, a few days before the evacuation, when Mr. Davis concluded to "decline housekeeping" and make a tour for his health. The coffee or tea sett in question is a perfect miniature or *facsimile* of a railroad locomotive, with tender attached; the locomotive boiler receives the coffee or tea, makes and discharges it through a spigot, a steam whistle indicating when [the] coffee or tea is ready. The boiler of

This elegant tea-and-coffee warmer, a gift from the French ambassador, belonged to Jefferson Davis and was sent to Abraham Lincoln after the capture of Richmond. Before it could reach Washington, Lincoln was assassinated, so the piece was commandeered by President Andrew Johnson. Later, after storage at the U. S. Treasury Department, it was returned to Johnson's daughter, Martha Johnson Patterson, in Greeneville, Tennessee. Johnson's great-granddaughter presented the historical piece to Tusculum College, Greeneville, Tennessee (courtesy Tusculum College, Department of Museum Program and Studies, Greeneville, Tennessee).

the same to Colonel Friedman, of Philadelphia, a gentleman well known in and out of the army. Colonel Friedman purchased the souvenir with a view of presenting the same to President Lincoln, and to save the public the trouble of an effort of inspecting the mechanism we have described, we may as well state that the rare article is on its way to Washington and the White House.

It may not be inappropriate to mention that upon the side of the locomotive, in miniature, is emblazoned "President Jefferson Davis," showing that the testimonial, locomotive and tender, were built expressly for his use or purpose. Upon the front, just above where the 'cow catcher' ought to be, appears the Confederate national banner and battle flag, entwined with the national ensign of France. Wonder if the whole affair wasn't a present from "Little Nap," as a testimonial of his "sincere regard and friendship," and as an offset to his entertainment of the kitchen

the locomotive is of porcelain, and the figure of the fireman, of the same material, appears on the locomotive, vigorously ringing the bell, which, we suppose, means the breakfast, dinner or supper bell. The tender, which is an admixture of brass and other metal, carries the sugar in an elegant sugar caisson, with a goblet for cognac and stunning small cut glasses. The sides of the tender are embellished with racks for cigars. The most curious contrivance of all is a secret music box located somewhere in the tender, which, being set, plays eight popular airs, sufficient in length to entertain a supper, dinner or breakfast table. It got obstreperous on Saturday and refused to play "Dixie." The whole establishment, engine and tender, rests upon two beautiful enameled waiters.

As we have said before, the article was disposed of at auction, and was purchased by an Italian, A. Barratti, who, several days ago, disposed of

waiters, Slidell and Mason, who were entertained at the back entry? However, the locomotive and tender are off the track, and all aboard are reported either killed, wounded or prisoner.

Little Nap is a short for "Little Napoleon," also known as General Ulysses S. Grant. John Slidell and James Mason were old friends of President Jefferson Davis and were Confederate politicians aiming to be ambassadors to France and England. Before this could happen, however, they were both taken off a British ship on the high seas in 1861 by the Union Navy and imprisoned in Boston. This incident was widely reported in Southern papers and caused a tremendous uproar in England; after consideration by all sides the two men were released.

19

TEXAS

*The Rosenberg Library,
2310 Sealy Avenue,
Galveston, TX
77550*

The Rosenberg Library was founded in 1871 and is the oldest public library in Texas. The map collection includes maps and charts of Texas, the Gulf of Mexico, the Caribbean Sea, and adjacent coasts, with maps dating from the sixteenth century to the present. Holdings of the museum department include historical artifacts pertaining to Galveston or early Texas, paintings of Galveston subjects and a sizable collection of Russian and Greek icons. The Fox Rare Book Room contains incunabula, first editions, and examples of fine printing.

Framed Baseboard Struck by Shell

A local Realtor and former Confederate officer preserved a small piece of the war. Souvenirs of the war were popular from its immediate aftermath.

BATTLE OF GALVESTON

As part of the Union blockade of the Texas coast, Commander William B. Renshaw led his squadron of eight ships into Galveston harbor to demand surrender of the most important Texas port on October 4, 1862. Brigadier General Paul O. Hébert, commanding the Confederate District of Texas, had removed most of the heavy artillery from Galveston Island, which he believed to be indefensible. The Fort Point garrison fired on the federal ships, which responded by dismounting the Confederate cannon with return shots. Confederate Colonel Joseph J. Cook, in command on the island, arranged a four-day truce while he evacuated his men to the mainland. The Union ships held the harbor, but 264 men of the 42nd Massachusetts Infantry, led by Colonel I. S. Burrell, did not arrive until December 25 to occupy Kuhn's Wharf and patrol the town.

When Major General John Bankhead Magruder replaced Hébert in the fall of 1862, the new district commander began to organize for the recapture of Galveston. For a naval attack, he placed artillery and dismounted cavalry from Sibley's brigade, led by Colonel Thomas Green, aboard two river steamers, the *Bayou City* and the *Neptune*, commanded by Captain Leon Smith. Magruder gathered infantry and cavalry, led by Brig. General William R. Scurry, supported by twenty light and heavy cannons, and planned to cross the railroad bridge onto the island to capture the federal forces ashore. To meet the attack, Renshaw had six ships that mounted twenty-nine pieces of heavy artillery.

The Confederates entered Galveston on New Year's night, January 1, 1863, and opened fire before dawn. Cook failed to seize the wharf because of the short ladders provided for his men, and naval guns helped drive back the

During the Battle of Galveston a shell fragment lodged in the center of this piece of baseboard, which was later framed and measures approximately 11½ × 14 inches. The baseboard was retrieved from Galveston's Hendley Building, built in 1859. The structure was located near Galveston harbor and served as a warehouse. The "H.M. [Henry Martyn] Trueheart" mentioned on the plaque was a successful local real estate agent and Confederate officer. The plaque was donated to the Rosenberg Library on February 7, 1912, by Trueheart's daughter, Sallie Trueheart Williams (courtesy the Rosenberg Library).

assault. Then, the Confederate "cottonclads"—so called because of the protection afforded by bales of cotton on their decks—struck from the rear of the Union squadron. The *Harriet Lane* sank the Confederate's *Neptune* when it tried to ram the Union ship, but men from the *Bayou City* boarded and seized the federal vessel despite the explosions from their own heavy cannon. Renshaw's flagship, the *Westfield*, ran aground, and the commander died trying to blow up his ship rather than surrender it. The other Union ships sailed out to sea, ignoring Confederate surrender demands, which could be enforced only upon the abandoned federal infantry in town.

Magruder had retaken Galveston with a loss of twenty-six killed and 117 wounded. Union losses included the captured infantry and the *Harriet Lane*, about 150 casualties on the naval ships, and the destruction of the *Westfield*. The port remained under Confederate control for the rest of the war.

20

VIRGINIA

The Arlington House Cemetery, Arlington National Cemetery, Arlington, VA

Arlington House was the home of Robert E. Lee and his family for thirty years and is uniquely associated with the Washington and Custis families. George Washington Parke Custis built the house to be both his home and a memorial to George Washington, his step-grandfather. It is now preserved as a memorial to General Lee, who gained the respect of Americans in both the North and the South. the house is operated as a memorial by the National Park Service.

Locks of Hair from General R.E. Lee and His Horse, Traveller

Preserved at Lee's family home are locks of hair from the general and his horse, handed down through the family. A tradition developed in Victorian times of saving a lock of hair from a recently deceased family member. These locks were fashioned into jewelry or framed, as here. This became an art form in the nineteenth century to help remember lost loved ones.

GENERAL ROBERT EDWARD LEE

Robert Edward Lee was born on January 19, 1807, at "Stratford" in Westmoreland County, Virginia. He was the fifth child born to Henry "Light-Horse Harry" Lee and his second wife, Ann Hill (Carter) Lee. He grew up in an area where George Washington was still a living memory, and young Robert had many ties to Revolutionary War heroes.

Educated in the Alexandria, Virginia, schools, he obtained an appointment to West Point in 1825. In 1829, Lee graduated second in his class without a single demerit against his name.

During the Mexican War, he was promoted to colonel based on his gallantry and distinguished conduct in performing vital scouting missions.

When Virginia withdrew from the Union, Lee resigned his commission rather than assist in suppressing the insurrection. He resigned just two days after General Winfield Scott offered him the position of chief of command of U.S. forces. After weighing the pros and cons of the crisis, he chose his love and allegiance to his home commonwealth of Virginia over his allegiance to the U.S. He proceeded to Richmond to become commander-in-chief of the military and naval forces of Virginia. When these forces joined the Confederate services, he was appointed brigadier general in the regular Confederate Army.

Lee returned to Richmond in March of 1862 to become the chief military advisor to President Jefferson Davis. In the field, Lee was a bold, unhesitating leader; when he developed a battle plan,

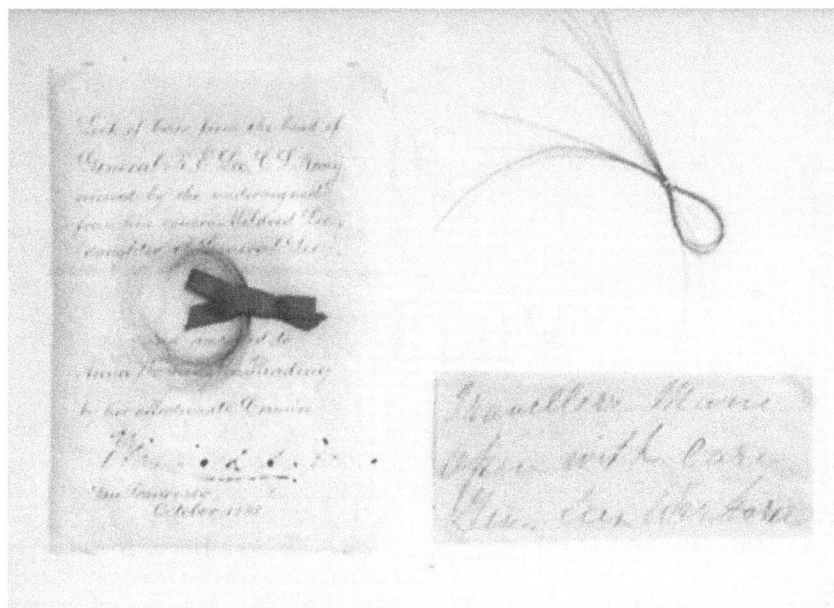

This card, attached to a sheet of notebook paper, contains a lock of Lee's hair, along with a few strands of mane from Lee's famed steed Traveller. The general's curled white lock is tied with red ribbon attached to the card that contains an explanation of its origin (courtesy Arlington House).

he took the initiative and acted at once. For example, he had Jackson cut off Union supplies and reinforcements at Seven Pines. He also stopped McClellan's threat to Richmond during the Seven Days' Battles (June 26–July 2, 1861). At the Battle of Second Manassas, Lee defeated Pope. At the Battle of Antietam, his Northern thrust was checked by McClellan, but he repulsed Burnside at Fredericksburg in December of 1862. In May of 1863, Lee defeated Hooker at Chancellorsville but was forced into a defensive strategy after Gettysburg in July. On April 9, 1865, Lee surrendered to Ulysses S. Grant at the village of Appomattox Court House.

After the surrender, Lee returned to Richmond. Soon after, he assumed the presidency of Washington College (now Washington and Lee University) in Lexington, Virginia. His exemplary conduct both in war and in peace made him a hero and a legend to thousands of ex–Confederates even before his death on October 12, 1870. Robert E. Lee is buried in Lexington.

Lee owned several horses that he rode during the Civil War, including Lucy Long, The Roan, and Ajax. But it was Traveller (spelled by Lee with two l's in the traditional English manner) who was his favorite and who would be most identified with him. Traveller was a nervous, spirited four-year-old colt when Lee purchased him from a Confederate officer in the spring of 1862. Soon, the two were inseparable as Lee rode him through the thick of battle after battle. In fact, Lee rode Traveller until the end of Lee's life. Not long after General Lee's death in October 1870, however, Traveller stepped on a rusty nail in his stall and died of tetanus. He is buried just yards from his master, outside the Lee Chapel in Lexington.

Lee's Pocket Bible

The pocket Bible was used by Lee during the Civil War. It is the King James Version and was printed in 1838. The flyleaf is signed, "R E Lee Lt. Colonel U.S.A." A card inside reads, "Bible — used by General R.E. Lee 1861–1865."

Accompanying the Bible is a bookmark with a note on lined paper that reads as follows:

"Xmas 1868; dear general; as evidence of my respect for you as a gentleman, soldier & patriot

Robert Edward Lee (courtesy Library of Congress).

Top: The pocket Bible that Lee carried with him throughout the Civil War (courtesy Arlington House). *Bottom:* Robert E. Lee served as commandant of West Point from 1852 to 1855, and this engraved, five-shot .28-caliber revolver was presented to him by arms manufacturer Samuel Colt at the end of Lee's tenure there. The cylinder is engraved with a dueling scene flanked on either side with trees. On the rear of the gun's grips is engraved, "Col. R.E. Lee, U.S. Army." The revolver's mint condition suggests that Lee rarely used it (courtesy Arlington House).

and in gratitude to you for many acts of reported, substantial kindness to one of my sons I send you this bookmark worked by my-self at my age of seventy seven years. I beg that it may mark the 13th of Corinthians 1st. with respect M.S. Baldwin"

West Point Commandant's Revolver

Samuel Colt presented a revolver to Lee at the end of Lee's stint as head of West Point. During his three-year tenure, he improved the buildings and courses and spent a lot of time with the cadets.

The gun was presented in this rectangular, maroon, velvet-lined case with two covered compartments, dividers, and a padded lid.

Library of Virginia, 800 East Broad Street, Richmond, VA

The Library of Virginia collections include books, magazines, newspapers, state and federal publications, county and city government records, state government records, architectural drawings and plans, Bible records, business records, organization records, personal papers, genealogical notes and charts, maps, rare books, broadsides, sheet music, posters, prints and engravings, postcards, paintings, sculpture and photographs.

Virginia's Ordinance of Secession

Each Confederate state ratified its own ordinance of secession between 1860 and 1861, typically by a special convention or a general referendum. Virginia's voters approved the ordinance — except in the northwestern part of the state, which led to the creation of West Virginia.

A HISTORIC
DOCUMENT REPATRIATED

The *Ordinance of Secession of Virginia* reads as follows:

AN ORDINANCE

to repeal the ratification of the Constitution of the United State of America by the State of Virginia, and to resume all the rights and powers granted under said Constitution.

The people of Virginia in their ratification of the Constitution of the United States of America, adopted by them in convention on the twenty-fifth day of June, in the year of our Lord one thousand seven hundred and eighty-eight, having declared that the powers granted under said Constitution were derived from the people of the United States and might be resumed whensoever the same should be perverted to their injury and oppression, and the Federal Government having perverted said powers not only to the injury of the people of Virginia, but to the oppression of the Southern slave-holding States:

Now, therefore, we, the people of Virginia, do declare and ordain, That the ordinance adopted by the people of this State in convention on the twenty-fifth day of June, in the year of our Lord one thousand seven hundred and eighty-eight, whereby the Constitution of the United States of America was ratified, and all acts of the General Assembly of this State ratifying and adopting amendments to said Constitution, are hereby repealed and abrogated; that the union between the State of Virginia and the other States under the Constitution aforesaid is hereby dissolved, and that the State of Virginia is in the full possession and exercise of all the rights of sovereignty which belong and appertain to a **free** and **independent State.**

And they do further declare, That said Constitution of the United States of America is no longer binding on any of the citizens of this State.

This ordinance shall take effect and be an act of this day, when ratified by a majority of the votes of the people of this State cast at a poll to be taken thereon on the fourth Thursday in May next, in pursuance of a schedule hereafter to be enacted.

Adopted by the convention of Virginia April 17, 1861

In 1865, this engrossed parchment, 36 inches by 24 inches, was "found among some old papers in the state house in Richmond, Virginia" and taken by Charles W. Bullis, a member of the 80th Regiment, New York Volunteers. In 1872, Bullis married and later revealed to his wife that he had the original *Ordinance of Secession of Virginia* that had been signed by 143 distinguished citizens of the Secession Convention. On October 19, 1877, Bullis's widow sold the document to Major George H. Treadwell. Fortunately, during these years the historic original ordinance had been placed into a metal cylinder that protected the somewhat yellowed document from the passage of time. The ordinance was inherited by George Curtis Treadwell, the son of George H., who kept it until 1930.

During all the intervening years its whereabouts had been an unsolved mystery for the people of Virginia, but students of history entertained the hope that the priceless manuscript would ultimately return home. And it did, as a gift from the aforementioned George Curtis Treadwell and his wife. The document, along with several notary public statements and affidavits, was mailed to the state librarian and received on December 31, 1930. After sixty-five years, the looted treasure of a Union soldier had returned home.

Lee's Confidential Dispatches

General Lee's correspondence to Confederate President Jefferson Davis returned to Virginia's archives in 1949.

WELL-TRAVELED PAPERS

As Richmond was being evacuated by the Confederate government, Robert E. Lee's confidential dispatches to Jefferson Davis were removed from the executive mansion in the top of a trunk belonging to Davis's secretary, Burton N. Harrison. The trunk was sent south in the train carrying Jefferson Davis and his executive staff, including his chief clerk with the appropriate name of Micajah H. Clark. Davis's train had chugged out of Richmond a few hours in front of the Confederate gold train and headed in the same direction. Because of the hot pursuit of the Union Army, Clark left Harrison's trunk containing Lee's confidential dispatches behind in Washington, Georgia. The valuable papers had been entrusted to Mrs. M.E. Robertson, wife of the cashier of the Bank of Georgia, and host to President Davis while he was in the Georgia town.

The presidential entourage hastily left Washington, proceeding, it was hoped, towards the safety of a Florida port and the open sea. Davis

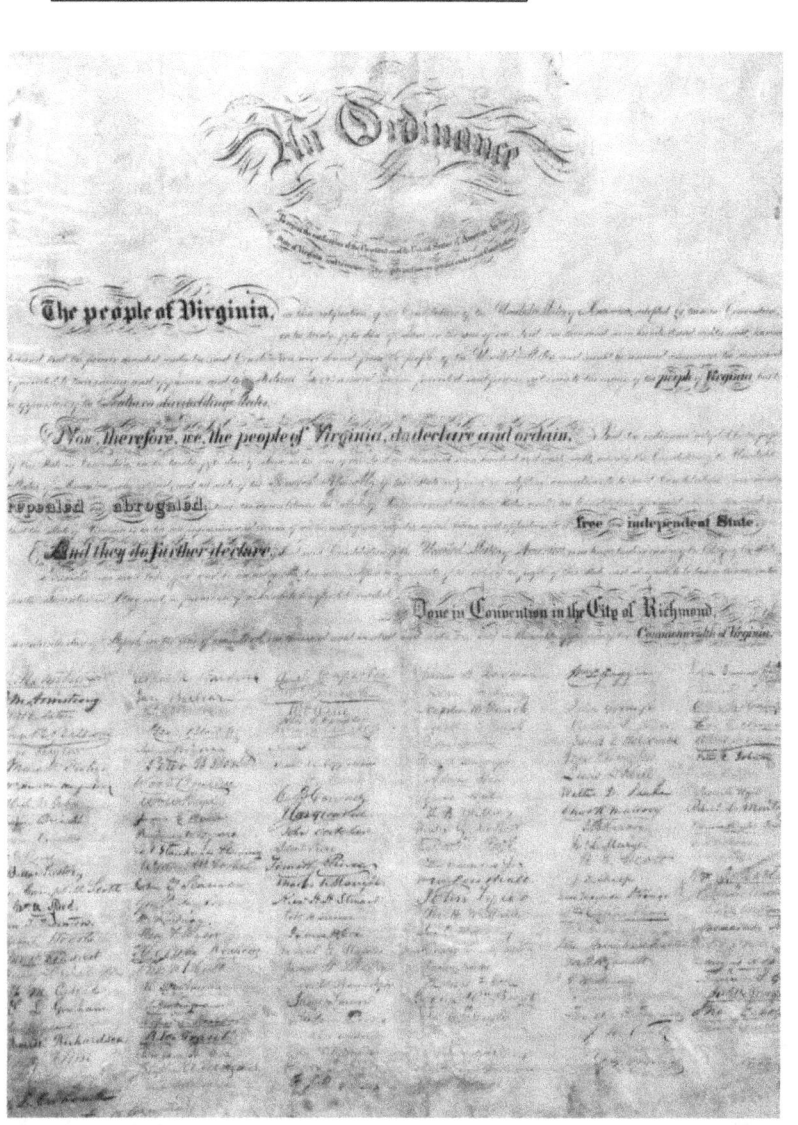

At the fall of Richmond, this yellowed historical document, *An Ordinance of Secession of Virginia*, was looted from the Capitol of the Confederacy by Charles W. Bullis, a Union soldier (courtesy The Library of Virginia).

After a long adventurous trip, Lee's confidential dispatches to Jefferson Davis are today stored safely in the Library of Virginia's vault. Boxes numbered 345 and 346 contain the dispatches, written on various kinds of paper, from the fine, thin, blue English paper which General Lee seemed to prefer, to the coarse "Confederate gray" sheets made in the South during the war (courtesy of the Library of Virginia).

removed himself from the wagon train, however, and was subsequently captured. Clark returned north to look after the safety of the records which had been left behind, but he soon learned that Union troops were occupying the Georgia town, and their presence deterred him from any attempt to retrieve Lee's dispatches.

After Burton Harrison was released from prison, his trunk with Lee's dispatches was sent to him in New York from Georgia by Mrs. Robertson. For several years Harrison stored the trunk in a warehouse.

In 1870, Harrison was persuaded to entrust the trunk to the care of a Southern lawyer, Colonel Charles C. Jones, now residing in Brooklyn, New York. Financially ruined by the war, Jones had moved his legal practice in 1866 to New York City, where he had made encouraging progress in mending his fortunes. He was unable to resist the temptation of publicizing the documents in his care, and in 1876 he published one of Lee's dispatches. This came to the attention of Davis, who sent his assistant to retrieve the papers. Jones denied that he had the dispatches and further lied by saying that the published dispatch had been borrowed from an unnamed person in Richmond. In 1877, he returned, dispatches in hand, to his native Georgia. Settling near Augusta at a small estate known as Montrose, he reestablished his law practice.

Charles C. Jones proceeded to earn a reputation as foremost Georgia historian of the nineteenth century. Also a noted autograph and manuscript collector and an accomplished amateur archaeologist, Jones in later years became a prominent memorializer of "The Lost Cause," and a critic of the New South. Over the next sixteen years he won increasing fame as a historian, collector, and orator. He died of Bright's disease at Montrose on July 19, 1893.

It was discovered at some point that Jones had sold the Lee dispatches to one Wymberley J. De Renne. Between 1844 and 1969, the first three generations of the De Renne family of Savannah made notable contributions to Georgia history by collecting materials relating to the state's past and by printing primary sources and other historical works relating to Georgia. This splendid collection was left to the Hargrett Rare Book and Manuscript Library at the University of Georgia.

From De Renne, the Lee dispatch collec-

General Bradley T. Johnson (*above*) preferred a sword formerly belonging to a Union sergeant. Today on display in the Museum of the Confederacy, the sword was originally taken from a sergeant in the Sixth Massachusetts Regiment when the regiment was attacked by a mob on April 19, 1861, while passing through Baltimore. An unidentified assailant jerked the sword and belt from the sergeant and ran him through with it. This was undoubtedly the first blood shed in the war. As captain of the Frederick Volunteers, Johnson reached Baltimore on the morning of April 20. He had an antiquated sword, so Marshal of Police George P. Kane gave him the one the police had seized the afternoon before from the Yankee sergeant's murderer. General Johnson wore the sword, as captain and major, up to and through Manassas (*Battles and Leaders of the Civil War*, De Vinne Press, Volume IV, page 521).

matters. A highly regarded elder statesman, Baruch was described as a man of immense charm and enjoyed a larger-than-life reputation that matched his considerable fortune. He is remembered as one of the most powerful men of the early twentieth century. Baruch's father, Simon, had served as a field surgeon on Robert E. Lee's staff, so Baruch was particularly interested in the collection of Lee's wartime dispatches, and on October 3, 1949, he presented the rare historical documents to the Library of Virginia.

Museum of the Confederacy, 12th and Clay Street, Richmond, VA

The Museum of the Confederacy houses the world's largest and most comprehensive collection of Confederate artifacts, including the personal belongings of many legendary Confederate generals and those of common soldiers. The museum boasts three floors of unique exhibits and houses the Eleanor S. Brockenbrough Library. The museum also serves as an international center of study on the role of the Confederacy in the American Civil War.

Sergeant's Sword of General Bradley T. Johnson

The sword later carried by General Bradley T. Johnson may have shed the first blood of the Civil War.

A RIOT IN BALTIMORE

The following remarkable document recorded for posterity the difficulties facing

tion came into the possession of Bernard Baruch, the famed financier, stock market and commodities speculator, statesman, and presidential adviser. After his success in business, Baruch devoted several decades to advising American presidents from Woodrow Wilson to John F. Kennedy on economic and financial

Union troops both in the South and in the border states such as Maryland:

Report of Colonel Edward F. Jones, Sixth Massachusetts Militia, regarding the April 19, 1861 Baltimore Riot.

In accordance with Special Orders, No. 6, I proceeded with my command towards the city of Washington, leaving Boston on the evening of the 17th April, arrived in New York on the morning of the 18th, and proceeded to Philadelphia, reaching that place on the same evening.

On our way John Brady, of Company H, Lowell, was taken insane, and deeming it unsafe to have him accompany the regiment, I left him at Delanco, N. J., with J. C. Buck, with directions that he should telegraph Mayor Sergeant, of Lowell, as to the disposition of him, and we proceeded thence to Baltimore, reaching that place at noon on the 19th. After leaving Philadelphia I received information that our passage through the city of Baltimore would be resisted. I caused ammunition to be distributed and arms loaded, and went personally through the cars, and issued the following order, viz:

> The regiment will march through Baltimore in column of sections, arms at will. You will undoubtedly be insulted, abused, and, perhaps, assaulted, to which you must pay no attention whatever, but march with your faces square to the front, and pay no attention to the mob, even if they throw stones, bricks, or other missiles; but if you are fired upon and any one of you is hit, your officers will order you to fire. Do not fire into any promiscuous crowds, but select any man whom you may see aiming at you, and be sure you drop him.

Reaching Baltimore, horses were attached the instant that the locomotive was detached, and the cars were driven at a rapid pace across the city. After the cars containing seven companies had reached the Washington depot the track behind them was barricaded, and the cars containing the band and the following companies viz: Company C, of Lowell, Captain Follansbee; Company D, of Lowell, Captain Hart; Company I, of Lawrence, Captain Pickering, and Company L, of Stoneham, Captain Dike, were vacated, and they proceeded but a short distance before they were furiously attacked by a shower of missiles, which came faster as they advanced. They increased their steps to double-quick, which seemed to infuriate the mob, as it evidently impressed the mob with the idea that the soldiers dared not fire or had no ammunition, and pistol-shots were numerously fired into the ranks, and one soldier fell dead. The order "Fire" was given, and it was executed.

In consequence, several of the mob fell, and the soldiers again advanced hastily. The mayor of Baltimore placed himself at the head of the column beside Captain Follansbee, and proceeded with them a short distance, assuring him that he would protect them, and begging him not to let the men fire; but the mayor's patience was soon exhausted, and he seized a musket from the hands of one of the men and killed a man therewith, and a policeman, who was in advance of the column, also shot a man with a revolver. They at last reached the cars, and they started immediately for Washington. On going through the train I found there were about one hundred and thirty missing, including the band and field music. Our baggage was seized, and we have not as yet been able to recover any of it. I have found it very difficult to get reliable information in regard to the killed and wounded, but believe there were only three killed.

As the men went into the cars I caused the blinds to the cars to be closed, and took every precaution to prevent any shadow of offense to the people of Baltimore; but still the stones flew thick and fast into the train, and it was with the utmost difficulty that I could prevent the troops from leaving the cars and revenging the death of their comrades. After a volley of stones some one of the soldiers fired and killed a Mr. Davis, who I have since ascertained by reliable witnesses threw a stone into the car; yet that did not justify the firing at him, but the men were infuriated beyond control. On reaching Washington we were quartered at the Capitol, in the Senate Chamber, and are all in good health and spirits. I have made every effort to get possession of the bodies of our comrades, but have not yet succeeded. Should I succeed I shall forward them to Boston, if practicable; otherwise shall avail myself of a kind offer of George Woods, esq., who has offered me a prominent lot in the Congressional burying-ground for the purpose of interment.

We were this day mustered into the United States service, and will forward the rolls at first opportunity after verification.

Edward F. Jones
Colonel Sixth Regiment, M. V. M.

Captain John Quincy Marr, a graduate of Virginia Military Institute, became the first Confederate soldier to die in battle as he and the men of the Warrenton Rifle Volunteers repulsed a pre-dawn attack at Fairfax Court House on June 1, 1861. The wound was directly over the heart, and there was a perfect circular suffusion of blood under the skin, somewhat larger than a silver dollar, but the skin was unbroken, and not a drop of blood was shed. It was the shock of impact that stopped his heart. The small bullet hole can be clearly seen on the pictured jacket, an artifact that brings home the horror of war even to the most callous individual (courtesy the Museum of the Confederacy, Richmond, Virginia; photograph by Tucker Hill).

John Quincy Marr (courtesy Virginia Military Institute, Lexington, Virginia)

If Baltimore was to become the focal point of Federal troops passing through Maryland to the District of Columbia, then the city needed a strong military presence to keep order and to deter Federal troops from occupying the area. To this end, Marshal George P. Kane, head of the Baltimore City Police, contacted several of the militia units scattered throughout the state. One such militia unit, the Frederick Company, was commanded by Captain Bradley T. Johnson, a local lawyer and politician.

After several days Baltimore settled down. Northern troops occupied the city in early May, and many Marylanders like Bradley Johnson who supported the

South made their way across the Potomac and offered their services to the Confederacy. In all, an estimated 20,000 Maryland men would fight for the Confederacy. But by war's end, some 40,000 Marylanders would serve the Union.

Uniform Coat of Captain John Quincy Marr

Marr was the first Confederate officer to die in battle. He was a graduate of Virginia Military Institute and a professor of math there. He also practiced law and served as sheriff of Fauquier County. His shako cap, jacket, epaulets, overcoat and sword are at the museum.

SHOT IN THE SHADOWS

John Quincy Marr was a tall man and strong, with black hair, dark eyes, and a perfectly smooth face. He was popular in his native town of Warrenton, Virginia, and its vicinity. When delegates were elected to go to a secession convention in Richmond in February 1861, the citizens of nearby Fauquier sent him there.

Marr returned to organize a company of infantry. These were the Warrenton Rifles, an extremely youthful group who were eventually to emerge as Company K of the 17th Virginia Regiment of Infantry.

On April 16, Marr marched his infantry to Dumfries beneath the flag that he had accepted in a "graceful" speech following its presentation by the ladies of Warrenton. From Dumfries, the Warrenton Rifles were directed back to Fauquier Springs, and then on to Bristow Station and to Centreville. And finally, late in May—with the captain just past his 36th birthday and informed that he would soon be commissioned a lieutenant colonel in the Virginia line—they bivouacked in the Methodist Episcopal Church building at Fairfax.

Fairfax was, in those latter days of May, more than the seat of the historic county from which it derives its name. Lying at the western apex of a triangle that placed it an equal distance of fourteen miles from both Washington, D.C., and Yankee-occupied Alexandria, it was an advanced position, a site of potential danger, and hence a post of honor.

About 3 A.M. on Saturday, June 1, a guard rushed into the church housing the Warrenton Rifles and shouted that the enemy's cavalry was approaching. The men were quickly roused by the crackling of small arms, the thunder of hooves, and the shouts of men up the Falls Church road as Union Lieutenant Charles H. Tompkins, 2nd U.S. Calvary, and his horsemen were galloping along the Alexandria Pike, which passed through the center of town, firing indiscriminately at buildings, persons, lights, and shadows. Marr was quickly afoot, and he hurried into the clover fields adjoining the structure and called for his men to form there. The Union troops easily overtook and captured four of the Prince William cavalry, and then went whooping westward. It all happened in an instant.

Afterwards, William Smith, the commander, found forty-two of the Warrenton Rifles men leaning against the inside of the fence that enclosed the clover fields.

"Boys," he asked, "where is your captain?"

"We don't know, sir," several replied. In the confusion, Marr had disappeared, as though swallowed up by the darkness, and half of his bewildered command had melted away.

It was clear that Lieutenant Tompkins would have to return by the same route that his calvary had gone. Accordingly, the remnant of the Warrenton Rifles were led west to Cooper's carriage shop, and Smith placed them behind strong post–and-rail fences bordering each of the pikes at that point.

Within thirty minutes Tompkins returned and attempted to force his way back through Fairfax. But when the head of his troop was opposite Zion Episcopal Church, forty yards from the carriage shop, it ran into stiff resistance. The frolicking was over. The Yanks withdrew, reformed, and went in again. Rifles spat, and lead whistled through the morning air, until finally Tompkins and his invaders withdrew, pulling down fences and making their escape through the fields, leaving the ground strewn with carbines, pistols, and sabers.

In the early morning light, Marr's body servant found him where he had fallen, face down in the clover fields, his sword gripped in his right hand. By one of those freak accidents with which all wars are replete, he had been dropped by a random spent bullet, probably fired when the blue coated riders were passing the courthouse 300 yards away.

Great Seal of the Confederacy

Delivered too late to be of any use to the Confederacy in the waning days of the war, the great seal remained a prized possession.

A SEALED FATE

On April 9, 1921, the *Richmond Times Dispatch* published an article saying that Jefferson Davis's coachman had died in Washington, D.C., and that the aged Negro took with him to his grave the whereabouts of the Great Seal of the Confederacy, which he hid when Davis was captured.

Throughout James E. Jones's long life, with his later years spent in government services in Washington, he would never reveal what became of the Confederate Great Seal. "Marse Jeff" had bidden that he never tell, and he never did. Veterans of the Union and Confederate armies, newspaper reporters, writers, curiosity seekers, and curio hunters from time to time urged Jones to reveal where he had buried the seal. They argued that the War Between the States was far in the past and that the seal should be produced for inspection by a younger generation dedicated to a united country. Always, Jones shook his head no and took the secret to his grave.

While it is not surprising that the death of James Jones should revive the myth that he alone knew where the Great Seal of the Confederacy was buried, it is remarkable, to say the least, that this absurd story should be published in Richmond, where the Great Seal always was, and is on exhibition and may be seen at any time by anyone who visits the Confederate Museum.

The Jones story was probably a fanciful illusion or a lie so often repeated that even Jones came to believe that it was fact. Jones may have seen the seal, but he certainly never had it in his possession. The facts were duly set forth in the Southern Historical Papers published in 1916, five years before the death of Jones.

By a joint resolution, approved April 30, 1863, the Confederate Congress adopted a seal for the Con-

The existence of the Great Seal of the Confederate States of America was shrouded in mystery for nearly half a century following the closing days of the Civil War. The Confederate provisional government had recognized the importance of having an emblem symbolic of its sovereignty and had adopted a simple seal portraying a scroll with the words "Constitution" written above it and "Liberty" beneath it. Later, the permanent Confederate government desired a more elaborate and artistic symbol. On April 30, 1863, the Confederate Congress commissioned the seal. The resulting Great Seal depicts the equestrian statue of George Washington erected in 1857 on the Capitol grounds in Richmond, flanked by a wreath of the chief agricultural products of the Confederacy: cotton, corn, tobacco, sugar cane, wheat, and rice. Around the outer edge of the seal are the words, "The Confederate States of America: 22 February 1862," the date that Jefferson Davis was inaugurated beneath the depicted statue, and the motto "Deo Vindice" ("God vindicates us") (courtesy Armed Forces History, Division of History of Technology, National Museum of American History).

federate States. This seal was to portray the equestrian statue of Washington in the Capitol square and was to be surrounded by a wreath showing the principal agricultural products of the Confederacy. Soon after the resolution was passed, Judah F. Benjamin, secretary of state, instructed James M. Mason, Confederate commissioner to England, to have the seal cut in silver. Mr. Mason in turn entrusted the work to J. S. Wyon, maker of the great seals of England. On July 6, 1864, Mason notified the State Department that the seal was ready and, with its equipment, was being shipped to Richmond. It sneaked past the blockade and arrived in September.

Here it remained until the evacuation of Richmond in April 1865. Secretary Benjamin entrusted the seal and archives of the Confederacy to William J. Bromwell, a clerk in the State Department. Bromwell reportedly hid the seal in a barn, and his wife later carried it, concealed in her dress, out of Richmond to Washington.

The seal next appeared in Washington City in 1872. Colonel John T. Pickett, a former officer on General Breckenridge's staff, acting as Bromwell's attorney, sold the Confederate Department of State archives to the United States government for $75,000. The U.S. agent for this transaction was Thomas O. Selfridge, captain, U.S.N., and as a "token of appreciation" to Captain Selfridge for his activity in promoting the sale of the papers, Pickett gave him the Great Seal. The gift was kept secret, however, and was not revealed until Pickett's personal papers were acquired by the Library of Congress. The library discovered through a careful search of manuscripts that Selfridge possessed the seal. Selfridge was by this time a retired rear-admiral and admitted that he had the seal. On May 14, 1912, Messrs. Eppa Hunton, Jr., William H. White, and Thomas P. Bryan of Richmond purchased the seal from Selfridge for $3,000. To remove all doubts of the seal's authenticity, the men shipped it back to England and had it meticulously inspected by Allan J. Wyon, nephew of the original engraver, who attested in writing that the seal acquired from Selfridge was indeed the original.

Thus, the Great Seal of the Confederate States, although never actually used by the Confederate government, came to reside in the Museum of the Confederacy in Richmond, where today it and the certificate of authenticity are proudly displayed.

Virginia Historical Society, 428 North Boulevard, Richmond, VA 23220

Collecting has been a vital function of the Virginia Historical Society from its beginning, with the first donations announced at the first annual meeting in 1833. Traditionally, most items have come to the Virginia Historical Society via gift or bequest. Some of the items in the exhibit are unique treasures. Examples include George Washington's personal diary from 1790 to 1791, Thomas Hariot's account of the "Lost Colony," a chair Dolley Madison bought in France, and a 1693 map of the Eastern Shore.

Window from Richmond's Libby Prison

The window returned to Richmond after being taken to Chicago and New York. The prison was demolished around 1888 and reassembled in Chicago. After the World's Columbian Exposition in Chicago in 1893, the building was again demolished, this time permanently, and the pieces were sold separately as souvenirs. One of the Chicago directors gave the window to a friend, George Goss Pittsford of Pittsford, New York, near Rochester. He in turn presented it to the local Union veterans' organization, E.J. Tyler Post 288, Grand Army of the Republic, at a ceremony attended by two former inmates of the prison. In 1915, the GAR donated it to the Rochester Municipal Museum, now the Rochester Museum and Science Center. In 1990, the museum in turn gave the window to the Virginia Historical Society. Made of rough Georgia pine with iron bars, the window is fifty-five inches by sixty-five inches and weighs about three hundred pounds. E.L.W. Baker, an imprisoned Union private from

Lansing, Michigan, carved his name and company, "21st Mich. Co. B.," into the frame.

OUT OF PRISON—
AND IN

Prior to his capture, Private Baker wrote the *Commercial Press*, a monthly newspaper in Pultneyville, New York, the following:

Chattanooga, Tenn., March 27, 1864
J.M. Reynolds,
Sir;

Your welcome little journal was received by me a few days since, and I am glad to say that I read its columns with a good deal of interest. You have my best wishes for the future; and may success crown all your efforts. We have had some very bad weather here for the past few days; snow fell on the 22, to a foot and a half deep, which the citizens say they have never seen before for a number of years. The Michigan Boys enjoyed it with pleasure, as they were continually snowballing until it was all gone. We are building a bridge in front of Chattanooga across the Tennessee River. I should be more happy to give you a glowing account, had I time.

Respectfully Yours
Edward L.W. Baker
Co. B, 1st Michigan Vol.

On an isolated site in Richmond, Virginia, bordered by the James River and empty lots, stood Libby Prison, garnering—but perhaps not deserving—an infamous reputation second only to that of Andersonville Prison. Formerly the Libby & Son Ship Chandlers & Grocers, this three-story, 45,000-square-foot brick building saw 125,000 Union officers, but no enlisted men, pass through its doors before May 1864.

By 1863 men were sleeping in squads, lined up on their sides to save space, turning only on the order of an elected leader. Prisoners complained of short rations, cold, and lice, yet many were able to buy extra provisions and receive packages from home. Black servants (captured Northerners) served the white officers, and there was running water and even primitive flush toilets.

Still, inmates' letters fueled Northern reports of inhumane conditions, especially after sentries were ordered to shoot anyone appearing at the windows, and hundreds of pounds of gunpowder were ominously placed in the cellar following a mass escape early in 1864.

Confederate authorities tried to head off the negative publicity by inviting in outside observers.

This a window from Richmond's notorious Libby Prison, where an estimated 125,000 Union soldiers were confined. An Illinois syndicate razed the building in 1888–89 and then reconstructed it in Chicago as the National War Museum to house Civil War relics (courtesy of Virginia Historical Society, Richmond, Virginia).

This structure, originally built as a warehouse for a tobacco merchant between 1845 and 1852, was being leased by Libby and Sons when the Confederacy took it over in 1862 to house Union prisoners (courtesy Library of Congress).

These observers reported the existence of plentiful books, games of whist, and classes in Greek. Effusive comments such as, "I ... found it kept scrupulously clean and well ventilated. There was not a bad smell about the place...," and "a picture of profusion met the eye. The rafters were thickly hung with hams of bacon and venison, beef tongues, bologna sausage, dried fish, and other substantials...." filled the press.

Manassas National Battlefield,
12521 Lee Highway,
Manassas, VA 20109

The park offers a wide array of activities along with scenic vistas, historic sites, and walking trails to interest the casual visitor or the dedicated Civil War history buff. *Manassas: End of Innocence* is a 45-minute film that gives viewers a good overview of both the First and Second Battles of Manassas. Artifacts and exhibits pertaining to the battles are on display, and exhibits include audiovisual presentations and a fiber-optic battle map presentation that describes troop movements during the battles.

THE BATTLE OF FIRST MANASSAS

Cheers of "On to Richmond!" rang through the streets of Washington on July 16, 1861, as General Irvin McDowell's army marched out to begin the long-awaited campaign to capture Richmond. A quick, powerful thrust would cast aside Southern resistance, topple the Confederate capital and end the war. Or so the common belief went. In truth,

McDowell's was an army of green recruits, few of whom had the faintest idea of the magnitude of the task facing them. But their swaggering gait showed that none doubted the outcome of the 100-mile march to Richmond. As excitement spread, many citizens, male and female, along with congressmen, carried wine and picnic baskets with them as they followed the army into the field to watch what all expected would be a colorful, circuslike show.

McDowell's lumbering columns were headed for the vital railroad junction at Manassas, Virginia. Here, the Orange and Alexandria Railroad met the Manassas Gap Railroad, which led west to the Shenandoah Valley. If McDowell could seize this junction, he would stand astride the best overland approach to the Confederate capital.

On July 18, McDowell's army reached Centreville. Five miles ahead a small meandering stream called Bull Run crossed the route of the Union advance, and there, guarding the fords from Union Mills to the Stone Bridge, waited the Southern troops under the command of General Pierre G.T. Beauregard. McDowell first attempted to move toward the Confederate right flank, but his troops were checked at Blackburn's Ford. He then spent the next two days scouting the Southern left flank. In the meantime, Beauregard asked the Confederate government at Richmond for help. General Joseph E. Johnston, stationed in the Shenandoah Valley, was ordered to support Beauregard if possible. Johnston gave an opposing Union force the slip and, utilizing the Manassas Gap Railroad, started his brigades toward Manassas Junction. Most of Johnston's troops arrived at the junction on July 20 and 21, some marching from the trains directly into battle.

On the morning of July 21, McDowell sent his attack columns in a long march north toward Sudley Springs Ford. This route took the Federals around the Confederate left. To distract the Southerners, McDowell ordered a diversionary attack where the Warrenton Turnpike crossed Bull Run at the Stone Bridge. At 5:30 A.M., the deep-throated roar of a 30-pounder Parrott rifle shattered the morning calm, and signaled the start of battle.

McDowell's new plan depended on speed and surprise, both difficult with inexperienced troops. Valuable time was lost as the men stumbled through the darkness along narrow roads. Confederate Colonel Nathan Evans, commanding at the Stone Bridge, soon realized that the attack on his front was only a diversion, and leaving a small force to hold the bridge, Evans rushed the remainder of his command to Matthews Hill in time to check McDowell's lead unit. Evans's force was too small, however, to hold back the Federals for long.

Soon, brigades under Barnard Bee and Francis Bartow marched to Evans's assistance. But even with these reinforcements, the thin gray line collapsed and the Southerners fled in disorder toward Henry Hill. Attempting to rally his men, Bee used General Thomas J. Jackson's newly arrived brigade as an anchor. Pointing to Jackson, Bee shouted, "There stands Jackson like a stone wall! Rally behind the Virginians!" Generals Johnston and Beauregard then arrived on Henry Hill, where they assisted in rallying shattered brigades and redeploying fresh units that were marching to the point of danger.

About noon, the Federals stopped their advance to reorganize for a new attack. The lull lasted for about an hour, giving the Confederates enough time to reform their lines. Then the fighting resumed, each side trying to force the other off Henry Hill. The battle continued until just after 4 P.M. when fresh Southern units crashed into the Union right flank on Chinn Ridge, causing McDowell's exhausted and discouraged young troops to withdraw.

At first the withdrawal was orderly. Screened by the regulars, the three-month volunteers retired across Bull Run, where they found the road to Washington jammed with the carriages of the congressmen and others who had driven out to Centreville to watch the fight. Panic now seized many of the soldiers and the retreat became a rout. The Confederates, though bolstered by the arrival of President Jefferson Davis on the field just as the battle was ending, were too disorganized to follow up their success. Daybreak on July 22 found the defeated Union army back behind the bristling defenses of Washington.

Cornerstones from Wilmer McLean's Barn

Wilmer McLean's barn, built in 1856, was used both as a hospital and as a prison during First Manassas.

Top: During the construction of a subdivision in the 1950s, this cornerstone from McLean's barn was recovered and donated to the Manassas National Battlefield Park. *Bottom:* "Wilmer McLean 1856, Enoch Rector, Builder," reads inscription on this large cornerstone from McLean's original large stone barn. One of Rector's descendants — also a Rector — is a builder in Manassas today (courtesy Manassas National Battlefield).

The Saga of Wilmer McLean

Nestled among cornfields and pasture lands in rural Prince William County was the 1,200-acre plantation known as "Yorkshire." Wilmer McLean and his wife had moved there in January of 1853, naturally completely unaware of the events that would transpire at their estate shortly after the beginning of the Civil War at First Manassas. Once war had touched their lives, however, and hoping to find a more peaceful setting, McLean moved to the southern Virginia community of Appomattox Court House in the fall of 1863. It turned out that fate would not allow the McLeans to escape the war, and they came face to face with one of the oddest coincidences of the great conflict, as we shall see later.

Relics of Mrs. Judith Henry

Elderly Mrs. Henry was the first civilian to die in the battle. The infirm women refused to leave her house, which ultimately was destroyed.

THE DEATH OF JUDITH HENRY

On Sunday, July 21, the day of the battle, Mrs. Judith Henry, her daughter Ellen, and a servant, Lucy Griffin, were living in the house today known as the Henry house. Eighty-five-year-old Judith was confined to her bed with the infirmities of old age. As the battle began, the Henry house stood right in the midst of it. One of the Confederate soldiers was planning on moving Mrs. Henry a safe distance from the house, but in the growing confusion this was out of the question: in the front hall the Confederate a shot Union soldier, who fell at the feet of the daughter, Ellen.

As cannon balls and rifle fire riddled the house, Ellen sought safety in the fireplace chimney as the servant Lucy Griffin hid under the bed. As the Union battery continued to shell the house to drive out Confederate sharpshooters, the bed on which Mrs. Henry lay was shattered by cannon fire, and she was thrown to the floor, wounded in the neck and side and had one foot blown partly off. She died later in the afternoon, the only civilian killed during the battle. Ellen suffered permanent injury to her eardrums, and Lucy Griffin was wounded

During the battle of First Manassas, McLean's very substantial barn (above) was used as a military hospital, as well as a prison for captured Union soldiers (courtesy Manassas National Battlefield).

These items associated with the death of Mrs. Judith Henry were donated in 1992 to the Manassas Battlefield Museum. They include a cloth purse with a green silk lining, a sawed-off section of a bedpost with a burn hole made by a shell fragment that killed Mrs. Henry, a carved ivory fan, and her Bible with leather cover.

in the right arm. The house itself was destroyed. The tragic incident serves as a testament to how civilians can get caught up in the terrors of war despite their innocence.

The 10th Virginia Infantry Flag

These flags or standards, tattered by winds, torn by cannonballs and rifle shot, and stained with the blood of dying heroes, were priceless treasures, more beloved than houses, land, riches, honor, ease, comfort, wives, or children. Were you to ask what was the dearest of all earthly things, there would be but one answer: "The flag! The dear old flag!" It was their pillar of fire by night, of cloud by day. The symbol of everything worth living for, worth dying for!

Shoe of Private George H. Lyles

At the start of the war, most troops had shoes. Many went barefoot by the end of the war.

The Henry house, pictured after its destruction during the Battle of First Manassas (courtesy Library of Congress).

The 10th Virginia Infantry Regiment carried this flag into the first battle of Manassas. The Virginia state seal is painted on the reverse of the canton. Ironically, perhaps, the flag is marked with "Horstmanns Phil," indicating that the flag was made in Philadelphia and then shipped south. The missing stars in the canton are the result of battle damage sustained during the fierce fighting. The Manassas Museum houses the flag (courtesy Manassas National Battlefield).

Hard Tack Souvenir

Hardtack is a crackerlike biscuit made of flour, salt, and water, and it was one of the most typical rations issued to soldiers by the U. S. government because it was relatively nutritious and unlikely to spoil easily. This hard-as-a-rock bread product was made in government bakeries in large cities and shipped in barrels to the troops. The adage is that an army travels on its belly, and the troops who had to eat this concrete army ration gave it such names as "tooth-dullers," "worm castles," and "sheet iron crackers." By far, the hardtack that Civil War soldiers received has been the source of more stories than any other aspect of their army life. Nothing demonstrates that better than this piece of hardtack, still in existence in the Manassas Battlefield Museum.

This resilient four-inch-square hard biscuit is cracked, forming three pieces, and two of its corners are missing. Amazingly, today's relic hunters can still discover hardtack when they are rummaging through old Civil War garbage dumps.

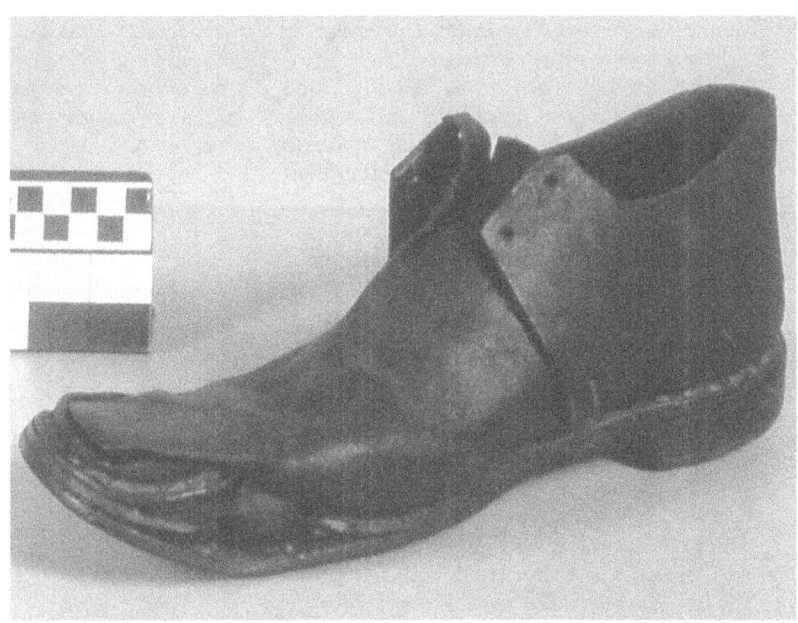

Private George H. Lyles was slightly wounded at Blackburn's Ford when a canister shot struck his foot and embedded itself in the sole of his shoe. Lyles was in the Mount Vernon Guards, Company E, 17th Virginia Infantry. As luck would have it, the 27-year-old Lyles's occupation was shoemaker. In a subsequent battle he was captured by Union troops. The shoe is on exhibit in the Manassas Museum (courtesy Manassas National Battlefield).

SECOND MANASSAS

In August 1862, Union and Confederate armies converged for a second time on the plains of Manassas. The naive enthusiasm that preceded the earlier encounter was gone. War was not the holiday outing or grand adventure envisioned by the young recruits of 1861. The contending forces, now made up of seasoned veterans, knew well the realities of battle.

During the Peninsula Campaign, the scattered Federal forces in northern Virginia were organized into the Army of Virginia under the command of General John Pope, who arrived with a reputation freshly won in the war's western theater. Lee knew that if he were to defeat Pope he would have to strike before McClellan's army arrived in northern Virginia. On August 25, Lee boldly started Jackson's corps on a march of over fifty miles, around the Union right flank to strike at Pope's rear.

Two days later, Jackson's veterans seized Pope's supply depot at Manassas Junction. After a day of wild feasting, Jackson burned the Federal supplies and moved to a position in the woods at Groveton near the old Manassas battlefield.

Pope, stung by the attack on his supply base, abandoned the line of the Rappahannock and headed toward Manassas to "bag" Jackson. At the same time, Lee was moving northward with Longstreet's corps to reunite his army. On the afternoon of August 28, Jackson ordered his troops to attack a Union column as it marched past on the Warrenton Turnpike, to prevent the Federal commander from concentrating his efforts at Centreville. This savage fight at Prawner's Farm lasted until dark.

On the 29th, Pope's army found Jackson's men posted along an unfinished railroad grade, north of the turnpike. All afternoon, in a series of uncoordinated attacks, Pope hurled his men against the Confederate position. In several places, the northerners momentarily breached Jackson's line but with each assault were forced back. During the afternoon, Longstreet's troops arrived on the battlefield and, unknown to Pope, deployed on Jackson's right, overlapping the exposed Union left. Lee urged Longstreet to attack, but "Old Pete," as he was known demurred. The time was just not right, he said.

The morning of August 30 passed quietly. Just before noon Pope erroneously concluded that the Confederates were retreating and ordered his army forward in pursuit. The "pursuit," however, was short-lived. Pope found that Lee had gone nowhere. Astonishingly, Pope ordered yet another attack against Jackson's line. Fitz-John Porter's corps, along with part of McDowell's, struck Starke's division at the unfinished railroad's so-called "Deep Cut." The Southerners held firm, however, and Porter's column was hurled back in a bloody repulse.

This turned out to be the decisive battle of the Northern Virginia Campaign. The Battle of Second Manassas, covering three days, produced far greater carnage, 3,300 killed, than the prior battle, and established the Confederacy as a fearsome power. Still, the battle did not weaken Northern resolve.

Field glasses of Major General Fitz-John Porter

Prism binoculars, invented in 1854, allowed for more distant viewing and better depth perspective, officers used them widely in the Civil War to follow troop movements and signals.

Major General Fitz-John Porter

Fitz-John Porter graduated from West Point in 1845 and his Civil War service began when he led a division to the Peninsula and participated in the siege of Yorktown, where George Washington received Cornwallis's surrender during the Revolutionary War. On the Peninsula, Porter made over 100 ascents in Thaddeus S.C. Lowe's observation balloon.

Written on the surface of this piece of hardtack in ink is the following: "Mrs M.J. Thurston/ Brought from the battlefield/ of Bull Run, July 21, 1861/ by Henry B(?)/ Lieut from (?) (?) Gen Sherman."

On an ascent in Yorktown, the rope attached to the balloon carrying Porter snapped, and he floated over the Confederate lines. He threw out enough ballast to rise high enough to avoid Rebel bullets. Fortunately, a countercurrent of air reversed the balloon's direction, and Porter came down in friendly territory. (During the Peninsula Campaign, incidentally, he developed a long-lasting friendship with his commander, George McClellan.)

These field glasses used by Major General Fitz-John Porter were donated to the Manassas National Park Service in 1989.

At Beaver Dam Creek and Gaines' Mill at the start of the Seven Days' Battles, Fitz-John Porter bore the brunt of Lee's furious offensive, operating his much smaller force in an exemplary fashion. At Malvern Hill he again played a distinguished role and covered the retreat of the Federal army to Harrison's Landing.

His command was sent to reinforce Pope in northern Virginia. At the Battle of Second Manassas, he was ordered to attack the flank and rear of Jackson's position, but could not execute the order because General James Longstreet's forces had come up and occupied the ground in front of him.

Blamed by Pope for the bitter loss at Second Manassas, Porter was removed from command; furthermore, he was arrested on a charge of disobedience of orders and misconduct in the face of the enemy. He was later court-martialed, and the fact that he was friends with McClellan—a scapegoat himself—and had said derogatory things about General Pope before the disastrous battle forced the tribunal to render a guilty verdict. He was dishonorably discharged from the army in January of 1863. He spent many years afterward trying to clear his name.

After years of claiming innocence at Second Manassas, Porter finally got a measure of justice. General John Schofield conducted an official inquiry in 1878 and found that Porter was indeed vindicated; he had actually saved the lives of many of Pope's troops by not committing to a useless assault that Longstreet would have crushed. Four years later, President Chester A. Arthur rescinded the sentence; Porter was re–commissioned by a special act of Congress in 1886, retroactive to May 1861. He was, however denied his back pay, no doubt a substantial cumulative sum.

Fredericksburg and Spotsylvania National Military Park (Fredericksburg)

Fredericksburg and Spotsylvania National Military Park is the second largest military park in the world and consists of five locations: a research center, two museums, and two interceptive shelters. Four separate battles two years apart were fought in Fredericksburg, Chancellorsville, Wilderness, and Spotsylvania, making this the bloodiest adjoining landscape in North America, as more than 85,000 men were wounded and 15,000 killed. No place has more vividly reflected the Civil War's tragic cost in all its forms.

The Fredericksburg Battlefield Visitor Center, 1013 Lafayette Boulevard, Fredericksburg, VA

The December 13, 1862, battle of Fredericksburg is generally accepted as General Robert E. Lee's easiest victory. The visitor center contains exhibits, and a 22-minute movie describes this battle. Just a few steps away is the famous stone wall at Marye's Heights. Historians lead a 35-minute walking tour along the Sunken Road. A five-mile driving tour beginning at the Fredericksburg Battlefield Visitor Center takes visitors through Prospect Hill and continues to the base of Marye's Heights.

Chatham Manor, 120 Chatham Lane, Fredericksburg, VA 22405

Chatham Manor is a historic building that served as a headquarters and hospital during the battle. Visitors can view both indoor and outdoor exhibits. This magnificent Georgian mansion with its various outbuildings and dependencies and the historic grounds which surround it represent a small preserve in which the entire scope of the Virginia heritage can be understood and appreciated. Five of the ten rooms contain exhibits and the rest of the building and its outbuildings are park offices.

Chancellorsville Visitor Center

From I-95, take exit 130A (Route 3) west for approximately seven miles. The visitor center is on the right, on the north side of the highway.

The Chancellorsville Campaign was fought on May 1–5, 1863, and is known as Robert E. Lee's greatest victory. A visitor center contains exhibits and a short film to help orient visitors to the battle. In the immediate area of the visitor center is a plaque marking the spot where Stonewall Jackson was mortally wounded. A seven-mile driving tour and several walking trails provide access to the key spots on the battlefield.

Wilderness Battlefield

From I-95 take exit 130 (Route 3) west for approximately eleven miles. Turn left at the traffic light at the intersection with Route 20. Proceed two miles. The shelter is on the right.

The Battle of the Wilderness was fought on May 1–6, 1864. It was the beginning of the Overland Campaign, the bloodiest campaign in American history and the turning point in the war in the eastern theater. An open air shelter provides orientation exhibits. Located a short walk from the shelter is Ellwood, a plantation home that became Federal headquarters during the battle. A five-mile driving tour and several walking trails provide access to key spots on the battlefield.

Spotsylvania Battlefield

The entrance to Spotsylvania Battlefield is on Route 613 (Brock Road) about two miles northwest of the town of Spotsylvania Court House.

On May 8, 1864, the Union army seized the initiative by moving from Wilderness to Spotsylvania Court House. That shift changed the course of the war as the armies began the rough road to Lee's surrender at Appomattox. An open-air shelter provides orientation exhibits. A five-mile driving tour and several walking trails provide access to key spots on the battlefield that includes the notorious Confederate salient that became known as the "Bloody Angle."

THE BATTLES OF FREDERICKSBURG AND CHANCELLORSVILLE

The battle for Fredericksburg was fought in December 1862 and again in April 1863, as

Union forces attempted to flank Lee's entrenched Fredericksburg defense. The unflappable Lee, though, boldly divided his army and attacked and defeated the Union forces in the battle of Chancellorsville, twelve miles west of Fredericksburg. The Union forces, under the command of General Joe Hooker, retreated to their original position on the north bank of the Rappahannock. Other Union armies under Generals Irvin McDowell, Ambrose Burnside, and Joseph Hooker, had tried to advance by the most direct route, 100 miles south to Richmond, and had found it blocked by determined Confederates under the Lee's command.

It had begun on November 19, 1862, as Ambrose Burnside's Army of the Potomac encamped on Stafford Heights, on the east bank of the Rappahannock River overlooking the city of Fredericksburg. They were waiting for the arrival of pontoon boats that would enable them to bridge the river and advance on Richmond. The pontoons finally arrived on November 25, but Burnside made no attempt to cross for nearly three weeks.

This unwise delay enabled Lee to unite the two wings of his Army of Northern Virginia, recently reorganized into two corps under James Longstreet and Stonewall Jackson. Rather than challenge the Federal crossing of the river, Lee chose to fortify the heights west of the city, which varied in distance from the river from one to two miles. Along a seven-mile front stretching from the Rappahannock on his left to Massaponax Creek on his right, he placed Longstreet on the left and Jackson on the right. Longstreet's position along a ridge known as Marye's Heights was further fortified by a sunken road and a stone wall at the base of the heights. An open plain about two miles wide lay between Jackson's position and the river.

Again showing an acute lack of judgment, Burnside decided to attack on December 13, having foolishly given Lee and the Confederates increased strength and a topographical advantage. All day long the Federals charged the almost impregnable Confederate position, only to be beaten back each time with heavy losses. Darkness mercifully put an end to the useless slaughter. Two days later, under cover of a violent rainstorm, the Army of the Potomac retreated across the river. They continue to skirmish for four more months, but Burnside turned his army over to its new commander, Joseph Hooker.

On the evening of April 30, 1863, Lee was struggling with the gravest strategic situation of his eleven-month command of the Army of Northern Virginia. Joe Hooker, the new commander of the Army of the Potomac, had encircled the Confederate left flank, ten miles behind Lee's lines at Fredericksburg, and General John Sedwick's VI Corps remained in the city to attempt a diversionary attack aimed at holding the Confederates in their defensive positions.

The aggressive Lee, leaving Jubal Early's division behind at Fredericksburg, advanced against Hooker's wing in the Wilderness, a large demonic landscape of scrub brush and oak trees.

On May 1, the Confederates in several columns marched westward. Federal officers were jubilant over the prospects of success and abandoned the Wilderness, tramping out into the open country. About two miles from the woodland, however, they encountered Stonewall Jackson's oncoming veterans, and skirmishing erupted along the lines. Hooker, who later admitted that he lost his nerve, ordered a sudden withdrawal back into the forbidding dense foliage; over the protest of his corps commanders, he abandoned the initiative to Lee. By choosing to make a stand in the Wilderness, Hooker neutralized the superiority of both his numbers and his artillery. The Federals withdrew into a line encircling the crossroad of Chancellorsville.

Lee reacted cautiously to this sudden retreat, but when J.E.B. Stuart's cavalry discovered that Hooker's right flank was unsupported, Lee decided to attack. That night he and Jackson, sitting on discarded Union cracker boxes, devised one of the most daring plans in military history. Defying accepted strategic and tactical laws, Lee again split his army, ordering Jackson to march beyond Hooker's vulnerable flank and attack while Lee assaulted Hooker along the Federal works.

Jackson's fourteen-mile march took nearly all of May 2 to complete. Federal scouts discovered the movement and notified Hooker, who in turn warned his flank commander, General Oliver O. Howard, XI Corps commander. Howard dismissed the vital intelligence. As twilight enveloped the woodland, Jackson's veterans stormed onto Howard's unsuspecting troops, and Howard's line collapsed under the lightning assault, his men fleeing two miles to the rear. Darkness and the combined Confederate commands prevented a full-scale pursuit.

While reconnoitering between the lines, Jackson was mistakenly shot—"friendly fire"—by members of the 18th North Carolina. Stuart assumed command of the infantry, and at daylight on May 3 launched another assault on Hooker's contracted lines. When the Federals abandoned a high point, Stuart moved fifty cannon up the commanding hill. Supported by this massed artillery fire, Stuart's and Lee's wings wrenched the Chancellorsville crossroads from the Federals. Hooker withdrew to a new line, its flanks firmly secured by the Rapidan and Rappahannock rivers.

Lee, meanwhile, was preparing to charge this new line when he learned that Hooker had ordered Sedgwick to seize Marye's Heights and then advance to attack Lee's right flank. Sedgwick did indeed charge the heights several times and was driven back by General William Barksdale's brigade of Mississippians, who had seen heavy fighting on the same ground five months earlier. Sedgwick attacked again with a daring and gallant bayonet charge that drove the Confederates off the heights and back toward Richmond. Pausing only long enough to regroup, Jubal Early proceeded west toward Chancellorsville.

When Lee learned that the heights had been lost and another Federal force was moving toward him, on May 3 he boldly split his army in Hooker's front and marched two divisions back toward Fredericksburg. Late that afternoon, Confederates under Lafayette McLaws met Sedgwick's advance division near Salem Church on the Orange Turnpike and halted it. The next day Early also came up. Attacked furiously on three sides, Sedgwick wisely abandoned any idea of joining Hooker; instead, he swung his corps around toward the Rappahannock to protect his flanks and that night crossed the Rappahannock River. Conversely, Hooker made no move to help Sedgwick at any time.

Following Sedgwick, Hooker withdrew his army across the Rappahannock. The general's boasting of a great victory to come before the campaign set him up for a spectacular fall. Whispers suggested that Hooker had been drunk during the battle. At cavalry headquarters, barely hours after the army had re–crossed the Rappahannock, young Captain George A. Custer wrote to George McClellan on May 6, 1863, about Hooker's alleged drinking. (One month later, Custer would become a 23-year-old general.) Custer summarized the Chancellorsville campaign for his former chief thus: What had ruined Hooker, the cavalryman reported, was "a wound he received from a projectile which requires a cork to be drawn before it is serviceable."

Board Pierced by Ramrod

MARYE'S HEIGHTS KNOWN TO FIRE THEIR RAMRODS

Captain Samuel D. Buck writes: "I always picked up any gun I found and fired it if it was loaded, and if the rammer was in the barrel I would fire it ramrod and all just the same." This embedded ramrod was received along with some other objects from the heirs of M.B. Rowe, owner of Brompton, the brick mansion that stood atop Marye's Heights that was a prominent landmark during the Battle of Fredericksburg. The Rowes were the last private family to own the property, and they sold the house to Mary Washington College in 1946. Unfortunately, there are no specific details about the ramrod and where it was found. It is assumed that it was found somewhere on the grounds surrounding the house.

Twice the focal point of major attacks by the Union Army, Marye's Heights ranks among the foremost landmarks in American military history. On December 13, 1862, during the Fredericksburg battle, Ambrose Burnside assailed the ridge with nine divisions. Confederate William Miller Owen watched as line after line of Union soldiers surged toward the ridge. "What a magnificent sight it is!" he marveled. "We have never witnessed such a battle-array before; long lines following one another, of brigade front. It seemed like a huge blue serpent about to encompass and crush us in its folds...." Miller's fears were unfounded. Not a single Union soldier reached the heights, though 8,000 fell in the attempt.

WITHDRAWAL

On the night of December 15, crying tears of frustration, Burnside gave the order for a careful withdrawal. Retreating across a river is a very dangerous military maneuver, but Burnside extricated his army unnoticed. Under the cover of darkness, in a rain storm, the artillery crossed first, followed by a thick cordon of soldiers, the echo of their footsteps muffled by the cold, heavy rain. When the morning fog dissipated, the Confederates discovered the flight of the Union troops which had taken place during the night. Hundreds of Union soldiers still lay where they had fallen. Once assured that the Yankees had indeed retreated beyond the river, the poorly clad Confederates scurried out and stripped the wool uniforms from the bodies that would no longer need them.

The town lay in ruins and nearly every house bore the scars of shells and bullets. Fredericksburg's citizens returned to their homes to discover looting, destruction, and an occasional dead soldier's body in their former homes.

This ramrod blasted through a piece of wood is on exhibit at the Fredericksburg Battlefield Visitor Center. It may have been fired accidentally from a rifle, or perhaps the rifleman, out of bullets, discharged the loading tool in an act of desperation (courtesy Fredericksburg and Spotsylvania National Military Park).

Painting of Residents' Return

Fredericksburg resident Jane Howison Beale wrote in her diary on May 14, 1862: "We are often compelled to listen to the enemy's excellent, firing of guns and loud strains of martial music in celebration of some triumph of their arms and superior numbers over our Spartan bands of which we know nothing except what their boasting tongues tell us. They invade our premises, find pretexts for thrusting unwelcome presence upon us at every turn and are 'surprised not to find more Union feeling among us...'"

"Handshake" Sword

A sword with a hand-painted scene showing the Lacy House is now on display at the former Union headquarters.

Photograph of the Stone Wall at Marye's Hill

Andrew Joseph Russell (1830–1902) was a member of the 141st New York Volunteers,

The battle at Fredericksburg left few homes unscarred. One house was hit by more than 130 cannonballs (courtesy Fredericksburg and Spotsylvania National Military Park).

who documented bridge-building and Union camps. He photographed at Fredericksburg, Petersburg and the fall of Richmond. After the war, he became one of the world's first photo journalists. He also was a painter.

Piece of Stonewall Jackson's Uniform

Like many other "relics" of the Civil War, this scrap of uniform was preserved, documented, and handed down to succeeding generations. Visitors to the Chancellorsville, Virginia, battlefield site can view the small, framed piece of Confederate General Stonewall Jackson's uniform. It was once a part of a large collection of Jackson memorabilia in the Jackson shrine that was transferred to the National Park Service from the R. F. & P. Railroad in 1937. As the photograph caption indicates, it was originally in the possession of Mrs. R. H. Alexander, who presented it to one Mr. W. L. Slaughter, believed to be the son of wartime Fredericksburg, Virginia, mayor Montgomery Slaughter.

THE DEATH OF AN ICON

Born in the town of Clarksburg in what is now the state of West Virginia, Thomas Jonathan Jackson already possessed a strong

---

Opposite top: This painting by David E. Henderson depicts some residents of Fredericksburg returning to their shattered home. The work is one of several displayed in the art section of the Fredericksburg Battlefield Visitors Center (courtesy Fredericksburg and Spotsylvania National Military Park). *Bottom:* Chatham is a plantation house once owned by J. Horace Lacy, a major in the Confederate Army. Known as the Lacy House by Union forces, it was occupied by the Union Army in April 1862. By the time the war ended in 1865, Chatham was in desolation. The restored house is the headquarters for the Fredericksburg and Spotsylvania National Military Park (courtesy Fredericksburg and Spotsylvania National Military Park).

This elaborate much-traveled sword is on display at the Chatham headquarters building. The engraving shows the Chatham house and a handshake between USA and CSA with this legend: "Lacy House opposite Fredericksburg Gen. Burnside Headquarters." The scabbard is decorated with a hand-painted scene of the "Lacy House" and Union and Confederate soldiers shaking hands. It was part of Doctor Chewning's large collection in Fredericksburg. The collection was sold and found its way across the country, then back to Fredericksburg, and finally to Florida where it was acquired for the Rosensteel collection of Gettysburg, Pennsylvania. In 1984, it was returned to Chatham for permanent display.

The most famous image from the Fredericksburg battle and perhaps from the entire Civil War is Andrew Joseph Russell's photograph of dead 18th Mississippians next to the famed stone wall. The photo was taken May 3, 1863, in the midst of actual fighting. Russell captured the stark scene even as Federals swarmed across the high ground (courtesy Fredericksburg and Spotsylvania National Military Park).

military background at the outbreak of the Civil War. His training in the U.S. Military Academy at West Point, his recognition as a hero in the Mexican War, and his experience as an instructor at the Virginia Military Institute led to his rapid rise through the officer corps and his justified rank of brigadier general at the first major battle of the Civil War near Manassas, Virginia. During that victory by the Confederacy, General Bernard E. Bee had famously proclaimed, "There is Jackson, standing like a stone wall," and a legend as well as a nickname was born.

By 1863, Jackson's military feats had ele-

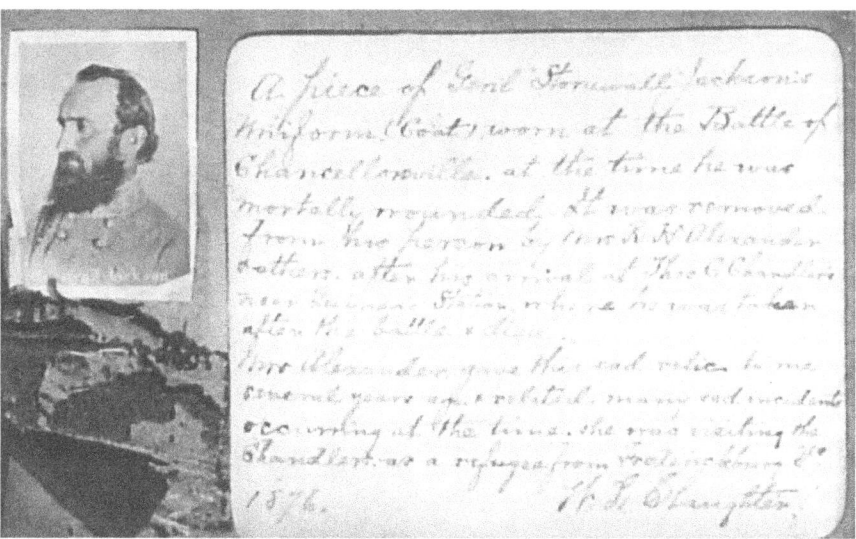

This framed fragment of a uniform worn by Stonewall Jackson is inscribed, "A piece of Genl Stonewall Jackson's uniform (Coat) worn at the battle of Chancellorsville at the time he was mortally wounded. It was removed from his person by Mrs. R H Alexander & others after his arrival at Thos G. Chandlers near Guinea's Station where he was taken after the battle and died. Mrs. Alexander gave this sad relic to me several years ago & related many sad incidents occurring at the time she was visiting the Chandlers as a refugee from Fredericksburg Va. W.L. Slaughter, 1876."

vated him to near mythical proportions by both Northern and Southern troops. Then, in the midst of one of his most brilliant battlefield maneuvers, he was mistakenly shot by his own men—"friendly fire"—on the night of May 2, 1863, at the Battle of Chancellorsville.

On Sunday, May 10, 1863, the doctors lost all hope of recovery as Jackson grew physically weaker. At the end, he was heard to say quietly, and with an expression as if of relief, "Let us cross over the river, and rest under the shade of the trees." Jackson's body was carried by train and canal barge to his present final resting place in Lexington, Virginia.

Photograph of Private George Murray

Murray was among the many men wounded at the Battle of Chancellorsville. The Chancellorsville Visitor's Center displays the photographs and uniforms of two young men who became casualties of that fierce battle. On May 3, 1862, Private George Murray, a Union soldier, and Confederate Sergeant George Hightower were engaged in the heavy fighting of that battle. Murray was with the 114th Pennsylvania Infantry and Hightower was attached to the 23rd Virginia Infantry. Their respective lines swayed back and forward through the woods as the armies contended for the same position.

For both of these young men it was a day of personal tragedy. Hightower was wounded in the left leg, and Murray, eighteen years old, was wounded in the left shoulder and survived the war.

Photograph of Union Major General A.W. Whipple

Whipple was killed by a Confederate sharp shooter during the Battle of Chancellorsville.

PICKED OFF

The story of A.W. Whipple's death is well told by Bigelow in his book, *Campaign of Chancellorsville*.

While standing near Ricketts' battery, directing the construction of some earthworks, he was

Jackson's chaplain, B. Tucker Lacy, had a brother who owned a house near the surgical tent at Wilderness Tavern, and thus he carried Stonewall's severed left arm to his brother's family cemetery for burial. Today four cedar trees maintain watch over Jackson's arm and several unmarked graves in the middle of a quiet cornfield.

mortally wounded by a sharpshooter sitting in a tree, who had been annoying the Federal officers with his fire directed especially upon them. General Sickles had sent instructions to Whipple to have Berdan detach a portion of his command to dislodge him. Whipple was on his horse writing an order to this effect when he was hit. The bullet passed through his belt and stomach, and came out at the small of his back close to the spinal column. The sharpshooter proceeded to load, but he never fired again. A lieutenant of Berdan's, carrying a loaded rifle, stalked across the Federal line of battle, crept through the line of skirmishers, and felt his way into the woods beyond till he caught sight of the Confederate marksman. Before the latter could finish reloading the lieutenant drew a bead on him and fired, bringing him down a corpse. On his return he exhibited as trophies an extra rifle, a fox skin cap, $1,600 in Confederate money, and $100 in greenbacks.

The best-known Union victim of a Confederate sharpshooter wielding a Whitworth sharpshooter rifle was Major General John Sedgwick, commander of the VI Corps of the Army of the Potomac, who was killed a year later on May 9, 1864, at nearby Spotsylvania Court House. Just moments before the fatal shot, to encourage his men, he had said, "Don't worry, boys. They couldn't hit an elephant at this dis...."

Richmond National Battlefield Park, Tredegar Street, Richmond, VA

Richmond's wartime story, as preserved by its National Battlefield Park, is not just the tale of two major campaigns to take it, the capital of the Confederacy — those being the 1862 Peninsula Campaign and the 1864 Overland Campaign. In addition, the park's documents a naval battle, a key industrial complex, the Confederacy's largest hospital, dozens of miles of elaborate original fortifications, and the evocative spots where determined soldiers stood paces apart and fought with rifles, reaping a staggering cost in lives.

The park contains cherished memorabilia concerning the four major actions of the Civil War leading to the eventual submission of Richmond.

Private George Murray, United States Army

THE PENINSULAR CAMPAIGN OF 1862 AND GRANT'S OVERLAND CAMPAIGN OF 1864

The Battle of Manassas in July 1861 had been a humiliating experience for the North, and it had proved conclusively that ill-trained recruits could not successfully prosecute the war. During the winter of 1861–62, therefore, the U.S. military augmented, reorganized, and intensively trained the forces defending Washington. By spring, these forces had been forged into a formidable instrument of war, more than 100,000 strong. It was called the Army of the Potomac and was commanded by General George B. McClellan.

The Northern press and populace were impatiently demanding action. The Peninsular Campaign was the answer to this demand. McClellan's plan was to transport his army by water from Washington to Fort Monroe at the tip of the peninsula that lies between the York and the James rivers, and then to march up the peninsula to Richmond, where he was to

Two soldiers' uniforms: The left leg of Confederate Sergeant George Hightower's trousers is missing; it was cut off in order to amputate his leg. He died after the operation, on May 21, 1863, at the age of 19.

be joined by General Irvin McDowell's corps from Fredericksburg, and together they would crush Richmond's defenders and capture the Confederate capital.

During March 1862, the waterborne movement to Fort Monroe was accomplished. Then McClellan commenced a slow advance northwestward up the peninsula. He pushed through the undermanned Confederate defense lines at Yorktown and Williamsburg and on May 15 established his base of operations at White House on the Pamunkey River, a tributary of the York.

To transport supplies, the Federals used great numbers of steam vessels, brigs, schooners, sloops, and barges, as well as thousands of wagons and the Richmond and York River Railroad.

Meanwhile, a fleet of Federal gunboats, led by the ironclads *Galena* and the famed *Monitor* had steamed up the James River to within eight miles of Richmond. Near-panic spread through the city before the heavy guns at strategic Fort Darling on Drewry's Bluff repulsed the Union fleet.

By the end of May, McClellan's advance up the peninsula had brought the Union Army so close to Richmond that observers in balloons could see the church spires of the city.

General Joseph E. Johnston, the Confederate Army commander, now believed that McClellan planned to stay north of the James River, and he decided to attack. He caught the Federal commander with his army split by the Chickahominy River, a low, marshy stream bordered by swamps. Heavy rains had made it almost impassable; thus, McClellan's forces were effectively divided. Employing his whole army, Johnston fell on the Federals south of the Chickahominy in the Battle of Seven Pines (Fair Oaks).

Although the battle itself was inconclusive, it produced significant effects on both armies. The already deliberate McClellan was made even more cautious than usual. More important, as a result of a wound sustained by General Johnston during the battle, Confederate President Jefferson Davis placed command of the defending forces in the hands of General Robert E. Lee.

McClellan, expecting General Irvin McDowell's corps to march overland from Fredericksburg to join him for the final assault on Richmond, stationed his right flank north of the Chickahominy to hook up with McDowell, but McDowell could not join McClellan. He had been recalled to protect Washington against Stonewall Jackson's threatening actions in the Shenandoah Valley. McClellan proceeded to sit on his hands, waiting for the roads to dry and the heavy siege guns to be brought up. In exasperation President Lincoln telegraphed: "Either attack Richmond or give up the job."

Aware of McDowell's withdrawal, Lee promptly brought Jackson down from the valley. On June 26, in a bold gamble, Lee struck forcefully at McClellan's exposed right flank with three-fourths of his command. To mount this attack, he had only about 20,000 troops left to hold the main part of the Federal army, 70,000 strong, away from Richmond.

This first of what became known as the Seven Days' Battles took place at Mechanicsville, or Beaver Dam Creek. Although the Confederates were repulsed, the appearance

Among the notable casualties of the May 4, 1863, fighting was Union Major General A.W. Whipple. The circumstances surrounding his death are featured in the Chancellorsville Visitor's Center (courtesy Fredericksburg and Spotsylvania National Military Park).

of Jackson's forces late in the day forced McClellan to fall back to a prepared position on Boatswain's Creek. The next day, the Battle of Gaines' Mill (First Cold Harbor), was fought there, the most vicious and costly of the Seven Days' Battles. When the Federal lines were finally broken that night, McClellan withdrew his right flank south across the Chickahominy and decided to change his base of operations from White House to Harrison's Landing on the James River, there to await reinforcements.

In an attempt to destroy the Union Army as it marched south to Harrison's Landing, Lee attacked again on June 29 and 30 at Savage Station and Glendale (Frayser's Farm), where bitter rear-guard actions took place. But a lack of coordination and proper timing on the part of Lee's subordinate generals, combined with McClellan's masterful organization for withdrawal, foiled Lee's strategy.

The last of the Seven Days' Battles was fought on July 1 at Malvern Hill. McClellan placed his artillery on the crest of this strong defensive position. As the Confederates charged up the slope, they were assailed by withering fire from these guns, and their gallant attack was broken. This led Confederate General D.H. Hill to remark: "Confederate infantry and Federal artillery, side by side on the same field, need fear no foe on earth."

The next day, the Army of the Potomac was safely encamped at Harrison's Landing under the protection of Federal gunboats on the James. Shortly thereafter, however, the army was recalled to Washington to support General John Pope's campaign in Northern Virginia.

The Seven Days' Battles cost the Confederates 20,614, and the Federals 15,849, in killed, wounded, and missing.

Grant's Overland Campaign began with the Battle of the Wilderness, May 5–7, 1864, in what proved to be the start of the final campaign against the Army of Northern Virginia. The Army of the Potomac, commanded by General George G. Meade and numbering approximately 118,000 troops, here fought the Confederate defenders of Richmond. Lee had about 62,000 men with him, while an additional 30,000 under P.G.T. Beauregard held the Richmond/Petersburg area. The battle resulted in a fearful loss of men on both sides, although the armies remained essentially intact. This was followed by an equally heavy series of engagements around Spotsylvania Court House from May 8 to 19.

Failing to destroy the Army of Northern Virginia in these battles, Grant moved the Army of the Potomac to the east of Richmond. He hoped to outflank the Confederate defenders by persistent night marches. Lee was not to be so easily outguessed, however, and after minor battles at the North Anna River (May 23) and Totopotomoy Creek (May 29), Grant

Balloon gondolas were used as observation platforms during the war. In 1928, J. Amber Johnston received a phone call asking him to come out to the Gaines Mill Battlefield, site of the Lowe balloon station. After arriving, Johnston was shown this valve that had been dug up about 18 inches below the surface by one of the workmen who had been hired to clean up the property (courtesy Richmond National Battlefield Park).

arrived at Cold Harbor, about eight miles east of Richmond. Lee's army stood between him and the city, and on June 3, two days after he arrived at Cold Harbor, Grant ordered a direct frontal assault. He was repulsed with horrific losses, so he decided to turn quickly to the south of Richmond and isolate the city and the defending troops by cutting the railroads which supplied it. To do this, he would need to attack Petersburg.

There are few months in the calendar of centuries that will have a more conspicuous place in history than the month of May 1864. It will be remembered for the momentous events which took place in one of the greatest military campaigns the world has ever seen. We cannot fully comprehend the endurance, the persistence, the grueling marching, the intense fighting, and the unrelenting, almost cheerful energy and effort that carried the Army of the Potomac from the Rappahannock to the James in a mere forty days, against the stubborn opposition of an army of almost equal numbers. There was not a day of rest, scarcely an hour of quiet. Morning, noon, and night, the booming of cannon and the rattling of musketry echoed unceasingly through the Wilderness, around the hillocks of Spotsylvania, along the banks of the North Anna, and among the groves of Bethesda Church and Cold Harbor. This one small section of Virginia became America's bloodiest battleground, as one out of every five soldiers killed in the entire Civil War died in three neighboring counties.

Lowe's Balloon Valve

Thaddeus S. Lowe turned his interest in ballooning into a Union strategic asset. President Lincoln appointed him chief aeronaut of the Union Army Balloon Corps in July 1861. Balloons allowed the army to observe troop movements.

The workman who unearthed the valve in 1928 claimed the valve as his own and wanted $25 for it. His employer told him the valve was not his, that he was working by the hour and that if he took it they would "set the law on him." After some argument, the employer agreed to give him $2.50 for the balloon gas line valve. This fourteen-inch valve is displayed at the Richmond National Battlefield Park.

A NEW MILITARY DIMENSION

The ability of Thaddeus Lowe's new field generators to produce the gas necessary to lift balloons provided the mobility needed by the opposing armies. A photograph shows Lowe's balloon *Intrepid* being inflated on Gaines Hill, June 1, 1862. Lowe is standing at right with his hand resting against the balloon. The politically savvy Lowe had an immense portrait of General McClellan painted in color on the yellow varnished cloth surrounding one of the balloons.

The ecstatic days of balloon observation occurred during the Peninsular Campaign, culminating in Richmond's two balloon camps, one at Gaines Mills, with the *Intrepid*, and the other, with the *Constitution*, near Mechanicsville, piloted by Assistant Aeronaut James Allen. The activity at these bases lasted about a month. The following are two reports regarding this engagement:

BALLOON CAMP,
Near Mechanicsville,
May 29, 1862—9.30 A.M.

Brig. General A.A. HUMPHREYS,
Chief of Topographical Engineers,
Army of the Potomac:

GENERAL: I ascended at 7.30 o'clock this A.M., near New Bridge; could discover no change in the position of the enemy in that vicinity. I then came to this point to get another view, which I have just obtained, and find the enemy quite opposite Mechanicsville.

A battery consisting of several guns is in position near the road on the opposite heights. There are troops lying in the shade of the woods along the whole line from below New Bridge to some distance above this point, the greatest number, however, opposite this point.

I have now on hand material sufficient to keep the two balloons in operation for about one week only.

Very respectfully,
your obedient servant,
T. S. C. LOWE, Chief Aeronaut,
Army of the Potomac.

BALLOON CAMP,
Near Doctor Gaines' House,
June 1, 1862—11 A.M.

Brigadier-General HUMPHREYS,
or General R.B. MARCY,
Chief of Staff:

My ascent and observations just completed show the firing of the enemy to be in the same posi-

Thaddeus S. Lowe organized the U.S. Army's Balloon Corps in the early days of the Civil War. Lowe's development of a field generator for inflating the balloons allowed for the practical application of balloons for observation during the Peninsular Campaign (courtesy Library of Congress).

tion. The road in the rear of the firing is filled with wagons and troops. About two miles still farther to the rear of Fair Oaks Station, and on the Williamsburg stage road, Charles City road, and Central road, are also large bodies of troops; in fact, I am astonished at their numbers compared with ours, although they are more concentrated than we are. Their whole force seems to be paying attention to their right. A regiment has just marched to the front, where we are preparing a crossing. Their large barracks to the left of Richmond is entirely free from smoke, and, in fact, the whole city and surroundings are nearly free from smoke, which enables me to see with distinctness the enemy's earth-works. Quite a large body of troops are on the other side of the river, about two miles from here, to our left.

The weather is now calm, and an excellent opportunity is offered for an engineer officer to accompany me.

The balloon at Mechanicsville is constantly up.

Your very obedient servant,

T. S. C. LOWE.

Lowe's savoir-faire did not last another year. His reports were over exaggerated as his observations missed large troop movements. Jubal Early wrote, "Professor Lowe's balloon reconnaissance so signally failed on this occasion and in the operations at Chancellorsville, that they were abandoned for the rest of the war." His daily salary of $10 and insistence on placing his father on his payroll were just two of Dr. Lowe's bones of contention with the army. His ego clashed with those of the lower-ranking Union officers, and his two main supporters, generals George McClellan and Fritz-John Porter, had been discredited. Finally, his mission was scrapped when Congress refused to appropriate funding for the Army Balloon Corps.

The Confederates also employed a reconnaissance balloon during the Yorktown Campaign and the Seven Days' Battles. The balloon at Yorktown was inflated by burning pine tree knots that created the hot gases necessary to carry it aloft. At Seven Pines, the

The Confederate gunboat *Teaser*. Unfortunately for the Rebels, a map of the underwater mines in the James River was carried aboard the Teaser and fell into the hands of the Union Navy (courtesy Library of Congress).

Confederate balloon was filled with gas from the city gas works overlooking Rocketts, the Confederate Navy Yard, and transported to the front lines east of the city on the Richmond & York River Railroad. When McClellan moved his army south and east of Richmond, the rail line no longer served as a useful vantage point for observing enemy movements. Colonel Edward Porter Alexander, the officer charged with making the balloon ascents, accordingly shifted operations to the James River. Alexander had the balloon filled at Rocketts and transported it on the gunboat *Teaser* to Drewry's Bluff. Just after midnight on the morning of June 30, 1862, Alexander made his first ascent from the vessel's deck. The balloon was sent back for more gas, and Alexander made a second airborne sortie later that day. His career as a balloonist ended without fireworks on the Fourth of July after only a few more nocturnal flights when the *Teaser* ran aground and was captured.

General James Longstreet had this to say regarding the capture of the balloon:

The Federals had been using balloons in examining our positions, and we watched with envious eyes their beautiful observations as they floated high up in the air, well out of range of our guns. While we were longing for the balloons that poverty denied us, a genius arose for the occasion and suggested that we send out and gather silk dresses in the Confederacy and make a balloon. It was done, and we soon had a great patchwork ship of many varied hues which was ready for use in the Seven Days' campaign.

We had no gas except in Richmond, and it was the custom to inflate the balloon there, tie it securely to an engine, and run it down the York River Railroad to any point at which we desired to send it up. One day it was on a steamer down on the James River, when the tide went out and left the vessel and balloon high and dry on a bar. The Federals gathered it in, and with it the last silk dress in the Confederacy. This capture was the meanest trick of the war and one that I have never yet forgiven.

Battle Sash of Major Luther Kieffer

The sash Kieffer was wearing when he took a fatal shot in the Cold Harbor assault during the Overland Campaign is on display in Richmond. The assault was a useless waste of Union lives. General U.S. Grant later said, "I have always regretted that the last assault at Cold Harbor was ever made ... no advantage was gained to compensate for the heavy losses we sustained."

AN ENTIRE FAMILY WIPED OUT

Luther Kieffer was a French immigrant who was born in 1820 and who later married into a prominent New York family. He served in the Mexican War and joined the great gold rush of 1849. After returning from the prospecting hills of California, he purchased a farm near Sedalia, Missouri.

In 1861, Kieffer joined the 1st New York Light Artillery and was appointed a major and commander of that artillery battalion at the battle of Chancellorsville, but his frustrations with General Joseph Hooker's leadership led to his resignation, and Kieffer returned home.

Having second thoughts, Kieffer a year later reenlisted in the 14th New York Heavy Artillery. He also persuaded his two grown sons, his brother, and a cousin to join him; he was now the commander of Company M and held the rank of captain. Kieffer and his immediate relatives survived the carnage of the battles of the Wilderness, Spotsylvania, and North Anna, but at the bloody massacre at Cold Harbor, Kieffer's luck ran out, and both he and his son William were killed. His other son, Theodore, was wounded and died from the injury twenty months later. The cousin, Abner, was taken prisoner that dreadful morning and died from his wounds in Libby Prison, Richmond. In effect, a complete family had been killed in the same battle. Neither Luther Kieffer's nor his son's body was recovered, but a Confederate soldier sent the captain's effects to his family in New York. These included a diary, and the last two entries follow:

Wednesday,
June 1, 1864
After 12 o'clock were ordered with Capt. Wilkie. The pickets were fired upon on my right & left & forced back occasional firing until midnight. Swung back the right of my co. The Division officer of the day assisted Capt. Wilkie to connect his co. with mine.

Wednesday,
June 2, 1864
Bernie [abrupt end]

In May 1864, Ulysses S. Grant, now in command of all Union armies, crossed the Rapidan River with George

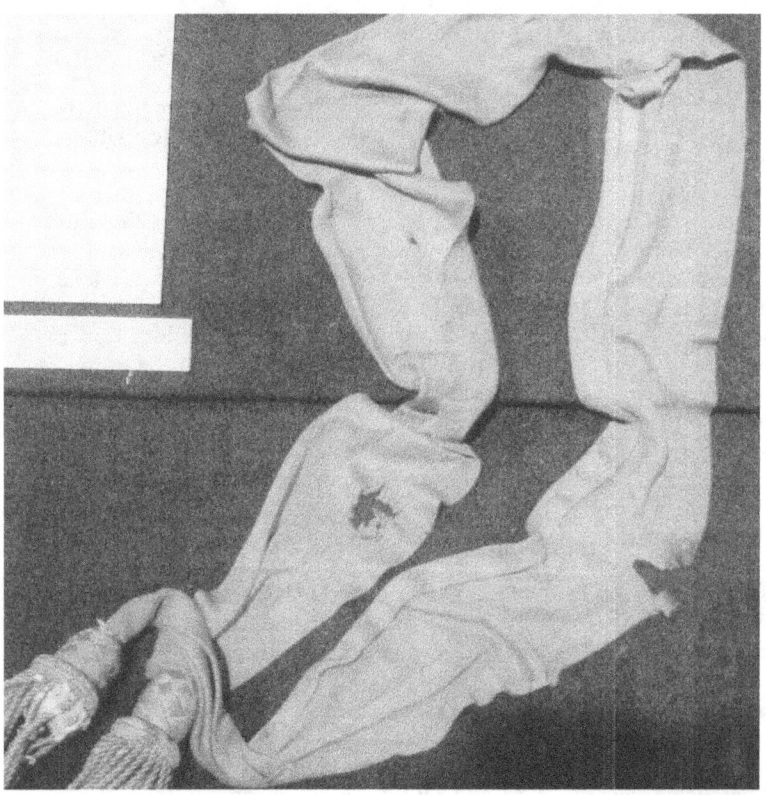

This battle sash, revealing bloodstains and the tear where a fatal round hit Major Luther Kieffer, was recently donated to the Richmond National Battlefield Park by his descendants.

Meade's Army of the Potomac. Grant had two objectives: destroy Lee's army and capture Richmond. The latter was to be a formidable task; for almost two years the Confederates had been strengthening the earthen forts and breastworks around the capital so that the city the city was practically encircled by three lines of defense. Lee's army was as ready as it would ever be.

After a month of fighting by day and marching by night, the Federals had left behind the bloody Wilderness and Spotsylvania battlefields, and on June 1, the Northern and Southern armies again came to grips at Cold Harbor, a strategic crossroads guarding the approaches to Richmond. After horrendous fighting which cost the Federals heavily, the Confederate lines were bent back in several places, but they were not broken.

Grant spent the next day, June 2, maneuvering troops into position for another frontal assault. Lee's men took advantage of the lull to entrench themselves, using the existing terrain so effectively that they were able to cover the Yankees' field of attack with a murderous fire. Furthermore, Grant's corps commanders had not properly reconnoitered these fortified positions, and thus the Union Army began what would prove to be a hopeless attack at 4:30 A.M. on June 3. It lasted fewer than thirty minutes but left over 7,000 killed and wounded lying

This lone stone monument at Cold Harbor commemorates the fallen comrades of the 2nd Connecticut Volunteer Heavy Artillery. Surprisingly, there are no other monuments to honor the numerous casualties suffered by both armies in this savage 1864 battle, where over 7,000 men were literally shot to pieces in half an hour.

between the trenches. Union General Martin T. McMahon rightly observed: "In that little period more men fell bleeding as they advanced than in any other like period of time throughout the war." The horror of the day was cruelly intensified when a hot sun rose to further torture the wounded men pinned down between the lines.

The battle of Cold Harbor saved Richmond for another ten months but proved to be Lee's last major victory. The battle had shown the futility of frontal assaults on the well-entrenched Confederates. Among the dead lay Luther Kieffer, his son, and his cousin; his second son would die later. Only Kieffer's bloodstained sash would survive.

Petersburg National Battlefield Park, 1539 Hickory Hill Drive, Petersburg, VA 23803

This battlefield contains 2,460 acres and is made up of six major units with battlefields, earthen forts, trenches, and the Poplar Grove National Cemetery. Collectively, they vividly remind visitors of the story of the longest siege in American warfare and of the experiences of the 150,000 soldiers from both sides of the trenches.

The visitor center offers exhibits and audiovisual programs that introduce the story of the siege and its place and impact on the course of the Civil War. A driving tour of the battlefields includes thirteen separate sites with three visitor centers along a thirty-three mile route. Plan on a full day to experience the entire battlefield park.

Wooden Grave Marker

A Georgia soldier named Vaughn was hastily memorialized by his brother after his death at Petersburg on July 30, 1864.

THE PETERSBURG SIEGE AND THE BATTLE OF THE CRATER

It was the task of the Army of the Potomac and the Army of the James to capture Richmond, crush the Army of Northern Virginia, and march south to hook up with Sherman. The story of the Army of the James in the early phase of the offensive is a brief one. General Benjamin F. Butler was ordered to advance upon Richmond from the south and threaten communications between the Confederate capital and the Southern states.

Employing some 40,000 Union troops, Butler began his advance. City Point, located at the junction of the James and Appomattox Rivers and soon to be the supply center for the attack on Petersburg, was captured on May 4, 1864. Within two weeks, however, a numerically inferior Confederate force shut up the Army of the James—"as if it had been in a bottle strongly corked"—in the Bermuda Hundred, a loop formed by the winding James and Appomattox Rivers. Butler tarried here while north of him the Army of the Potomac and the Army of Northern Virginia were engaged in a series of bloody battles.

The battle of Cold Harbor saved Richmond for another ten months and proved to be Lee's last major victory. The battle had shown the hopelessness of frontal assaults on the well-dug-in Confederates. Grant was compelled to change his strategy from maneuvers to siege tactics. During the night of June 12, he secretly moved his troops out of the trenches at Cold Harbor, and by June 15 the main body of his army had crossed the James to begin the siege of Petersburg.

The blockade was punctuated by another surprise from Grant three months later. In the predawn darkness of September 29, he quietly slipped two corps back across the James River in a sudden attack on Forts Gilmer and Harrison, two strongly fortified positions in the Richmond defenses. His purpose was to prevent Lee from sending reinforcements to Jubal Early in the Shenandoah Valley. Fort Gilmer successfully resisted the assault, but Fort Harrison was captured and renamed Fort Burnham by the Federals.

The next day, with Lee looking on, the outnumbered Confederates failed in repeated attempts to retake the fort. Then, they proceeded to build new fortifications to compensate for their loss. The Union forces, to protect their position further and to neutralize Confederate gunboats, constructed Fort Brady a few miles south of Fort Burnham (Harrison) on a high bluff overlooking the James River.

After weeks of preparation, on July 30 the Federals tunneled beneath the Confederate encampment and exploded the notorious mine beneath Pegram's Salient, blowing a gap in the Confederate defenses of Petersburg and creating the famous Petersburg crater which, though smaller now through almost 140 years of weathering, is still visible. After the initial

The crude grave marker in the photograph was carved by the brother of a Confederate officer killed at The Crater.

shock of the stunning, unexpected explosion, everything deteriorated rapidly for the Union attackers. Unit after unit charged into and around the crater, where soldiers scurried around in total confusion. The Confederates quickly recovered and launched several counterattacks, led by Major General William Mahone. The break was sealed off, and the Federals were repulsed with severe casualties. Edward Ferrero's division of black soldiers was badly mauled. This could have been Grant's best chance to end the Siege of Petersburg early and save lives but instead, the opposing forces settled in for another eight months of dreaded trench warfare. General Burnside was relieved of command for his role in the debacle.

The entrenched armies faced each other day after day until Grant finally broke Lee's lines at Petersburg on April 1, 1865, forcing the Confederates to abandon Richmond.

Upon evacuation of the Southern capital, the Confederate Government authorized the burning of warehouses and supplies, resulting in considerable destruction to factories and houses in the business district. The end of the war was imminent; before the charred ruins of Richmond had cooled, Lee brought his remaining army west and surrendered to Grant at Appomattox Court House on April 9, 1865.

Fused Minié Balls

During the war, the North and South both used a great variety of small arms ammunition, but the type most often employed was the famed Minié ball. Prior to the development of the Minié ball, rifles were not used in combat because of the difficulty of loading them effectively. The ammunition used by rifles was the same diameter as the barrel in order for the bullet to engage the grooves of the rifled barrel, and as a result the ball had to be forced into the barrel. The Minié ball, originally designed by Captain Claude-Etienne Minié of France and improved on by manufacturers in the United States, changed warfare dramatically. Since the Minié ball was smaller than the diameter of the barrel, it could be loaded quickly by easily dropping the bullet down the barrel. This innovative lead bullet featured either two or three grooves

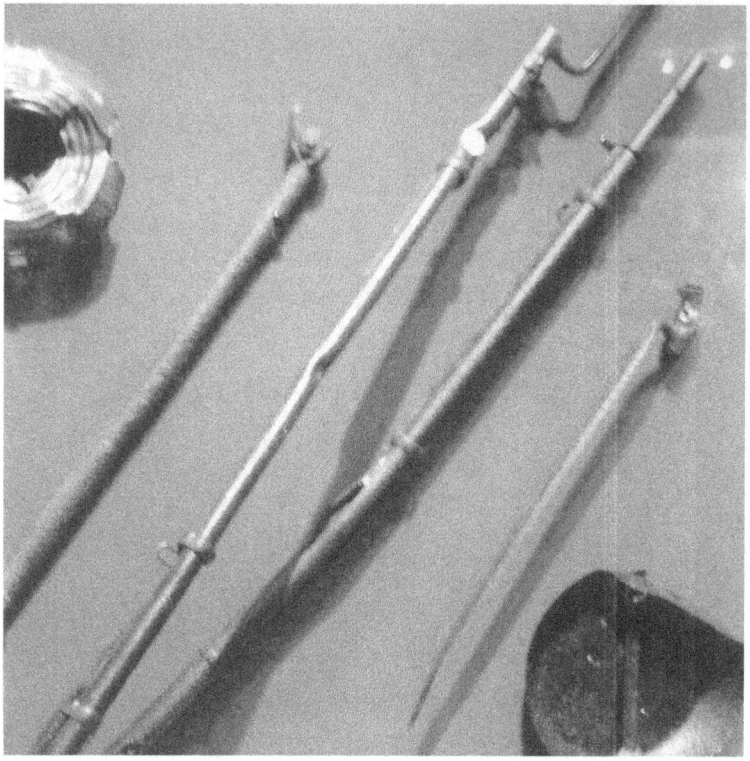

These weapons were excavated at the site of the Battle of the Crater.

and a conical cavity in its base. When the rifle was fired, the rapidly expanding gases formed by the exploding powder expanded the base of the bullet so that it instantaneously engaged the rifling in the barrel. Now, rifles could be loaded quickly and fired accurately.

City Point National Park, Cedar Lane, Hopewell, VA

At Grant's former headquarters at City Point, you will learn about the Union's massive supply base and large field hospital operation. You can also learn about the Appomattox plantation, the Eppes family, and their slaves, who were here before the war's arrival. For nearly ten months this site served as the main logistics and supply base of the Union army then surrounding Petersburg. Roam the grounds where Grant discussed both war and peace with President Lincoln, and enjoy the video presentations and ranger talks.

Grant's Headquarters' Cabin Door

General U.S. Grant used a specially-constructed cabin for his headquarters at City Point. The door is on display there today.

A PRIME LOCATION

During the siege of Petersburg, General Grant's headquarters were maintained at the small port town of City Point, Virginia, eight miles behind Union lines. Located at the confluence of the James and Appomattox rivers, City Point had been connected to Petersburg by railroad prior to the war. Its strategic position next to the railroad bed and the two rivers offered Grant easy access to points along the front, as well as good transportation and communications with Fort Monroe, Virginia, and Washington, D.C. When he arrived at City Point on June 15, 1864, Grant at first established his headquarters in a tent on the east lawn of Dr. Richard Eppes's plantation, also known by the Native American name of Appomattox. As the battle stalemated, Grant had carpenters build the cabin shown in the photograph.

Even more important than being the headquarters for the United States Armies, City Point was the supply base for the Union forces fighting at Petersburg. Overnight the tiny village became one of the busiest ports in the world as hundreds of ships arrived bringing food, clothing, ammunition, and other supplies for the Union army. On an average day, for example, the Union army had stored in and around City Point 9,000,000 meals for the men and 12,000 tons of hay and oats for the horses

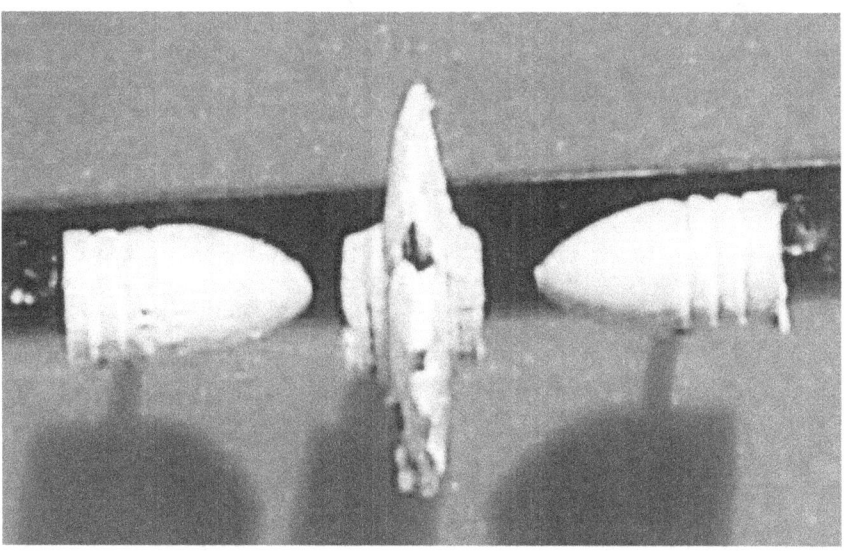

Defying all odds, two Minié balls from opposing sides met head-on during fierce fighting at the Battle of the Crater, and fused into a disk. The display above illustrates the ways the two balls collided into a perfect circle in the center.

The above Minié ball oddity is displayed at the Petersburg National Battlefield. Bullets occasionally would indeed collide or penetrate a bullet already on the ground merging into a distorted mass of lead.

and mules. The only food not imported from the North was bread, which the army produced on site. In a bakery built on the grounds, commissary personnel produced 100,000 rations of bread a day for the hungry soldiers fighting in the trenches. In this respect, the Union army had a huge advantage over the supply-poor Southern troops who were getting by on what they could.

Suppliers sent bread and other necessities to the front by train and by wagon. The U.S. Military Railroad Construction Corps rebuilt the line west to Petersburg, and then extended it southwest behind Union lines. Twenty-five locomotives and 275 railroad cars were then brought to City Point by barge from Washington, to provide rolling stock for the line. In a breathtaking twenty-two days, the army had completed the first stage of the railroad and had trains operating on a full schedule. At Petersburg victory rode the rails.

"Essence of Coffee"

In the second year of the war, the Union commissary began to distribute a mixture of coffee extract missed with sugar and milk that looked like axle grease. This was to fight a coffee shortage fueled by war commodity speculators. According to one source, the men would not drink it and it was discontinued.

This coffee can label advises that the four-ounce tin container "will go as far as four pounds of coffee." On the right side of the 3-inch by 2.5-inch container in large bold characters is printed the number "5000," insinuating

The door to the cabin that General Grant had constructed at City Point was given to the Fredericksburg National Battlefield Park by Edward T. Stuart in 1939. Stuart was the son of George H. Stuart, who had been in charge of the United States Christian Commission during the Civil War. That same year the door was shipped to Petersburg National battlefield, being the most appropriate place for its display.

that this tin of "instant coffee" could brew 5,000 cups. "Of all articles of diet afforded the soldier, none is more important or popular than his coffee," said the *Manual for Cooks*, 1862.

Detonator

A detonator similar to one on display at City Point used clockworks to time an explosion.

CITY POINT
SABOTAGE

At City Point Battlefield Park, park official Jim Blankenship would tell visitors about Grant and Lincoln, the place's military history, and about the fateful day in August when twelve pounds of powder in a box ignited 80,000 pounds of powder loaded into a barge, creating an earthshaking, thunderous, thirty-second explosion. The resulting black smoke could be observed thirty miles downriver. Those who saw it thought that Petersburg or Richmond was burning.

Blankenship did not know much more about the explosion and the man responsible, John Maxwell, until a hot summer day in 1990 when a lady named Alice Westmore Evans paid him a call. She asked Mr. Blankenship if he knew anything about the explosion. He responded in the affirmative, but he was about to learn much more. Evans told Blankenship that John Maxwell was her grandfather and although she had known him only when she was girl, she had something very interesting to show Blankenship—a small, odd-looking mechanical device. Mrs. Evans then donated to the National Park Service the horological torpedo, the same type of mechanism Maxwell had used in the explosion. When Blankenship excitedly gave the device to a detonation expert to examine, "he said this would still be considered a class A detonator today, and it works."

John Maxwell had been born in Paisley, Scotland, and came to Virginia as a young man, for reasons unknown to his family. An adventurous spirit, Maxwell enlisted in 60th Infantry Regiment (also called 3rd Regiment, Wise Legion) on April 19, 1861—nine days after Fort Sumter. He later became a Confederate raider, joining a small band of soldiers who tried to capture Union ships.

Maxwell was eventually captured and at first sentenced to be hanged, but he was later freed in a prisoner-of-war exchange. He then went to work for a Confederate Secret Service division organized by Zebekiah McDaniel. In July 1864, when he was thirty-one years old, Maxwell embarked on a clandestine mission to destroy enemy vessels in Virginia waters.

According to Maxwell's own report, he left Richmond on July 26, heading for the James River with a guide named R. K. Dillard. The pair arrived in Isle of Wight County on August 2, where they found out about the "immense supplies of stores being landed at City Point." The Union supply depot seemed the perfect place to execute Maxwell's plan, so he and Dillard struck out for the point.

They traveled by night, crawling on their knees to pass through the Union picket line

A close inspection of 1864 photographs of Grant's cabin provided proof that the door at Petersburg is indeed the cabin's original door. The nail patterns and knotholes match up exactly with the door in the pictures (courtesy City Point National Park).

undetected. The sun had not yet risen when they at last neared City Point on August 9. Maxwell told his companion to wait for him and advanced the last half-mile alone, carrying the detonator and powder in a medium-sized box. Maxwell surveyed the wharf from the overlooking bluff and watched the captain of one of the three docked barges leave his craft and come ashore. As Maxwell advanced to the wharf, a sentinel stopped him. Maxwell told the guard that the captain had ordered him to take a box to his cabin. As Maxwell surreptitiously activated the detonators, he flagged down a sailor from the barge and handed the lethal box to the man, with the instruction to carry it aboard. "Rejoining my companion," Maxwell wrote, "we retired to a safe distance to witness the effect of our effort. In about an hour the explosion occurred."

That morning, Union physician James Otis Moore had come to City Point to load a train car with medical supplies for the Third Division hospital near Petersburg. After a few minutes of mild arguing, he and a colleague boarded the last car on the train. Moore's friend, a Dr. Merryweather, wanted the two of them to ride on top of the train. Moore didn't want to, pointing out that it was a hot day. The only open car left contained a pile of cowhides that smelled none too fresh, but Moore persisted, and Merryweather reluctantly got in.

They were chatting about the similarity of the smell of the hides to that of the hospital dissecting room when they heard what Moore called "a terrific noise." They quickly peered out the open door toward the river, about sixty yards away, and as they did, a cloud of hot cinders slammed into their faces. The startled doctors instinctively flung themselves on the floor of the car. When the booming noise subsided, they ran out to see what had happened.

The first thing they spied was "a man lying flat on his back, dead, on the top of one of the cars," Moore wrote the next day in a letter to his wife. "We went a little further and there lay the lower half of the trunk & about

On any given day in the bustling harbor of City Point, 150 to 200 schooners, steamships, and barges were waiting to unload military supplies (courtesy City Point National Park).

half of the thighs of a man. We proceeded up the hill where our hospital used to be & all along the road we saw detached portions of the human body. A foot, hand, pieces of the scalp—large pieces of muscle & flesh lay scattered all around. We dressed some of the most hideous & ghastly wounds which falls to the lot of Surgeons to dress." Had the two surgeons been atop the train as Dr. Merryweather had wished, they themselves could have been victims.

The explosion aboard the powder barge destroyed more than half of the 400-foot wharf and caused a whopping $2 million in damage. Debris flew half a mile in every direction. One account describes the hideous scene of barrels of human flesh fragments collected after the explosion. The official tally

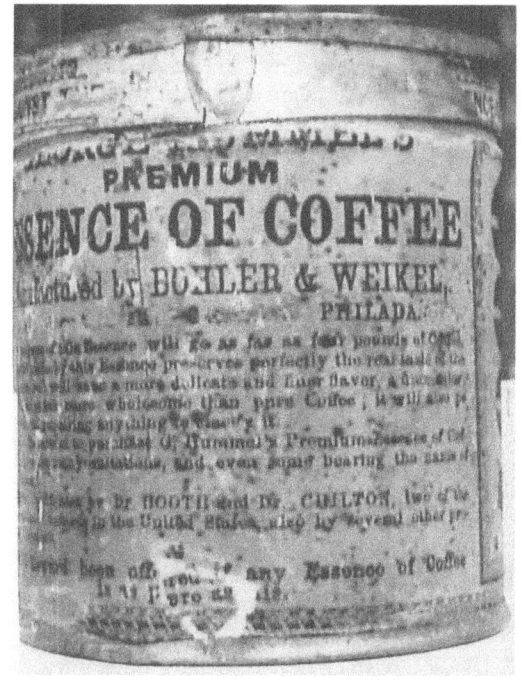

Wooden boxes of Essence of Coffee were among the tons of supplies arriving daily at City Point. Printed on this brown paper label is "Essence of Coffee, manufactured by BOHLER & WEIKEL, PHILADA."

The triggering device for a terror weapon of the times — a horological torpedo — meaning literally, a "time bomb."

listed forty-three persons who died instantly, including the depot's lemonade vendor, who was killed when a flying saddle hit him in the stomach. One hundred twenty-six more people were wounded. "I really believe more people were killed in this thing than are known," Blankenship says. The majority of the victims were recently freed black dockworkers, whose names were likely never written in any muster rolls. The explosion also rained shells, balls, and debris upon the hillside tent camp of the black workers and their families.

Debris also showered Grant's camp on the bluff, injuring some of his staff and killing one mounted courier. Surrounded by splinters and various kinds of ammunition, Grant, who had been sitting under a sycamore and reading the newspaper, was nevertheless unharmed. Several horses and the mounted orderly were killed as Grant's staff rushed to the edge of the bluff overlooking the wharf. Oddly, perhaps, General Grant was the only one of the party who remained unmoved; he did not even leave his seat to run to the bluff with the others to see what had happened. Five minutes after the explosion, he wired a telegraph to Washington describing the event.

Most people at the time assumed that the explosion was the result of an accident, perhaps a dropped shell, but of course the real cause was the contents of Maxwell's package, the one he'd carried so far: a delicate little device nestled in twelve pounds of black powder. The maker had taken the insides of a clock—the windup mechanism and fine-toothed gears—and affixed two small cylinders. The cylinder on the left held a spring, the one on the right a percussion cap. When the clockworks reached a preset detonation time, the action moved a lever, which released the spring, which smashed the percussion cap.

Maxwell, hiding a short distance away, saw and felt the terrific explosion. He escaped injury but his companion, Dillard, received serious ear damage. Maxwell later collected some Union newspaper articles describing the carnage and enclosed them in his report to his commander. He expressed no regret for the effects of his deadly device, except to note that some accounts (now believed to be false) claimed that "a party of ladies" had been killed. "It is saddening to me to realize the fact that terrible effects of war induce such consequences," Maxwell wrote, "but when I remember the ordeal to which our own women have been subjected, and the barbari-

City Point before the explosion (courtesy City Point National Park).

ties of the enemy's crusade against us and them, my feelings are relieved by the reflection that while this catastrophe was not intended by us, it amounts only, in the Providence of God, to just retaliation."

His mission accomplished, Maxwell helped a party of Confederates board and capture a Union ship and its crew in the James. Later attempts to raid Union vessels failed, and Maxwell soon found himself running from Union soldiers who had landed at Smithfield to pursue the Confederate pirates. He then beat a retreat to Richmond.

Grant appointed a board of officers to investigate the explosion. Several days were spent taking testimony from anyone who had witnessed the catastrophe, and the board employed every possible means to probe the massive explosion. All of the men in the close proximity of the boat had been killed. The investigation concluded that the explosion occurred because of careless handling of ammunition by the laborers who were unloading the ship. It was years before Confederate records revealed the true cause of the disaster.

After the war, Maxwell became a blacksmith, working in wrought iron. He had a shop at 1006 East Cary Street in the heart of Richmond, and in late 1865, he married Elizabeth "Lizzie" Cance, a Scottish woman who was also from Paisley. Lizzie died in 1898, and ten years later, Maxwell went to live in the Robert E. Lee Camp Confederate Soldiers' Home, located at the corner of Grove Avenue and The Boulevard. In 1916, as another great war raged in Europe, John Maxwell, age eighty-four, contracted pneumonia and died soon after.

Staunton River Battlefield State Park, Route 600, Clover, VA

The Staunton (pronounced "Stanton" by Virginians) visitor's center opened on June 10, 1995. Exhibits focus on Wilson's Raid, the battle of "Old Men and Young Boys," and

City Point after the devastating explosion that closed the port down for nine days (courtesy City Point National Park).

home life in Southside Virginia during the war. A large relief map of the surrounding countryside highlights battlefield features and the Randolph and Mulberry Hill plantations. The center also features extensive displays on the generation and use of electrical energy. Two displays of special interest are the banjo of Robert Leonard Skelton and a Union officer's sword.

Union Sword

A Union officer gave his sword to 9-year-old Donald McPhail when the child's pony was commandeered.

THE BATTLE OF STAUNTON RIVER BRIDGE

On June 22, 1864, the cavalry divisions of Union generals James Wilson and August Kautz were dispatched from the Petersburg lines to disrupt Confederate rail supply lines. General Grant knew that if these supply lines could be destroyed, Robert E. Lee would have to abandon Petersburg. Federal troops left Petersburg with over 5,000 cavalry troops and sixteen pieces of artillery. As they moved west, pursued by Confederate General W.H.F. "Rooney" Lee and his cavalry, Wilson's own cavalry tore up sixty miles of track and burned two trains and several railroad stations.

Just south of Roanoke Station (present-day Randolph, Virginia) was a long, covered railroad bridge over the Staunton River, Wilson's final objective. The bridge was defended by a battalion of 296 Confederate reserves under the leadership of Captain Benjamin Farinholt.

On June 23, at 10 P.M., Captain Farinholt received word from General Lee that a large detachment of enemy cavalry was moving his direction to destroy the bridge and that he should "make every possible preparation immediately." That night, Captain Farinholt sent off circulars urging the citizens of Halifax, Char-

In June of 1864, Union cavalry forces moved south on the Richmond & Danville Railroad toward the Staunton River bridge, commandeering any animals and supplies they deemed useful, including young Donald McPhail's pony. When the boy started to cry, a sympathetic Union officer gave him this sword to help ease the loss. The sword hung in the Mulberry Hill Plantation home until April of 2000, when it was donated to the Staunton River Battlefield State Park by the James Butler family.

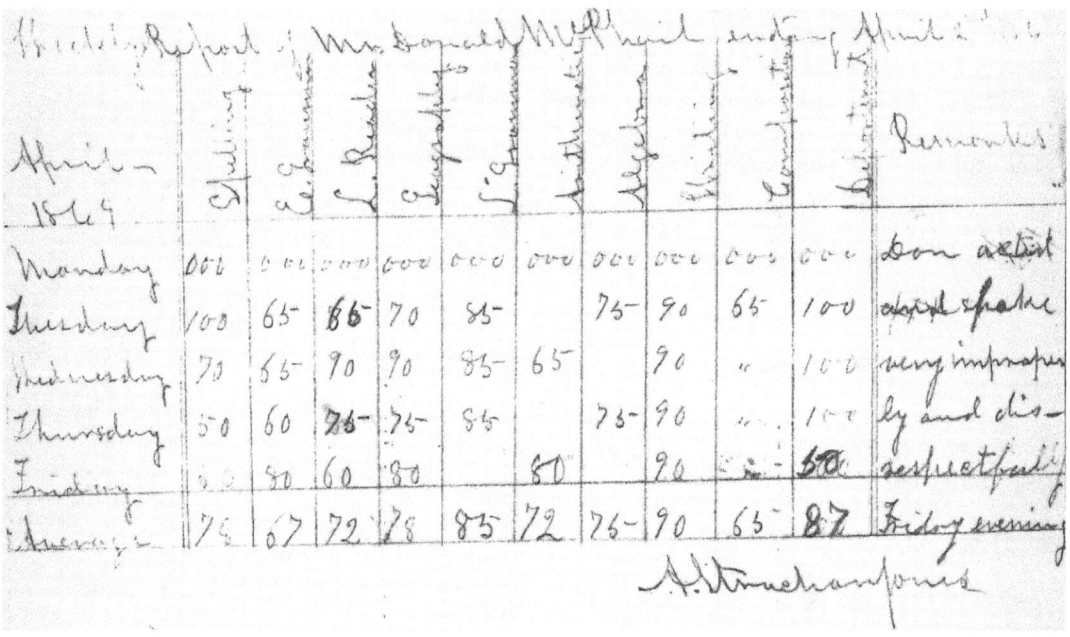

Donald McPhail's weekly report card ending April 2, 1869, indicates that he was an active normal boy. Under remarks: "Don acted and spoke very improperly and disrespectfully Friday evening."

General Wilson's raid, when the Union soldier "appropriated" nine-year-old Donald McPhail's pony, apparently left no lasting scars on the boy's psyche. His tombstone, found under leaves in a remote and abandoned graveyard, indicates that he went on to become a medical doctor.

lotte, and Mecklenburg counties to assemble for the defense of the bridge, and ordering all local companies to report immediately.

As a result of his circulars, by June 25 Captain Farinholt's command had increased to 938 men, including 492 citizens. Farinholt was still badly outnumbered, though. He had only six pieces of artillery: four were in the earthwork fort on the hill just east of the bridge, and two were situated in a small fortification west of the bridge. Between these artillery positions and the river was a line of trenches, and across the bridge there was another line of hastily constructed but well-concealed rifle trenches. Confederate Captain James A. Hoyt with his two companies of regulars were on the east side of the bridge, and Colonel Henry Eaton Coleman's "Old Men and Young Boys" were on the west side. Scouts and pickets were posted north of the bridge near Roanoke Station.

Mulberry Hill plantation was located on a commanding hill near the battlefield, and the grounds of the house served as the Union headquarters and field hospital during the battle. (It is claimed that Mrs. McPhail, the lady of the house, told the Federals that 10,000 Confederates lay in wait for them beyond the breastworks and that every train was bringing more.)

The Union cavalry arrived on a hill above the battlefield about 3:45 P.M. and immediately opened with rifled Parrotts and 12-pounder Napoleons. The shells striking the thin roof of the bridge made a fearful racket, scaring some of the small boys into fits of weeping.

General Kautz's cavalry troops were dismounted north of the span under attack and formed up to cross the open fields toward the bridge. They were receiving heavy fire from the Confederate artillery on the other side of the river. Colonel Samuel R. Spear's 1st D.C. and 11th Pennsylvania approached along the east side of the railroad and Colonel Robert M. West's 5th Pennsylvania and 3rd New York along the west side.

The Union troops reached a shallow drainage ditch some 150 yards north of the bridge, and organized for what was to be the first of four separate charges, all of them repulsed by the badly outnumbered but determined Confederate forces. When the Union forces left the drainage ditch for their first assault on the bridge, they were met by intense fire from Colonel Coleman's Old men and Young Boys and the regulars who had been hidden from view in their shallow trenches around the bridge.

It was during the fourth charge, when there were some misgivings about the results, that Confederate General W. H. F. Lee and his division struck the rear-guard of the Federals, causing them to have to fight in two different directions.

Finding that the Staunton River Bridge could not be carried without severe loss, if at all, the Confederate cavalry being at their rear and the Staunton River too deep for fording, Union General James H. Wilson decided to discontinue the battle and return to Petersburg. The withdrawal started around midnight.

The next morning, the Confederates advanced their line of skirmishers half a mile and discovered that the enemy had left quite a number of their dead and some wounded on the field. Eight Union soldiers were captured and forty-two were buried. The reported Confederate losses were a mere ten killed and twenty-four wounded.

The antebellum Mulberry Hill Plantation also expired, in a sense. In its prime, the plantation covered 2,800 acres and worked more than 100 slaves. After the war, the plantation was subdivided among the family and sections sold off. In 1982 the heirs of Mulberry Hill Plantation sold their shares to Butler Lumber Company, which in turn sold the farmland. Today, the plantation home and its immediate acreage are a part of Staunton River Battlefield State Park.

Appomattox Court House National Historical Park, Route 24, two miles northeast of Appomattox, VA

Appomattox Court House National Historical Park comprises twenty-seven original historic structures on approximately 1,700 acres in rural Southside Virginia. Two different fifteen-minute slide programs are presented on an hourly schedule. The documentary program covering the campaign is always shown on the half hour. The second program, "Soldiers' Diaries," consists of excerpts from the diaries of soldiers who were present at the site in 1865, and it is always shown on the hour.

The McLean house is located within the historic village approximately 150 yards west of the visitor center. The three-story structure is furnished with mid–nineteenth century furnishings, and the parlor where the surrender took place is furnished with a combination of original and reproduction items. The outbuildings are also open, including the former slave quarters, exterior kitchen, and outhouse.

Exhibits include many original artifacts associated with the events surrounding the surrender of the Confederate Army of Northern Virginia. Artifacts range from the pencil used by General Lee to make corrections in the surrender terms to documents and military artifacts.

THE APPOMATTOX CAMPAIGN

By February of 1865, Lee's concerns stretched beyond the Confederate capitol to Federal actions elsewhere in the South. Two Union armies, one under Sherman and the other under Major General John M. Schofield, were moving through the Carolinas. If they could not be stopped, then they could sever Virginia from the rest of the South, and if they joined Grant at Petersburg, Lee's men would face four armies instead of two. Realizing the danger, Lee wrote the Confederate secretary of war on February 8, 1865: "You must not be surprised if calamity befalls us."

By the time he wrote this letter, Lee knew he would have to leave the Petersburg lines; the only question was when. Muddy roads and the poor condition of the horses forced the Confederates to remain in the trenches throughout March.

Once again, Ulysses S. Grant seized the initiative. On March 29, Philip Sheridan's cavalry and the V Corps began moving southwest toward the Confederate right flank and the South Side Railroad. On the first of April, 21,000 Federal troops smashed the 11,000-man Confederate force under Major General George Pickett of "Pickett's Charge" fame, at an important road junction known locally as Five Forks. Grant followed up this victory with an all-out offensive against Confederate lines on April 2.

With his supply lines cut, Lee had no choice but to order Richmond and Petersburg evacuated on the night of April 2–3. Moving by previously determined routes, Confederate columns left the trenches that they had occupied for ten months. Their immediate objective was Amelia Court House, where forces from Richmond and Petersburg would concentrate and receive the now-meager rations sent from Richmond.

Once his army was reassembled, Lee planned to march down the line of the Richmond and Danville Railroad with the hope of meeting General Joseph E. Johnston's Army of Tennessee coming from North Carolina. Together, the two armies could establish a defensive line near the Roanoke River and assume the offensive against Sherman.

The march from Richmond and Petersburg started well enough. Many of the Confederates, including Lee, seemed exhilarated at being in the field once again, but after the first day's march signs of weariness and hunger began to appear.

When Lee reached Amelia Court House on April 4, he found to his dismay that the rations for his men had not arrived. Although a rapid march was crucial, the hungry men of the Army of Northern Virginia needed supplies. While awaiting the arrival of troops from Richmond who had been delayed by floods, Lee decided to halt the march and send wagons into the countryside to gather provisions. Local farmers, though, had little to give and the wagons returned practically empty. The major result of this effort was a lost day of marching. This delay allowed the pursuing Federals time to catch up, which proved to be the turning point of the campaign.

Leaving Amelia Court House on April 5, the columns of Lee's army had traveled only a few miles before they found Union cavalry and infantry squarely across their line of retreat at Jetersville. Rather than attack the entrenched federal position, Lee changed his plan. He would march his army west, around the Federals, and attempt to supply his troops at Farmville along the route of the South Side Railroad.

The retreating Army of Northern Virginia was under constant Federal pressure. Union cavalry attacked the Confederate wagon train at Paineville, destroying a large number of wagons. Tired from lack of sleep (Lee had ordered night marches to regain the day he lost) and hungry, the men began falling out of the column, or breaking ranks searching for food. Weakened mules and horses collapsed under their loads.

As the retreating columns grew more ragged, gaps developed in the line of march. At Sailor's Creek a few miles east of Farmville, Union cavalry exploited such a gap to block two Confederate corps under Generals Richard Anderson and Richard Ewell, until the Union VI Corps arrived to crush them. Watching the massacre from a nearby hill, Lee exclaimed, "My God! Has the army been dissolved?"

Nearly 8,000 men and eight generals were lost in one stroke, killed, captured, or wounded. The remnants of the Army of Northern Virginia arrived in Farmville on April 7, where rations at last awaited them, but the Union forces followed so quickly that the Confederate cavalry had to make a stand in the streets of the town to allow their fellow troops to escape.

Blocked once again by Grant's army, Lee again swung west, hoping that he could be supplied farther down the rail line and then turn south. Just north of Farmville, Lee turned west onto the Richmond-Lynchburg Stage Road. The Union Corps followed. Unbeknownst to Lee, however, the Federal cavalry and the V, XXIV, and XXV Corps were moving along shorter roads south of the Appomattox River to cut him off.

While in Farmville on April 7, Grant sent a letter to Lee asking for the surrender of his army. Lee, in the vicinity of Cumberland Church, received the letter and read it. He then handed it to one of his most trusted corps commanders, Lt. General James Longstreet. Longstreet's reply was a terse "Not yet!"

As Lee continued his march westward, though, he knew the desperate situation his army faced. He reasoned that if he could reach Appomattox Station before the Federal troops, he could receive rations sent from Lynchburg and then make his way to Danville via Campbell Court House (Rustburg) and Pittsylvania County. If not, he would have no choice but to surrender.

On the afternoon of April 8, the Confederate columns halted a mile northeast of Appomattox Court House. That night, artillery fire could be heard from Appomattox Station, and the red glow from Union campfires foretold that the end was near. Federal cavalry and the Army of the James, marching on shorter roads, had blocked the way south and west.

Lee consulted with his generals and determined that one more attempt should be made to reach the railroad and escape. At dawn on April 9, General John B. Gordon's Corps attacked the Union cavalry blocking the stage road, but after an initial success, Gordon sent word to Lee around 8:30 A.M. "that my command has been fought to a frazzle, and unless Longstreet can unite in the movement, or prevent these forces from coming upon my rear, I cannot go forward."

Receiving the message, Lee replied sadly, "There is nothing left for me to do but to go and see General Grant, and I would rather die a thousand deaths."

On April 9, 1865, after four years of Civil War, approximately 630,000 deaths and over one million casualties, General Robert E. Lee surrendered the Confederate Army of Northern Virginia to Lieutenant General Ulysses S. Grant at the home of Wilmer and Virginia McLean in the town of Appomattox Court House, Virginia. General Lee arrived at the McLean home shortly after 1 P.M., followed a half-hour later by Grant. The meeting lasted approximately an hour and a half. The surrender of the Army of Northern Virginia allowed the Federal government to bring increased pressure to bear in other parts of the South, which resulted in the surrender of the remaining field armies of the Confederacy over the next few months.

It is most ironic that Wilmer Mclean found himself in the unenviable position of seeing both the beginning and the end of the Civil War on his own property. The improbable coincidence is best told by Confederate artillerist E.P. Alexander:

> He was a short, stout little fellow & with a face easily remembered. I said, "Hello McLean, why what are you doing here?" He replied, "Alexander, what the hell are you fellows doing here? I stood it on Bull Run till, backwards & forwards, between you, my whole plantation was ruined & I sold out & came way off here over 200 miles to this out of the way place where I hoped I never would see another soldier of either side, & now just look at this place"—& he pointed around to his yard full of tents & his fields stretching off low from [being] trampled & fences burned in the numerous camp fires, for the last guns were fired on his lands & in his house General Lee surrendered to General Grant. So the very first & the very last headquarters & the very first & last collisions of these two great armies in a four year's war had taken place in the house & on the premises of the same individual—who fleeing from the turmoil & danger had moved meanwhile over 200 miles.

Wilmer McLean fell on hard times after the surrender and paid to have his Appomattox house photographed so that the prints could be sold. McLean used early connections to ask Robert E. Lee to pose for a portrait by a New York artist so that copy prints could be made and sold for a profit for McLean. Lee's reply was immediate, icy, and negative.

McLean returned to the Manassas area, joined the Republican Party, supported the Union, and obtained a job as a treasury clerk. None of these moves endeared him to his former Confederates, but they saved his family from financial ruin. Wilmer McLean died on June 5, 1882.

Lula McLean's Doll

The doll belonging to the 7-year-old child of Wilmer McLean, whose house provided the venue for the surrender, was taken along with other items from the parlor as a souvenir of Appomattox.

THE "SILENT WITNESS"

While the generals met, and the room was packed tightly with the entourage that was Grant's staff, the rag doll remained in the room where Lula had left it. When the meeting ended, Union officers—anxious to obtain souvenirs of the event—plundered the McLeans' parlor, appropriating items that included Lula's rag doll. Colonel Horace Porter of General Grant's staff wrote: "A child's doll was found in the room, which the younger officers tossed from one to the other, and called her the 'Silent Witness.'" One of the cavorting Federal staff officers was Captain Robert Todd Lincoln, son of the president of the United States. The doll was taken from the home by Capt. Thomas W.C. Moore, aide-de-camp to General Sheridan. For well over a century, the Moore family kept the doll as a "war trophy" of sorts. Poor Lula never saw her beloved rag doll again.

Lula's descendants remembered the doll

as "lovingly handmade by a doting mother." The body of the doll was made of coarse unbleached cotton and stuffed. Inked on the simple, round face were eyes and nothing more. Printed cotton fabric was stitched together to fashion a bodice, skirt, and leggings.

The doll was taken by Captain Moore to his home in Mt. Kisco, New York, and was placed in a glass case in the Moores' library; it remained in the family until the death of Richard Moore in 1992. Moore's widow Marjorie thought Appomattox would be the best place for the doll. Accordingly, she took a trip to the Appomattox Battlefield Park to check out the place and make sure that it would indeed be a good home. After the visit, she telephoned the park and said she wished to donate the "silent witness" to the park. The doll was presented to the Appomattox Court House National Historical Park on December 17, 1992, and is now on permanent exhibit.

THE SEIZURE OF FURNITURE USED BY GRANT AND LEE AT APPOMATTOX

The marbletop table General Lee used for signing the surrender terms was taken from the parlor by General Edward O. C. Ord, who claimed that he paid forty dollars for it. Ord offered the table to Mrs. Grant, who modestly declined it and insisted that Mrs. Ord should become it possessor. In his role as commander of occupation, Ord then took the table to Richmond. (He took over Jefferson Davis's home, the "Confederate White House," for his command post.)

The marbletop table was later stored at Fort Monroe until 1887. After Ord's death, his widow sold it to Charles F. Gunther, the owner of a dime museum in Chicago. The relic was

The child's doll taken from the McLean House.

later purchased from his estate by the Chicago Historical Society and is today in Chicago's Historical Society Museum.

The brass candleholders were taken from the McLean House parlor by U.S. General George Sharpe, who paid ten dollars. They are currently on loan from Senate House Museum, Kingston, N.Y., and have been exhibited in the Appomattox Park Museum since June 1999.

General Ord stands beside his wife and child on the veranda of Jefferson Davis's mansion in this attention-grabbing photo. The marble top table used in the South's surrender is in the immediate background, evidence that Ord most likely considered the photographic documentation of the table very important (courtesy Library of Congress).

Colonel Michael Sheridan, the general's brother, took the stone inkstand.

Other items and their subsequent disposition are as follows:

Secretary-bookcase: This item now rests in the Smithsonian Institution. It was sold in 1904 by Nannie Spillman to Caroline Stokes of New York, who presented it immediately to the Smithsonian.

Vases: These are of English polychrome design and were acquired from the family in 1989. They are on exhibit in the McLean House at Appomattox Court House National Historical Park.

Sofa: This typically Victorian horsehair-and-mahogany couch was acquired from a Mrs. Campbell (a McLean granddaughter) for $1,000 in 1952. It is on exhibit in the McLean House at Appomattox Court House National Historical Park.

Pictures: Nothing definite is known about them.

Carpeting: A wool ingrain carpet is shown in the lithograph produced by Wilmer McLean in 1867 (on exhibit in the park visitor center/museum) and in the Guillaume painting (on exhibit in the park visitor center/museum). A reproduction carpet remains on exhibit in the McLean House at Appomattox Court House National Historical Park.

Curtains: Reports from family members indicate that there were large, draped red curtains tied back with heavy cords and tassels. The tassels are on exhibit in the park visitor center/museum.

Washington and Lee University, Jefferson Street, Lexington, VA

Construction began on the chapel in 1867 at the request of Robert E. Lee, who served as president of what was then Washington College, from 1865 to 1870. Lee died on October 12, 1870, and was buried beneath the chapel. The remains of his beloved horse, Traveller, are also interred in a plot outside the museum entrance.

Lee's office is preserved much as he left it for the last time on September 28, 1870. The rest of the lower level became a museum in 1928, exhibiting items once owned by the Lee and Washington families.

Lee's Last Order — General Order Number 9

At the university museum is General Robert E. Lee's final transmission to his men, after the surrender at Appomattox. The text follows:

> Hdqrs. Army Northern Va.,
> April 10th 1865
> Gen'l Order
> No. 9
>
> After four years of arduous service, marked by unsurpassed courage and fortitude, the Army of Northern Virginia has been compelled to yield to over-whelming numbers and resources.
>
> I need not tell the brave survivors of so many hard-fought battles, who have remained steadfast to the last, that I have consented to this result from no distrust of them. But feeling that valor and devotion could accomplish nothing that would compensate for the loss that must have attended the continuance of the contest, I determined to avoid the useless sacrifice of those whose past services have endeared them to their countrymen.
>
> By the terms of the agreement, officers and men can return to their homes and remain until exchanged. You will take with you the satisfaction that proceeds from the consciousness of duty faithfully performed, and I earnestly pray that a merciful God will extend to you His blessing and protection.
>
> With an unending admiration of your constancy and devotion to your country and a grateful remembrance of your kind and generous consideration for myself, I bid you all an affectionate farewell.

U.S. Army Quartermaster Museum, Building 5218, A Avenue and 22nd Street, Fort Lee, VA

Since 1957, the Quartermaster Museum has preserved the history and heritage of the U.S. Army Quartermaster Corps, the Army's oldest logistic branch. The museum collects, preserves, exhibits and interprets the history of the Quartermaster Corps from its birth in

General Lee's last order, General Order No. 9 (courtesy Washington and Lee University).

1775 to the present. To this end, the museum has collected over 23,000 artifacts relating to the Corps's history, along with thousands of relevant documents.

General Ulysses S. Grant's Saddle

The Grimsley saddle was in common use prior to the Civil War, but was replaced as standard issue by the simpler and cheaper

McClellan saddle. The Grimsley had numerous and same what complicated accessories, but it was the saddle used by General U.S. Grant.

> ### WHO HAD GRANT'S SADDLE?
>
> Head Quarters Armies
> of the United States
> Washington D.C.
> May 19th 1865
>
> Colonel A. H. Markland
> Spl. Agt. P.M. Dept.
>
> Colonel:
> I take great pleasure in presenting you the "Grimsley Saddle" which I have used in all battles from fort Henry Tenn. In February 1862, to the battles about Petersburg Va., ending in the surrender of Lee's army at Appomattox C. H. Va., on 9th of April, 1865.

In 1861, Colonel A.H. Markland was assigned the position of first assistant postmaster general and given the duties of superintendent of the distribution of mail for the army under General Grant's command. In the West, this included the men under the command of generals Sherman, Sheridan, and Thomas. Markland's establishment of post offices and supervision of the delivery of the mail after the battles at Cairo, Vicksburg, Chattanooga, Charleston, and Savannah, to quote Grant, "was marvelous." Grant was so pleased with Markland that he continues the above provenance as follows:

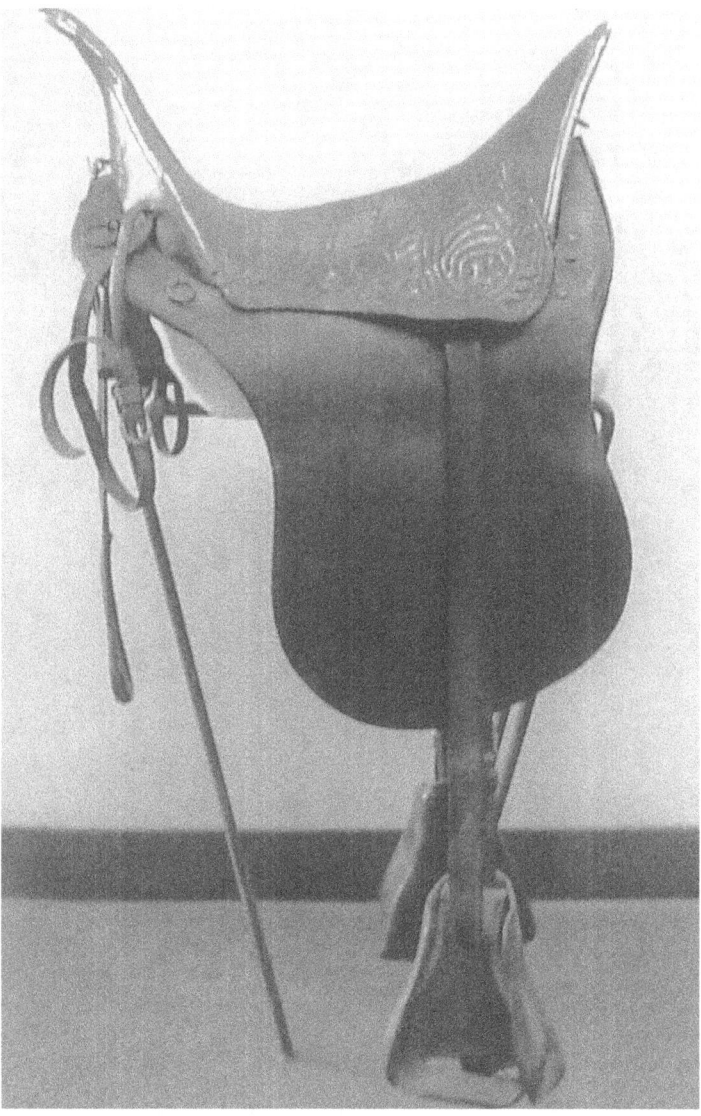

This priceless, brown leather Grimsley saddle used by Grant is displayed in the U.S. Army Museum at Fort Lee, Virginia. The documentation of its provenance is kept in a highly secure location.

> I present the saddle, not for any intrinsic value it possesses, but as a mark of my friendship and esteem, after continued service with you through the great rebellion. Our services commencing at Cairo, Ill., in the fall of 1861 and continuing to the present day, I hope that our friendship, if not our service together will continue as heretofore.
>
> Yours truly
> U.S. Grant. Lt. Gen

On December 12, 1872, Colonel Markland loaned the saddle to the Soldiers' Home in Dayton, Ohio. There was no doubt about the saddle until April, 1885, the twenty-first anniversary of the surrender of General Lee when the *Cincinnati Enquirer* printed the following article:

General Grant and his warhorse Cincinnati at Cold Harbor, Virginia, on June 4, 1864. The Grimsley standard issue saddle is pictured on the horse (courtesy Library of Congress).

"Chicago, April 8—The Illinois Commandery of Military Order of the Loyal Legion received to-day from Colonel Fred Grant the saddle used by General Grant when he rode to the surrender of Lee. The commandery raised $42,341 for the Grant Monument fund."

Of course Markland asked the paper to write a history of the saddle and "cause it to be printed in the Cincinnati Commercial or such other paper as you may think fit." In Markland's mind there was no question about his ownership of Grant's saddle.

But now a third Grant saddle enters the picture. On April 20, 1897, Hempstead Washburne donated Grant's saddle to the Chicago Historical Society. The provenance stated: "The saddle and bridle was presented through my father Elihu B. Washburne to my grandfather Israel Washburne of Maine." The following saddle provenance was a letter written by Hempstead Washburne's father, Elihu Washburne: "This is the saddle on which General Grant rode during the entire war of the Rebellion and which he presented to Israel Washburn, Senior at the close of the war."

During the Civil War, Elihu B. Washburne was a member of Congress from the Galena Congressional District in Illinois, General Grant's district. Washburne introduced a bill creating the new grade of lieutenant general, with the implied understanding that General Grant would fill this position. Washburne paid several visits to Grant's military headquarters, and on March 10, 1885, he arrived at City Point with a gold medal commemorating Grant's victories. Washburne had been commissioned by Congress to present the medal.

Would Grant have given Washburne's father a saddle? After all, Grant, like many military men, had two horses, Cincinnati and Jeff Davis, the latter a horse captured in Mississippi from the plantation of Joe Davis, the brother of Jefferson Davis. Did Grant have two saddles? There would normally be no question that he did except that in *The Personal Memories of Ulysses S. Grant*, Grant writes briefly that Elihu B. Washburne visited him at his headquarters at the Wilderness and presented as a literary gentleman, a Mr. Swinton. Grant "expressed an

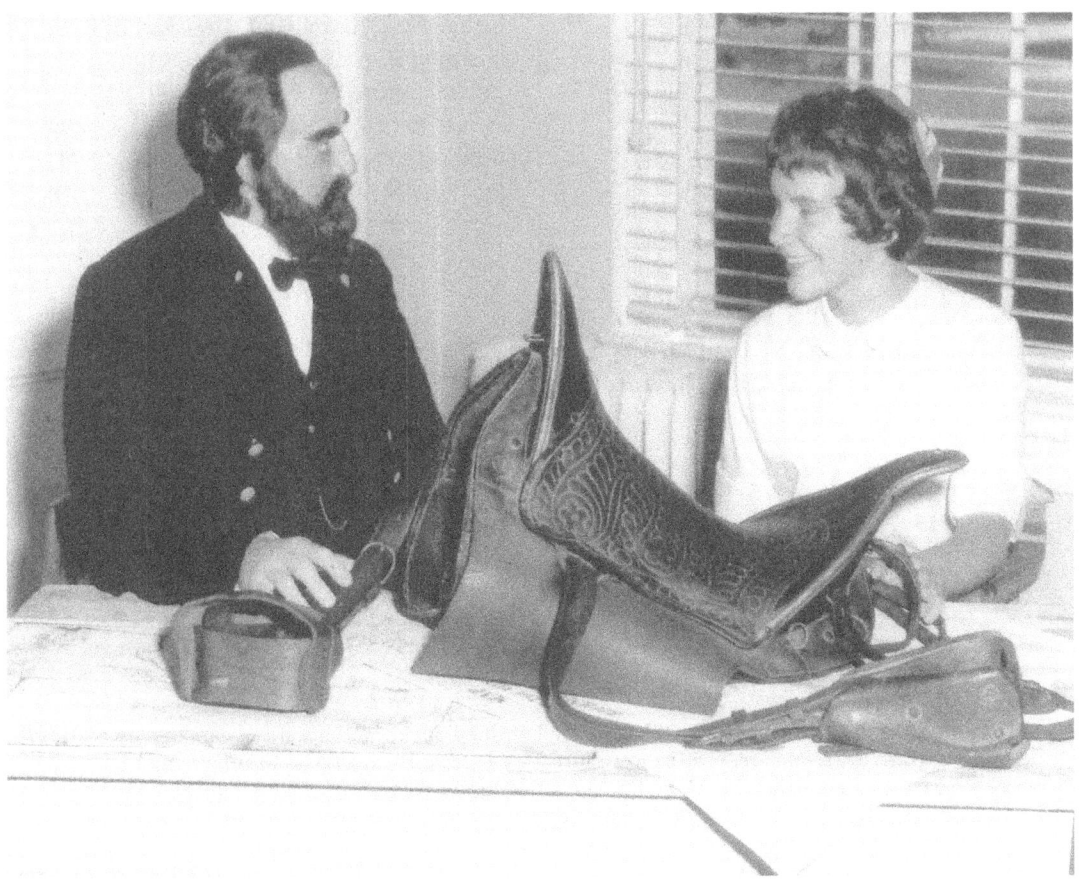

On September 6, 1968, Frances Will's sister, Mrs. William E. Pritchard, permanently donated Grant's controversial saddle to the U.S. Army Quartermaster Museum (courtesy U.S. Army Quartermaster Museum).

entire willingness for him (Swinton) to accompany his army," and then Grant expands on two pages, explaining that Swinton was a Rebel spy. General Meade ordered Swinton to be executed, but Grant rescinded the orders and had Swinton released and expelled from the Union lines. Other than this uncomplimentary reference, Elihu B. Washburne is excluded from Grant's autobiography. Had they been close friends, he would have mentioned Washburne, and the gift of a treasured saddle would have made more sense.

The saddle presented to Colonel Markland remained at the Soldiers Home for fifteen years, until June 1887. Markland then decided to loan the saddle to the Smithsonian Institution because Grant's "other relics" were housed at the museum. Markland wrote the home, praising it for the care it had provided for the saddle and stated, "I prize it beyond measure because it was and is a testament to me from a schoolboy friend." Indeed, Markland and General Grant had been schoolmates at the Maysville (Kentucky) Academy.

The Smithsonian wrote Markland that it would be very happy to receive the saddle and that the saddle "will always be at your disposal to withdraw, should you at anytime so desire." It seemed that the saddle had found a permanent home on September 20, 1887. On the death of Colonel Markland in May 1888, however, the title to the historic item passed to Miss Fanny Beall. In 1899, she appealed to the Smithsonian, and ownership of the saddle was recorded in her name, although the saddle itself remained in the museum. Upon her death, the saddle became the property of Mrs. Alice Beall Will, who died in 1962 and left her trust to her three grandchildren, one being Miss Frances Beall Will. She, with the consent of her brother and sister, had the saddle removed from the Smithsonian and placed in Appomattox Manor, the home of the Richard Eppes family and headquarters of General Grant during the Petersburg siege.

It moved once more, in 1968, to the museum at Fort Lee.

Engraved Walking Stick

President Ulysses S. Grant first received this stick made from a piece of the ruined Fort Sumter during a visit to Charleston, S.C.

his famous "contraband" decision, by which escaping slaves reaching Union lines would not be returned to bondage.

It remains an active military base, now used for soldier training and development of operational doctrine.

Benjamin Butler's Tiffany mess kit

Union General Benjamin Butler traveled in style with a silver-plated neess kit made by Tiffany in New York.

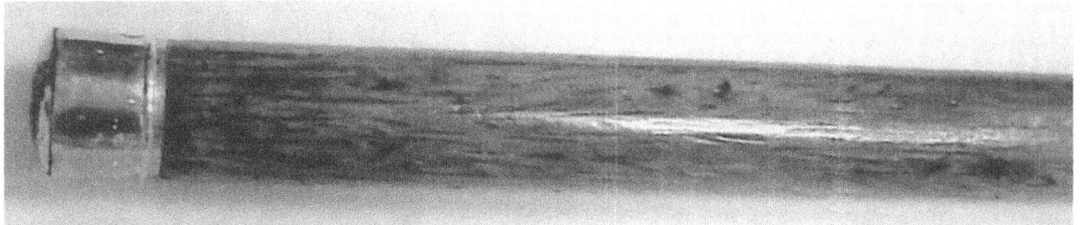

The engraved gothic lettering in the 18k gold head of this wooden walking stick bears the inscription, "From the ruins of Ft. Sumter." The cane was presented to President Ulysses Grant during a trip to the harbor of Charleston, South Carolina. On May 12, 1920, the treasured item was presented to the secretary of war and then subsequently transferred to the Quartermaster Museum at Fort Lee, Virginia.

Casemate Museum,
Fort Monroe, VA
23651

Fort Monroe was built between 1819 and 1834, and its mission was to protect the entrance to Hampton Roads and the several port cities that had access to its waters.

During the Civil War, Fort Monroe was quickly reinforced so that it would not fall to Confederate forces. In cooperation with the Navy, troops from Fort Monroe extended Union control along the coasts of the Carolinas. Several land operations against Confederate forces also were mounted from the fort, notably the battle of Big Bethel in June 1861, George McClellan's Peninsula Campaign of 1862, and the Siege of Suffolk in 1863. In 1864, the Army of the James was formed at Fort Monroe. Fort Monroe is also the place at which Major General Benjamin Butler made

POLITICS MAKES
STRANGE COMMANDERS

Before the war he was all for peace, but after war was declared, he quickly switched to being a "war Democrat." A mere three days after Fort Sumter surrendered, Benjamin Butler became a brigadier general with the Massachusetts Volunteers, assigned to the post of commanding Fort Monroe, Virginia, and the surrounding district.

Later, in March of 1862, he commanded the ground forces assigned to capture New Orleans. As events would have it, he was deterred from winning any personal glory because the Navy captured it unaided, but he managed to keep himself in the newspapers. He hanged a man who ripped down the U.S. flag; he was involved in a scandal, accused of stealing silver spoons; he continued to make money, mostly by kickbacks on smuggled cotton, until December 1862. Before long, Lincoln had had enough of the opportunistic Butler and removed him from command.

The resilient general, however, had built

Butler's extravagant three-foot-long mess kit and engraved Tiffany tableware are symbolic of his opulent but inadequate military lifestyle. Butler really did not care that he was a bad general; he was first and foremost a good politician and knew that he had to at least appear to be a general to have the sort of post-war political career he wanted — his ambition was to be president of the United States.

too much political clout to be fired, so Lincoln felt obliged to find Butler another job. After a year "on the shelf," he was reassigned to the southern Virginia/North Carolina border in late 1863. There wasn't much to do, but Butler once more took care that his name appeared regularly in the newspapers. Eventually, he was promoted to command the Army of the James, still based at Fort Monroe. Butler was evidently a man who made a good first impression; Grant was impressed enough at their first meeting to give Butler a simple but vital job: strike at Richmond while he, Grant, pinned down Lee's forces further north.

Butler fumbled every

aspect of his orders. He moved too slowly and lost the battles as well. He could have had his pick of Richmond, Petersburg, or the railway in between. Instead, his two corps were bottled up by Beauregard's 5,000 men. He had a chance to redeem himself by moving on Petersburg, but he bumbled another surprise attack, and the Petersburg militia held off the veterans. From then on, Grant made sure Butler had plenty of adult supervision.

Lincoln must have felt the need to keep Butler pacified politically as well, else there is no doubt that a man with such a track record would have been sacked. There was a *quid pro quo*: Butler backed Lincoln for a second term, and Lincoln reciprocated by keeping Butler in a job. But re-election success and Butler's unique brand of incompetence ended the tenuous compact. Lincoln no longer needed Butler, and Butler failed badly in his command during the capture of Fort Fisher, North Carolina. In January 1865, he was permanently removed from command.

Union Major General Benjamin Butler was Commander of the James River Army of 1864 (courtesy Library of Congress).

Cell of President Jefferson Davis

Fort Monroe has preserved the cell where the former Confederate president was initially taken to await a trial that never took place.

THE INCARCERATION OF JEFFERSON DAVIS

After his capture, Jefferson Davis and his family were taken to Savannah, Georgia. Davis and several other Confederate officials boarded the *Clyde* and were sent north to be held in prisons. When the ship dropped anchor off Hampton Roads, Virginia, on May 19, 1865, some of the Confederate officials were transferred to ships that took them to prisons at Fort Delaware near Philadelphia and Fort Warren in the Boston harbor. Military officials delayed three days before taking Davis to Fort Monroe.

In the summer of 1866, the government removed Davis from his basement-like cell and gave him more comfortable quarters in Carroll Hall, a commodious house at the fort. By this time the government allowed him to receive visitors. Finally, Washington decided to discharge the former Confederate president; on May 11, 1867, a federal court in Richmond accepted a writ of habeas corpus from his attorneys and released him on $100,000 bail. Following the advice of several legal experts, the federal government finally resolved not to try Davis. He lived as a free man for another twenty-two years before he died in New Orleans, age eighty-two, on December 9, 1889.

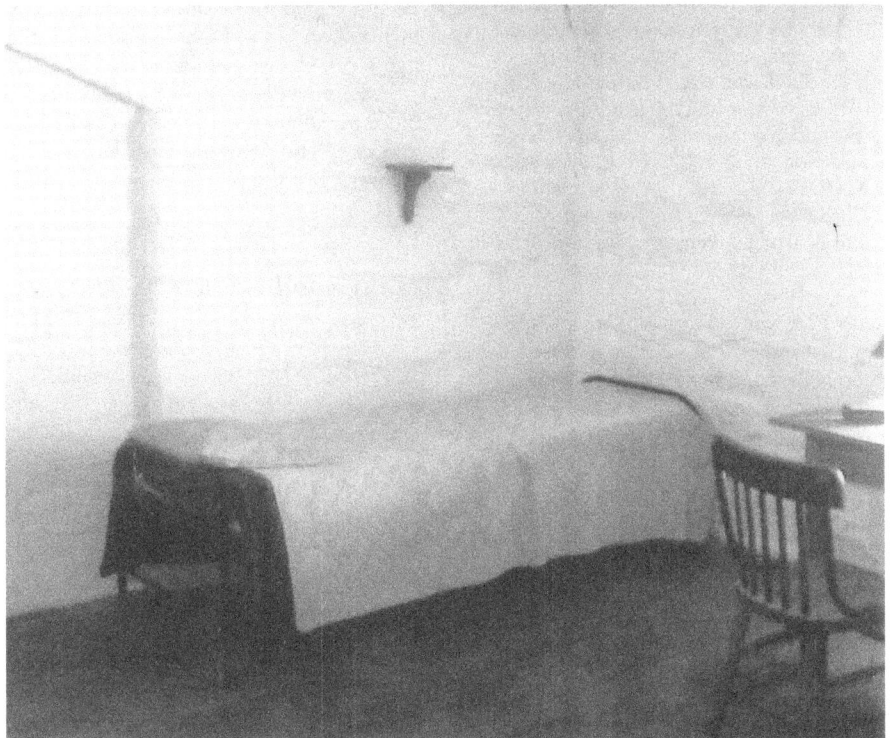

Upon his arrival in prison, Jefferson Davis was placed in a casement compound that faced Hampton Roads. Surrounding the fort was a moat, and beyond the moat was a water battery protecting the fort. In the former Confederate president's cell the only furnishings were a couch and a rustic chair.

Jefferson Davis's Pipe

Stolen from the museum in 1977, the egg-and-talon-shaped pipe is once again on display.

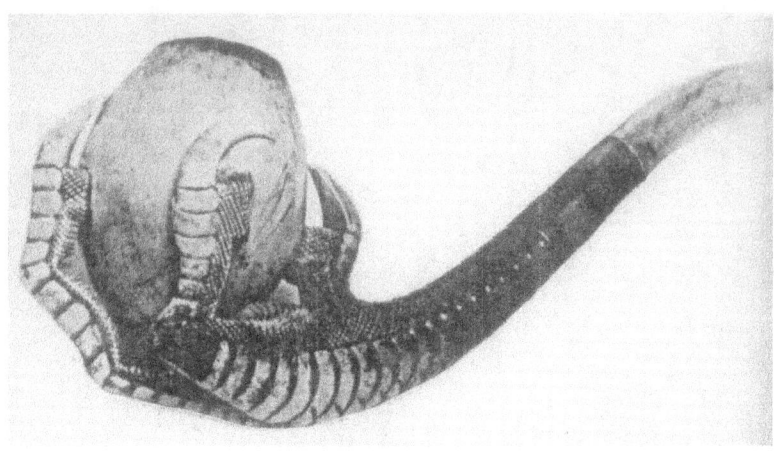

Jefferson Davis' priceless smoking pipe, stolen from the Casemate Museum.

A TEMPTATION TO THIEVERY

At Fort Monroe, George W. Reifsnyder, Company D, Third Pennsylvania Heavy Artillery, was one of Jefferson Davis's guards. In a newspaper article in 1905, Reifsnyder told a reporter:

> Mr. Davis had a fine meerschaum pipe, with a long stem that was his constant companion and which I had my eyes on. I wanted it for a souvenir of my standing guard in his cell. For a long time I debated the question with myself, but finally realized orders to show courtesy to Mr. Davis were so rigid that I would be harshly dealt with if the theft was placed on me, and I knew that if Mr. Davis reported the matter, as undoubtedly he would, it would rest with one of the three who had stood guard in his cell that day. All this time Mr. Davis was lying on the couch asleep, but I finally stole over to his coat and cut a button from it, which I kept as a souvenir until it was lost.

Reifsnyder wanted to steal Davis's pipe but restrained himself; more than a hundred years later, however, on the Monday morning of May 8, 1977, someone did steal the priceless pipe from the Casemate Museum at Fort Monroe. Using the noisy activities of forty sixth-graders to cover his crime, the thief forced open a Plexiglas case and removed the eight-and-a-half-inch long meerschaum pipe. The bowl was intricately carved into the shape of an egg held in the upturned talons of an eagle's claw. The bowl had turned brown from frequent use and the stem bore the imprints of Davis's teeth.

By midmorning the pipe was discovered missing, and suspicion was focused on the local schoolchildren, whom officials thought might be playing an unappreciated prank. The Casemate Museum was sealed off, and the Army's Criminal Investigation Division called in. Officers questioned each and every one of the school kids. They all denied any knowledge of the missing pipe.

The FBI was then called, and Fort Monroe officials immediately offered a substantial award for the return of the pipe, which had been donated to the museum in the early 1960s by Jefferson Hayes Davis, grandson of the former Confederate president.

Five days later, the FBI announced that its office in Augusta, Ga., had recovered the pipe and case. The Army gives no details about the recovery, but the pipe is once again on display.

Hollywood Cemetery, 412 South Cherry Street, Richmond, VA 23220

Hollywood Cemetery was laid out by John Notman in 1848. It is a fascinating site and is the final resting place of over 75,000 persons, including many notable Virginians such as presidents James Monroe and John Tyler, General J.E.B. Stuart, and writer Ellen Glasgow, as well as Jefferson Davis, president of the Confederate States. Also buried here are the remains of over 18,000 Confederate dead. The cemetery takes its name from the groves of holly trees on the grounds.

The Confederate Monument was created

in 1869 by the efforts of the women of the Hollywood Memorial Association. Not content merely to tend the graves of the Confederate dead, the women decided to raise money to erect a monument. A successful two-week bazaar raised over $18,000 in 1867. Charles Dimmock's design is a dry stone pyramid made of James River granite. It took nearly a year to build and is ninety feet tall. The 18,000 Confederate dead are buried around its base.

Headstone of Private William Morgan

On May 26, 1930, the War Department authorized Confederate headstones of marble with a pointed top and the Confederate Cross of Honor an on the front face, along with the standard inscription of the soldier's name, rank, company, and regiment.

The Veterans Administration will provide a headstone for veterans of the blue and gray free of charge — but only if the deceased has no private marker already.

A FINAL RESTING PLACE

The stories of death and grieving are perhaps best described by way of a despairing observation by Constance Cary Harrison in her article, *Richmond Scenes in '62*, which appeared as follows:

> Day by day we were called to our windows by the wailing dirge of a military band preceding a soldier's funeral. One could not number those sad pageants: the coffin crowned with cap and sword and gloves, the riderless horse following with empty boots fixed in the stirrups of an army sad-

The finest and brightest of the South, many slain at Antietam, Gettysburg, and Cold Harbor, are buried in Hollywood Cemetery, Richmond, Virginia. Private Morgan's headstone reveals that his death occurred at the Battle of the Peninsula. The plaque in the Confederate section of Hollywood Cemetery is etched with the words "Fate denied them victory but gave them a glorious immortality — Furled but not forgotten." Since its first burial in 1849 the famed cemetery became the final resting place for 25 Confederate generals, CSA President Jefferson Davis, and thousands of Confederate soldiers.

dle; such soldiers as could be spared from the front marching after with arm reversed and crape-enfolded banners; the passers-by standing with bare, bent heads. Funerals less honored outwardly were continually occurring. Then and thereafter the green hillsides of lovely Hollywood were frequently upturned to find resting-places for the heroic dead. So much taxed for time and for attendants were those who officiated that it was not unusual to perform the last rites for the departed at night. A solemn scene was that in the July moonlight, when, in the presence of the few who valued him most, we laid to rest one of my own nearest kinsmen, of whom in the old service of the United States, as in that of the Confederacy, it was said, "He was a spotless knight."

In spite of its melancholy uses, there was no more favorite walk in Richmond than Hollywood, a picturesque beautiful spot, where high hills sink into velvet undulations, profusely shaded with holly, pine, and cedar, as well at by trees of deciduous foliage. In spring the banks of the stream that runs through the valley were enameled with wild flowers, and the thickets were full of May-blossom and dogwood. Mounting to the summit of the bluff, one may sit under the shade of some ample oak, to view the spires and roofs of the town, with the white colonnade of the distant Capitol. Richmond, thus seen beneath her verdant foliage "upon hills, girdled by hills," confirms how an old writer felt called to exclaim about it, "Verily, this city hath a pleasant seat." On the right, below this point, flows the rushing yellow river, making ceaseless turmoil around islets of rock whose rifts are full of birch and willow, or leaping impetuously over the boulders of granite that strew its bed. Old-time Richmond folk used to say that the sound of their favorite James (or, to be exact, "Jeems") went with them into foreign countries, during no matter how many years of absence, haunting them like a strain of sweetest music; nor would they permit a suggestion of superiority in the flavor of any other fluid to that of a draught of its amber waters. So blent with my own memories of war is the voice of that tireless river, that I seem to hear it yet over the tramp of rusty battalions, the short imperious stroke of the alarm bell, the clash of passing bands, the gallop of eager horsemen, the roar of the battle, the moan of hospitals, the stifled note of sorrow!

J.E.B. Stuart's Grave

Stuart was born February 6, 1833, and received his primary education in the home of his birth in Patrick County, Virginia. He entered the U.S. Military Academy in 1850, graduating thirteenth in his class. Lieutenant Stuart remained in the U.S. Army until Virginia seceded from the Union. As Captain Stuart, he resigned his U.S. Commission on May 10, 1861, and accepted a commission as a lieutenant colonel in the Virginia Infantry. During the Battle of First Manassas, his bravery led to his appointment as brigadier general. During the Peninsular Campaign, Stuart was assigned to scouting duty and in the process led his cavalry around McClellan's entire Union Army. This was Stuart's finest hour, and he was promoted to major general on July 25, 1862.

He served creditably at the Second Battle of Manassas, Antietam, and Fredericksburg. At the Battle of Gettysburg, however, Stuart followed his own plans and reached that battle on the second day, thus depriving the Confederate army of critical cavalry support.

For the remainder of his career he heeded the hard-earned lesson of Gettysburg and kept in close communication with the Confederate infantry. On May 11, 1864, at Yellow Tavern on the outskirts of Richmond, Stuart was mortally wounded in a clash with General Philip Sheridan's cavalry.

The Confederate Pyramid Monument

This plain but powerful monument is built of local granite.

HONORING THE CONFEDERATE DEAD

The funds for the construction of the pyramid were raised by the women of the Hollywood Memorial Association. They raised the $18,000 by bazaars and an auction that included letters written by Civil War generals, inkstands made from the bones of horses killed in battle, and buttons from the uniform coat of General Stonewall Jackson. Contributions were sent from as far away as England and France.

The cornerstone was laid on December 3,

1868, and it contained a variety of Confederate memorabilia, including Confederate buttons, money, postage stamps, the first Confederate flag made in Richmond, Federal musket balls found within two miles of Richmond, a fragment of the coat worn by Stonewall Jackson the day he received his mortal wound, copies of the Bible, and many other items of Southern sentimental value.

The monument was constructed from granite blocks taken from the nearby James River and took almost a year to complete. The capstone was set in place on November 6, 1869, and it required someone to climb to the top of the ninety-foot tall edifice and guide the stone into position as it was lowered by a derrick. While onlookers looked on, a convict working with the construction crew climbed to the top, and while they cheered loudly, he guided the stone into its final resting place.

With this task completed, the women of the Hollywood Memorial Association set one additional goal, the return of the remains of Confederate soldiers who had fallen at the battle of Gettysburg. Following the battle, the dead of both sides were buried in the immediate area of their demise. Thousands were buried in the long trenches that had shielded them during the actual combat phase.

On October 27, 1863, weeks after the battle, the federal government began disinterment of Union soldiers and five months later had transferred 3,534 to the Soldiers' National Cemetery. An elaborate dedication ceremony attended by President Abraham Lincoln took place on November 19. The federal government

Major General James Ewell Brown, or "JEB," Stuart, the "Cavalier of Dixie," is buried in Hollywood Cemetery.

still regarded the dead Confederates as traitors, and placed them in unmarked graves on hostile soil. Farmers plowing their fields frequently exposed skeletons that lay strewn about. This disrespect towards Confederate remains by Pennsylvania farmers rankled Southerners, who urged that something be done. The women of the Hollywood Memorial Association raised funds, and in 1871 they hired Rufus Weaver to remove the bodies from Gettysburg and send them to the Hollywood Cemetery. He began exhumations on April 19, 1872, nine years after the battle, and on June 20, the first shipment

This pyramidal Civil War monument in Hollywood Cemetery was erected in 1869 in the soldiers' section, where over 18,000 unknown Confederate soldiers are interred.

of Gettysburg dead arrived at the wharf in Richmond. The boxes containing the dead were draped in white and black and covered with flowers and Confederate flags. Crowds gathered to watch the wagons as they left the wharf for Hollywood Cemetery. They were led by the saber-flashing Richmond Howitzers and by 400 men of the 1st Virginia Regiment, their colors furled and wrapped in crepe. The wagons carrying the Confederate dead followed, escorted by members of the Southern Cross, an association of Confederate veterans. At the rear of the procession were four Confederate generals leading more than 1,000 former Confederate soldiers in a tribute to their fallen comrades. The final shipment arrived at Hollywood Cemetery in October 1873, for a total of 2,935 disinterments from Gettysburg.

The graves of rank-and-file unknown heroes are situated among the burial places of such luminaries as Jeb Stuart, whose stainless sword is sheathed forever; A.P. Hill, who lay down his life at the call of duty; the gallant George E. Pickett of the Gettysburg charge; and John Pegram, the boy artillerist whose last words were, "I have done my duty, and now I turn to my savior."

According to the keepers of the Hollywood Cemetery, "These men's lives, together with those of their Northern counterparts, were given to forge a single and better nation. Their bloodshed in battle gave birth to a new America, one that in another century would restore and protect freedom around the world."

21

WEST VIRGINIA

Harpers Ferry National Park, U.S. Route 340, Harpers Ferry, WV

Harpers Ferry National Historical Park commemorates the historic events that occurred at or near Harpers Ferry. Programs include ranger-guided education programs, self-guided history searches, living history hands-on classroom experiences, science field studies, civic leadership workshops, and self-guided hikes and walks.

Mountains, rivers, and human endeavors have created over 200 years of significant stories at Harpers Ferry National Historical Park. Pioneers, inventors, soldiers, and civil rights leaders struggled here to change the face of America. This restored nineteenth-century industrial village and its surrounding natural setting offer many opportunities for visitors to witness history in a unique and personal way.

Drawing of the Design for a .58-Caliber Minié Ball

This was one of many papers recovered from a home in Winchester, Virginia, belonging to former armorer at Harper's Ferry.

THE HARPERS FERRY TREASURE BOX

These priceless historical papers were discovered in Winchester, Virginia, during restoration of an historic home. The documents had belonged to the head of the U.S. Armory, stationed there in the mid–1800s.

The home in Winchester, Virginia, was undergoing restoration under the watchful eye of Mr. Donald Griffin, a specialist in such refurbishments. He was inspecting the home's basement when he decided to venture into a small crawlspace. Working his way into the dust-filled opening, he made an unexpected find: a walnut-wood box about two feet long, two feet wide, and eight inches high. As surprising as the discovery was, Griffin was to be even more astounded by what was inside the box.

It turned out to be a drawing box, the kind used by draftsmen and engineers, and when Griffin opened it, he saw that it contained aging documents, including drawings and sketches of armory buildings and machinery, rifles, bayonets, and other equipment. The box even contained a walnut T-square and triangle dating from the mid–1800s. Griffin rushed to check the authenticity of the documents and learned that the papers were linked to the U.S. Armory at Harpers Ferry, West Virginia. He then put in a call to the historian at the Harpers Ferry National Historical Park. Griffin was asked to come right away.

To the Harpers Ferry folks, seeing this unprepossessing box for the first time was like finding buried treasure. Up to this time, the National Park Service knew very little about the

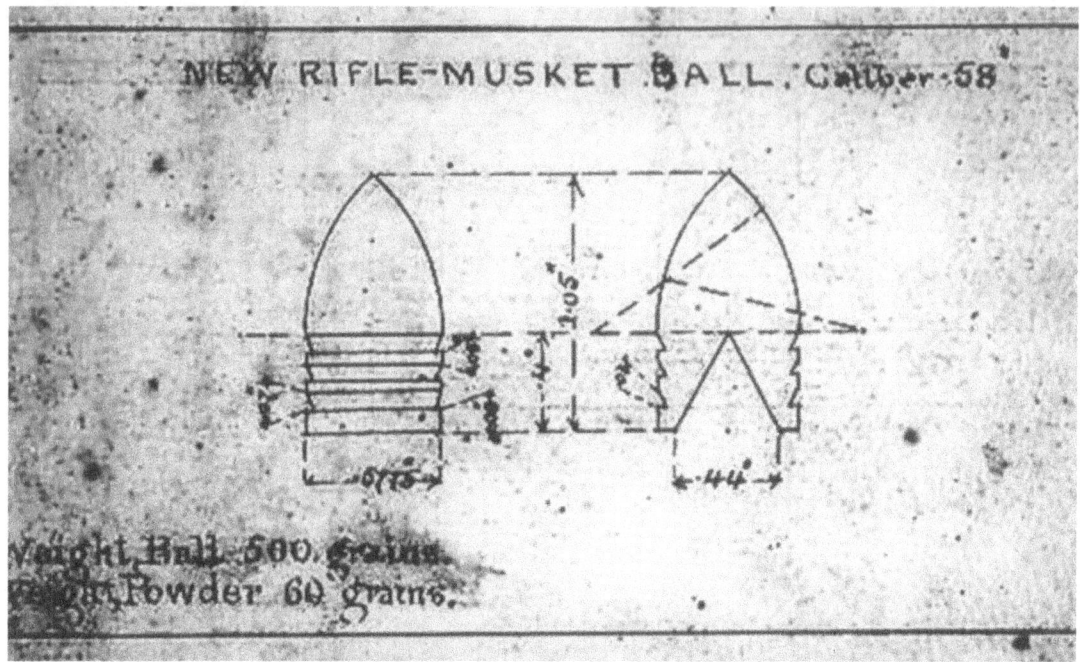

James H. Burton conducted experiments at the Harper's Ferry Armory during the early 1850. One result was this hefty .58-caliber version of the famous Minié ball, a type of bullet used extensively during the Civil War (courtesy Harpers Ferry National Park).

history and activities of the U.S. Armory itself at Harpers Ferry—its fame lay, of course, in the capture of John Brown and his fanatical abolitionist group. Moreover, Park Service officials had no idea that these rare and valuable papers even existed, because in April 1861, Confederate troops had burned the Harpers Ferry Armory, destroying all of the documents stored there, or so it was believed.

Donald Griffin sold the papers for an undisclosed amount to the Harpers Ferry Historical Association, which in turn donated them to the Harpers Ferry National Historical Park for all to enjoy.

What makes the documents so intriguing to students of the Civil War is the attention to detail that the creator displays, giving the observer a picture of the planning of some of the armaments central to Civil War fighting. The drawings and notes were penned by James H. Burton, the master armorer at Harpers Ferry from 1849 to 1853. Burton's job was to inspect all weapons produced at the armory to ensure that they met government standards, and to produce the aforementioned drawings and writings to document the goings-on at the armory. The pen-and-ink drawings are exquisite in both penmanship and line quality. Among them are drawings of rifles, bayonets, and the machinery used by the gunsmiths. There is a drawing, too, of a steam boiler for powering the heating plant.

Perhaps most exciting are the drawings illustrating the modification of the famous Minié ball. In fact, Burton's modification of the Minié ball was one of his most famous achievements. He reshaped the ball and refined it to the more accurate and more deadly bullet used by thousands of troops during the Civil War. The rifle as we know it today had not been used much because of the difficulty of stuffing a bullet the same diameter as the rifle bore down the barrel. The Frenchman Minié had developed the conical bullet smaller in diameter than the rifle bore; Burton perfected this by creating a large bullet with a concave base and two or three grooves on the outside. Now, this smaller-than-bore "Minié ball" could be dropped easily down a barrel; when the rifle was fired, the hollow base of the bullet expanded and the ball caught the rifling inside the barrel and zipped out of the muzzle with increased accuracy.

Burton was born in what is now Jefferson

County, West Virginia, in 1823. He was educated in Pennsylvania and at age sixteen traveled to Baltimore to learn the machine shop trade. He began work at the Harpers Ferry Armory in 1844. When war broke out, he sided with the Confederacy but ended up moving to England, where he remained after the war. His next move led him to Russia, where he directed the manufacture of weapons. Finally, perhaps feeling more secure in going back to his homeland even though he had been at odds militarily with its government, Burton returned to America and settled down on a Virginia farm. When he died at his home in Winchester on October 18, 1894, his obituary in the *Winchester Times* referred to him as "one of the most prominent citizens of this section."

22

WISCONSIN

The Wisconsin Historical Society, 816 State Street, Madison, WI 53706

The Wisconsin Historical Society is both a state agency and a private membership organization. Founded in 1846, two years before statehood, and chartered in 1853, it is the oldest American historical society to receive continuous public funding. By statute, it is charged with collecting, advancing, and disseminating knowledge of Wisconsin and of the trans-Allegheny West.

Tiffany Punch Bowl

The ingenuity of Wisconsin's Lieutenant Colonel Joseph Bailey saved a stranded Union fleet during the Red River Campaign in the Civil War. As a result of his efforts, Bailey became a national hero, was promoted to the rank of Brigadier General, and received this lavish silver punch bowl by Tiffany & Company from his fellow officers.

THE RED RIVER CAMPAIGN

In the spring of 1864, Union forces attempted to seize control of Texas and its valuable cotton resources. First, though, commanders desired to capture Shreveport, Louisiana. Army units marched on Shreveport while Union naval forces under Rear Admiral David Porter traveled up the Red River. On land, the army met strong resistance as the determined Confederates repelled the attack. As a result, Porter decided to turn his ships around and retreat to the Mississippi River. Because of unseasonably low water, however, the fleet became stranded at the falls above Alexandria, Louisiana. With encroaching Confederate forces and diminishing supplies, the fleet faced the danger of capture and destruction.

Bailey, a Wisconsin lumberman and engineer before the Civil War, convinced Union commanders to execute his plan to dam the Red River, which would raise the water level and allow the vessels to escape over the falls. Under Bailey's supervision, construction began on April 30, 1864. Led by ex-lumberjacks of the 23rd and 29th Wisconsin regiments, Union soldiers hastily constructed a series of crude dams in fewer than two weeks. When the water level rose enough to allow safe passage, the dam was breached. On May 12, the last Union ship cleared the falls and sailed for the safety of the Mississippi River. Even though the Red River Campaign failed, Bailey's ingenuity saved the North from far greater losses.

Bailey received the Tiffany punch bowl sometime between the Red River episode and his death in 1867. It is believed that grateful officers contributed part of their pay in silver coinage to be melted down for the creation of the bowl. An intricate engraving on one side depicts the Red River scene while the reverse carries the inscription, "Presented to Brigadier General Joseph Bailey by Rear Admiral Porter and The Officers composing the Red River Expedition as a mark of their esteem and as a memento of an event so creditable to the skill and energy of General Bailey. The Construction of the dam which saved to the nation a valuable squadron."

Wisconsin Veterans Museum, 30 West Mifflin Street, Madison, WI

The Veterans Museum offers instructive exhibits that highlight important events in Wisconsin military history from the Civil War to the present. It also operates a Research Center where books, photographic materials, oral histories, and archival collections can be accessed. The museum also cares for and safeguards a large collection of artifacts associated with Wisconsin's military history.

This Tiffany punch bowl was presented to Wisconsin's Joseph Bailey in honor of his service during the Civil War (courtesy of Wisconsin Historical Society).

Photograph of Old Abe the War Eagle

A mascot of the 8th Wisconsin Volunteers, this bald eagle survived 37 engagements and lived for 20 years.

A LIFE—AND—DEATH OF SERVICE

The most famous eagle in America—"Old Abe"—was hatched in 1861 and taken from his nest as a mere eaglet by one Ahgamahwegezhig (Chief Big Sky) of the Flambeau Band of the Ojibwa Indians. Big Sky later traded the bird to the McCann family of Chippewa County, Wisconsin. Later in 1861, when President Abraham Lincoln called for troops in Wisconsin to fight the seceding Confederacy, the McCanns sold Abe to the Eau Claire militia for $2.50. The militia traveled to Madison, becoming part of the 8th Regiment of the Wisconsin Volunteer Infantry. Captain John E. Perkins named the growing eagle "Old Abe" after the newly elected president.

Old Abe soon became a regular fixture around the 8th Regiment campgrounds during the troops' training at Camp Randall in Madison. When the regiment headed south, Abe accompanied it. Many outfits during the war, both North and South, adopted mascots as symbols of the units, but it is doubtful if any were as graceful and awe-inspiring as Old Abe as he soared over the men gathered below. As the mascot of the 8th Regiment, Abe saw action in thirty-seven battles and skirmishes, including some of the bloodiest fighting at Vicksburg and Corinth. During encampment, Abe would perform various crowd-pleasing stunts for the soldiers, and his celebrity grew with his morale-raising flights over the camps.

Top: One of the vessels from Admiral David Porter's fleet escaping through Bailey's dam along the Red River as depicted in *Frank Leslie's Illustrated Newspaper*, July 16, 1864 (courtesy Library of Congress).
Bottom: An "autographed" photograph of "Old Abe." He used his sharp beak to peck out a "signature" (courtesy of Wisconsin Veterans Museum).

At the end of the war, Old Abe "retired" and was presented to the state of Wisconsin. For fifteen years he lived in an "eagle department" in the basement of the Wisconsin State Capitol in Madison, attracting thousands of visitors. During this period Old Abe also served as the star attraction for many fundraising events, earning politicians and charities thousands of dollars.

Old Abe's long life of twenty years ended tragically on March 26, 1881, when he died from smoke inhalation suffered during a fire near his "department" in the Capitol. His remains were mounted by a taxidermist, and for the next twenty years he remained on display in the rotunda of the capitol building. When a new State Historical Society building was constructed in 1901, Old Abe was housed briefly at that facility before being moved back to the Capitol in 1903 by order of Wisconsin Governor Robert LaFollette, the famed progressive reformer. Sadly, Old Abe's remains themselves were destroyed when the Capitol burned down on February 26, 1904.

"Old Abe," the war eagle, was the mascot of the 8th Regiment, Wisconsin Volunteer Infantry, during the Civil War. He is shown at the battle of Vicksburg (courtesy Library of Congress).

Major Courtland Larkin's Mother's Poem

The poem given the young man by his mother and a photograph he carried bear the marks of the bullet that wounded him at Petersburg.

A MOTHER'S LOVE

Mrs. Larkin's poem expresses a mother's anguish over her child's military service and the fear that he may not return. She reminds him that at home she will watch and pray. Mrs. Larkin explains her fears, saying that she knows that the battlefield is not for her: "This din of war, and clatter/all this carnage and distress/all this bootless wholesale slaughter/is but murder, nothing less."

She recognizes that her son's military service is a result of his patriotism and duty, and that Courtland's "manly zeal" will allow him to fight well, honorably, and bravely.

Larkin first enlisted for Civil War service in 1862, serving four months before illness forced him to resign. After recuperating at home in Milwaukee for nine months, he reentered military service, joining the artillery and leaving Milwaukee carrying his mother's poetic prayer for safety, along with her photograph. He also carried five carte de visite portraits, including one of his mother.

Mrs. Larkin's wish that "heaven shield thee, guard thee, and protect thee" held true until Courtland, now a major in the 38th Wisconsin Infantry, fought at Petersburg, Virginia.

On June 17, 1864, the 38th Wisconsin was in a cornfield under heavy artillery fire when officers learned that the rest of the line had fallen back. Larkin was severely wounded by a musket ball while leading his men to cover in a ravine.

This injury was the cause of his discharge later in 1864. After the war, Larkin returned to

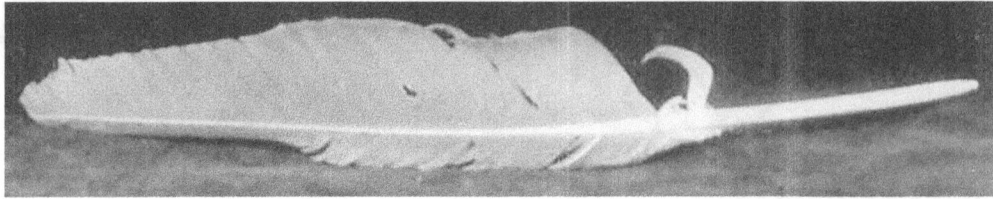

This one remaining feather on view at the Wisconsin Historical Society is all that remains of the once fearless Civil War veteran, "Old Abe the war eagle." Twelve-year-old Ida Karne picked up the feather when visiting Abe in 1868. Today, it represents one of the few remaining souvenirs of the proud bird who became famous not only for his Civil War exploits, but also as a symbol of valor and freedom in the post–Civil War era (courtesy of Wisconsin Historical Society).

Milwaukee where he lived and practiced law until his death in 1920.

Roster with Note Concerning the Capture of Jefferson Davis.

This note and other stories perpetrate the legend that Davis was dressed in women's clothes when captured.

THE LAST DITCH OF CHIVALRY, OR A PRESIDENT IN PETTICOATS?

As early as April 10, 1865, General William Tecumseh Sherman made a dire prediction to his wife Ellen: "It looks like the end of the war is approaching, but don't think so—Jeff Davis will sacrifice every man in the South & even his wife & child before he will give up his pride—He & at least 100,000 men in the South must die or be banished before we can think of Peace. I know them like a book. They can't help it any more than Indians can their wild nature but still it is a truth as with many others in Nature." Sherman's prediction was not far from being the truth.

Confederate President Jefferson Davis was captured by Union troops of the 1st Wisconsin and 4th Michigan Calvary near Irwinville, Georgia, on May 10, 1865. In the gray of early morning, in the midst of a futile, last-ditch effort to elude capture, Davis had "mistakenly" donned his wife's raincoat, and she had hastily draped her shawl around his head and shoulders against the morning cold. Federal troops swarmed through the captured camp, plundering through tents, saddlebags, and trunks. Bibles, prayer books, gold, and jewelry were thoroughly looted by the victorious Yankees. Davis's baggage was searched. John Reagan's $5,500 in gold coins in his saddlebag was taken, along with Liverpool Acceptances bonds. Davis, maintaining his dignity, watched the looting and commented, "You're an expert set of thieves." Davis's wife Varina later wrote: "It [Regan's $5,500] was probably appropriated by the drunken fellow Hudson who was recognized as Adj. of the Michigan Regiment and who Regan told me got his saddle-bags." "Hudson" was Captain Charles T. Hudson of the 4th Michigan Calvary.

The story in the North was that Davis had tried to evade capture by intentionally donning a female disguise. Predictably, the press exploited this turn of events, which grew more exaggerated with the telling. Inevitably, the print market began producing images showing Davis at the point of capture ignominiously dressed in bonnet and skirts. In this cartoon, while Davis utters protests indicating that he is but a poor defenseless woman, a pursuing Union soldier shouts "It's no use trying that shift, Jeff, we see your Boots!"

The following telegraph about Davis's capture was sent to the secretary of war by one of the youngest generals in the U.S. Army, twenty-eight-year-old Major General James H. Wilson. He was the cavalry general in command of the units that captured Davis.

MACON, GA., May 13, 1865 —
  9.30 A.M.
(Received 12.30 A.M. 14th.)
Honorable E. M. STANTON,
  Secretary of War:

Lieutenant-Colonel Harnden, commanding the First Wisconsin Cavalry, has just arrived from Irwinville... He pushed on at 3 A.M., and had gone but little more than a mile when his advance was fired upon by the men of the Fourth

Michigan. A sharp fight ensued, both parties exhibiting the greatest determination. Fifteen minutes elapsed before the mistake was discovered. The firing of this skirmish was the first warning that Davis received. The captors report that he hastily put on one of Mrs. Davis's dresses and started for the woods, closely pursued by our men, who at first thought him a woman, but seeing his boots while running suspected his sex at once. The race was a short one, and the rebel President was soon brought to bay. He brandished a bowie-knife of elegant pattern, and showed signs of battle, but yielded promptly to the persuasion of the Colt revolvers without compelling our men to fire. He expressed great indignation at the energy with which he was pursued, saying that he had believed our Government more magnanimous than to hunt down women and children. Mrs. Davis remarked to Colonel Harnden, after the excitement was all over, that "the men had better not provoke the President or he might hurt some of them" ...The party was evidently making for the coast. I look for them here by 3 P.M., and shall send Davis, A. H. Stephens, and Clay forward by Savannah. A boat is now waiting at Augusta. What must I do with the women and children?

J. H. WILSON,
Brevet Major-General.
MACON, GA., May 13, 1865—
   2.30 P.M.

In *The Personal Memories of Ulysses S. Grant*, Grant writes the following: "Much was said at

"Old Abe" perches proudly atop the Wisconsin State Memorial in Vicksburg, Mississippi. The memorial features bronze tablets with the names of 9,075 Wisconsin soldiers who fought during the siege of Vicksburg. The 122-foot-tall monument was constructed from South Carolina granite and was dedicated May 22, 1911 (courtesy Vicksburg National Park).

the time about the garb Mr. Davis was wearing when he was captured. I cannot settle this question from personal knowledge of the facts, but I have been under the belief, from information given to me by General Wilson shortly after the event, that when Mr. Davis learned that he was surrounded by our cavalry he was in his tent dressed in a gentleman's dressing gown."

Davis posed in these clothes in 1869 for a

For Country

1st Lieut. Heavy Artillery
Co. [illegible]

To my son, may Heaven direct thee
And shed blessings on thy head,
Shield thee, guard thee, and protect thee
From the dangers 'round thee spread

I have not the vaunted daring
Of the storied dames of yore,
To bid thee forth with regal bearing
Only sighing to give more —

To me, this din of war, and clatter
All this carnage and distress
All this bootless wholesale slaughter
Is but murder — nothing less —

Courtland Larkin was nineteen years old when he left Milwaukee, Wisconsin, in October, 1863, as a member of the 1st Wisconsin Heavy Artillery. The youth carried with him the poem entitled "For Country," a plea for his safety written by his mother (courtesy of Wisconsin Veterans Museum).

Before reaching Larkin, a bullet pierced his mother's folded poem and the five *carte de visite* photographs he carried in his left pocket (courtesy of Wisconsin Veterans Museum).

This roster of the 1st Wisconsin Cavalry unit has a dubious note on the back claiming that Jeff Davis was dressed as a woman when the Cavalry apprehended him (courtesy of Wisconsin Veterans Museum).

On of the many merriment cartoons lampooning the capture of Jefferson Davis; he is pictured as a fleeing coward disguised in a dress (courtesy Smithsonian Institution).

series of photographs to prove that he was not wearing women's clothing. His wife Varina donated the suit to the Museum of the Confederacy in 1899, and the museum's founders then sent photos of it to the Boston Athenaeum and other places that displayed cartoons of Davis in petticoats. One does have to question whether Jefferson Davis was dressed this formally at three A.M. on a dark, cold morning.

An 1869 photograph of Davis in these clothes does not validate the issue. It only brings on more doubt. Regardless, no one knows for certain, but once circulated, the account of Davis's capture in women's clothing gained a life of its own and has been retold for decades.

According to Jefferson Davis himself, he was wearing this coat and vest when he was captured (courtesy Library of Congress).

Appendix: Same Battles, Different Names

The North generally named a battle after the closest natural river, stream, or creek, but the South tended to name battles after towns or railroad junctions, hence the Confederate named "Manassas" after Manassas Junction, and the Union named the same battle "Bull Run" after the nearby Bull Run creek.

Date	Confederate	Union
July 21, 1861	First Manassas	Bull Run
Aug. 10, 1861	Oak Hills	Wilson's Creek
Oct. 21, 1861	Leesburg	Ball's Bluff
Jan. 19, 1862	Mill Springs	Logan's Cross Roads
Mar. 7–8, 1862	Elkhorn Tavern	Pea Ridge
Apr. 6–7, 1862	Shiloh	Pittsburg Landing
May 31–June 1, 1862	Fair Oaks	Seven Pines
June 27, 1862	Gaines's Mill	Chickahominy
Aug. 29–30, 1862	Second Manassas	Second Bull Run
Sept. 1, 1862	Ox Hill	Chantilly
Sept. 14, 1862	Boonsboro	South Mountain
Sept. 17, 1862	Sharpsburg	Antietam
Oct. 8, 1862	Perryville	Chaplin Hills
Jan 2, 1863	Murfreesboro	Stones River
Apr. 8, 1864	Mansfield Sabine	Cross Roads
Sept. 19, 1864	Winchester	Opequon Creek

NOTES

Alabama

Alabama Department of Archives and History (Montgomery): Cynthia Luckie, archivist, Alabama Department of Archives, E-mails, 07/29/2005, 09/15/2005, and 09/22/2005.

The Inauguration Bible of Jefferson Davis: Alabama Department of Archives and History; Patricia L. Faust, *Historical Times* (New York: Harper Collins, 1986).

Battle of Perryville and Stones River: Alabama Archives; Stones River National Battlefield.

Arkansas

Prairie Grove Battlefield State Park (Fayetteville)
Battlefield Sword: Alan Thompson, Prairie Grove Battlefield State Park, E-mails, 11/30/2005, 12/01/2005, 12/14/2005, 12/15/2005, 12/16/2005.

The Conciliation Quilt: Alan Thompson, Prairie Grove Battlefield State Park, E-mails, 12/08/2005, 12/09/2005.

Washington, D.C.

Library of Congress (Washington, D.C.): Text source, Library of Congress.

A Sharp-Shooter on Picket Duty: National Park Service, U.S. Department of the Interior, *1862 Peninsula Campaign* (guidebook).

Confederate Department of State records: Library of Congress control number, mm 78016550, call number: 0319M; Southern Historical Society Papers, 1916.

National Museum of Health and Medicine (Washington, D.C.): Armed Forces Institute of Pathology, Washington D.C.

Smithsonian (Washington, D.C.)
Spotsylvania's Bloody Angle: Horace Porter, *Campaign with Grant*, 1897.

Furniture from Appomattox Court House: Donor, Mrs. Elizabeth B. Custer, Acc 124419, no date, Appomattox National Historical Park; text from files at the park; Horace Porter, *Campaign with Grant*, 1897, pp. 486, 487.

Florida

Museum of Florida History (Tallahassee); Text courtesy of museum's Web page, www.museumoffloridahistory.com.

National Park Service Gulf Islands National Seashore (Pensacola): Text courtesy National Park Service, Gulf Islands National Seashore.

Georgia

The Georgia Campaign: *The War of the Rebellion: A Compilation of the Official Records of the Union and Confederate Armies* (hereafter referenced as "OR"), Series 1, Volume 38, Part 1, p. 3.

Southern Museum of Civil War and Locomotive History (Kennesaw): Stan Cohen and James Bogle, *The General & The Texas* (Colorado: Pictorial Histories Pub-lishing, 1999); OR, Series 1, Volume 38, Part 1, pp. 137–139.

Chickamauga and Chattanooga National Military Park (Chattanooga, Tenn.): National Park Service, U.S. Department of the Interior, *The Battles of Chickamauga and Chattanooga* (guidebook).

The Cannonball House, (Macon)
The Massenburg's Battery (Jackson Artillery) Flag: T.L. Massenburg, "How I Lost My Battery," *Macon Telegram*, December 5, 1863; Greg Seamands, "Georgia Thunder," undated article; Dorene Buchanan McElwain, The Cannonball House, E-mails, 02/02/2006, 02/06/2006.

Kennesaw Mountain Battlefield (Kennesaw)
Napoleon 12-Pounder: Retha W. Stephens, museum curator, letter July 27, 2005; George N. Bernard, *Photographic Views of Sherman's Campaign*.

Georgia Capitol Museum (Atlanta): Timothy Frilingos, curator of exhibits, E-mail 11/20/2005.

The Atlanta History Center—The DuBose Civil War Collection (Atlanta): Captain Samuel D. Buck, *With the Old Confeds* (Baltimore, H.E. Houck, 1925), p. 46.

Fort Pulaski National Monument (Savannah): Fort Pulaski National Monument's Web page, www.nps.gov/fopu/historyculture/siege-of-fort-pulaski.htm.

National Infantry Museum (Fort Benning): Text courtesy of National Infantry Museum.

The Mary Willis Library (Washington)
The Confederate Gold Train: Apparently working from his original papers, Micajah Clark's "Full Statement of Disposition of the Confederate Coins," written on January 10, 1882, to the editor of the *Courier-Journal* gives a detailed account of the disposition of the gold and silver coins. It is most interesting to note that Clark never mentions James A. Semple, the naval officer that received $86,000. He refers

to him only as a trusted officer of the Navy. Other sources include J. Hanna, *Flight into Oblivion* (Richmond, 1938, pp. 90–92); William H. Parker, *Recollections of a Naval Officer* (New York, 1883); James Morris Morgan, *Recollections of a Rebel Reefer* (Boston, 1917); Basil Duke, *Reminiscences*; Avery's *History of Georgia*, pp. 325–327; Southern Historical papers Vol. 12, p. 79; Publications of the Southern Historical Association Vol. 5, no. 3, 188–227; House Committee on Claims, 40th Congress, 1st session, 1886; Walter Scott, *Old Mortality*; Otis Ashmore, *Georgia Historical Quarterly*, Vol. 2, 119–133, 171–179 (story of the Virginia banks); Micajah Clark, Southern Historical Society Papers, Vol. 9, 542–556; John F. Wheless, Southern Historical Society Papers Vol. 10, 138–141; Parker, Southern, Historical Society Papers Vol.121, 304–312.

Illinois

Rock Island Arsenal Museum (Rock Island): Patricia Faust, *Historical Times* (Harper Perennial, 1986); Kris Leinicke, Rock Island Arsenal Museum, E-mail, 12/21/2005.

Iowa

State Historical Society of Iowa (Des Moines)
Samuel H. M. Byers escape: Bill Johnson, State Historical Society of Iowa, E-mail, 08/26/2005.

Kentucky

Simpson County Archives and Museum (Franklin): OR, Series 1, Volume 52, Part 1, page 355; Gayla Coates, Simpson County Archives and Museum, E-mails, 11/28/2005, 12/07/2005, 12/14/2005, and 12/19/2005; Simpson County Archives and Museum's Web page, www.simpsoncountykyarchives.com.

Louisiana

Louisiana State Museum (New Orleans)
The mysterious submarine: Greg Lambousy, "A Mystery of the Deep," *Louisiana Life*, Summer 2001; "Last Drawings Identify the Pioneer," Louisiana Endowments for the Humanities, Fall 1999; "Monster of the Deep," Louisiana Endowments for the Humanities, Spring 2005; Greg Lambousy, director of collections, E-mails, 08/08/2005, 08/22/2005, 09/19/2005, and 02/23/2006.

Maryland

Antietam National Battlefield (Sharpsburg)
The Battle of Antietam: National Park Service, U.S. Department of Interior, *The Bloodiest Day of The Civil War* (guidebook); Ted Alexander, staff historian, E-mails, 08/18/2005, 08/24/2005, 10/4/2005, 10/5/2005.
Stonewall Jackson's breakfast: Clifford Dowdey, *The War Time Papers of R. E. Lee*; Christopher Phillips, Department of History, University of Georgia, Letter, August 15, 1989.
The Pry House: Papers in the Antietam National Battlefield Archives.
Jared Wheeler: Deed of Gift, Antietam National Battlefield Archives, August 24, 1982.
Barefooted soldiers: Papers in the Antietam National Battlefield Archives; Clifford Dowde/y, *The War Time Papers of R. E. Lee.*
The Maryland Historical Society (Baltimore)
Shadowbox: Jeannine A. Disviscour, curator, associate director of satellite museums, E-mail, 08/23/2005.

Fort Foote National Park (Prince George County): Web page, www.nps.gov/fofo/historyculture/.

Minnesota

Minnesota History Center Museum (St. Paul)
The 28th Virginia Volunteer Infantry: The Associated Press, March 29, 2001.

Mississippi

Vicksburg National Military Park (Vicksburg)
The Vicksburg Campaign: Patricia L. Faust, *Historical Times* (HarperCollins, 1986).
U.S.S. Cairo: park Web page, *www.nps.gov/vick/u-s-s-cairo-gunboat.htm*; Elizabeth H. Joyner, supervisory museum curator, letter, October 4, 2000.

New Mexico

Pecos National Historical Park (Pecos): Martin H. Hall, *Sibley's New Mexico Campaign* (Albuquerque: University of New Mexico Press, 2000); *The New Mexican*, March 27, 2004.

North Carolina

North Carolina State Archives (Raleigh)
General Robert E. Lee's Special Order 191; Finding Aid V.C. 6 — The North Carolina State Archives; Clifford Dowdey, *The War Time Papers of R.E. Lee.*
The letter of Isaac Avery: Excerpts from *The Future of Our History* written and presented by Representative Daniel W. Barefoot at the Leadership Conference on Access to Special Collections, High Point, North Carolina, March 2, 2000.
Bennett Place (Durham): Mark L. Bradley, *This Astonishing Close*, p. 171; text courtesy Bennett Place State Historical Site.

Oklahoma

45th Division Infantry Museum: Text courtesy, Michael E. Gonzales, curator.

Pennsylvania

Gettysburg National Military Park (Gettysburg)
Pickett's Charge: The New York Times, November 16, 2005.
The Civil War & Underground Railroad Museum of Philadelphia (Philadelphia)
George G. Meade: Patricia L. Faust, *Historical Times* (Harper Collins, 1986); text courtesy of the museum.
Soldiers and Sailors National Military Museum and Memorial (Pittsburgh)
Dog Jack: Josh Fox, curator, E-mails, 12/9/2005, 12/12/2005, 12/19/2005, 12/20/2005, 12/21/2005.

South Carolina

Fort Sumter National Monument (Charleston)
Garrison flags: Richard Hatcher, historian, E-mails 08/01/2005, 08/08/2005.
The Citadel Archives and Museum
General Beauregard and the Fifteen Inch Hollow Shot: Oliver J. Bond, *The Story of The Citadel*, 1936; archives.

Tennessee

Stones River National Battlefield (Nashville)
Battle of Perryville and Stones River: Stones River National Battlefield Museum catalog records.

Lookout Mountain Battlefield (Chattanooga): National Park Service, U.S. Department of the Interior, *Chickamauga and Chattanooga* (guidebook).
Andrew Johnson National Historic Site (Greeneville): Elaine R. Clark, curator, E-mails 08/011/2005, 12/03/2005, 12/12/2005.
The President Andrew Johnson Collection (Greeneville): Richmond Whig, April 17, 1865.

Texas

The Rosenberg Library: Alwyn Barr, "Texas Coastal Defense, 1861–1865," *Southwestern Historical Quarterly* 65 (July 1961); Eleanor Clark, Rosenberg Library, E-mails, 12/12/2005, 12/13/2005, 12/16/2005, 12/19/2005.

Virginia

The Arlington House (Arlington): Mary Troy, The Arlington House, Robert E. Lee Memorial, E-mails, 08/04/2005, 08/05/2005, 08/08/2005, 09/10/2005.
Library of Virginia (Richmond)
Virginia's Ordinance of Secession: The Richmond News Leader, January 30, 1930.
Lee's confidential dispatches: "The Fate of the Confederate Archives," Reprinted from *The Historical Review,* Vol. 44, No. 4, pages 823–825, July 1939.
Museum of the Confederacy (Richmond)
Baltimore Riot — Sergeant's Sword of General Bradley T. Johnson: OR, Series 1, Volume 2, Part 1, page 7.
John Quincy Marr: OR, Series 1, Volume 2, Part 1, pages 60–61; Author unknown, "Reconnaissance through Fairfax," *Virginia Cavalcade,* Summer 1956.
Great Seal of the Confederacy: Richmond Times-Dispatch, April 9, 1921; *The Richmond News Leader,* April 9, 1921; Southern Historical Society Papers, 1916.
Virginia Historical Society (Richmond): Text courtesy of Richmond National Battlefield Park and The Virginia Historical Society.
Manassas National Battlefield Park (Manassas)
The battles of First and Second Manassas: National Park Service, U.S. Department of the Interior, *Manassas* (guidebook).
Wilmer McLean: Martin E. Wack, Manassas National Battlefield Park.
Judith Henry: Elenea Henry, *Some Events with the Life of Judith Carter Henry,* undated.
The 10th Virginia Infantry flag: Charles C. Carleton, *The Boys of 61,* Estates and Lauriat, Boston, 1883.
Major General Fitz-John Porter: Manassas National Battlefield Park Museum catalog records.
Fredericksburg and Spotsylvania National Military Park (Fredericksburg)
The Battles of Fredericksburg and Chancellorsville: Text courtesy of park Web page, *www.nps.gov/frsp/fredhist.htm;* Robert Kirk, *Chancellorsville: Against the Odds,* Series Archive, March 09, 2002; Janice Frye, park historian/curator, E-mail, 10/16/2005, 10/18/2005, 02/17/2006.
Marye's Heights: Captain Samuel D. Buck, *With the Old Confeds* (Baltimore, H.E. Houck, 1925), pp. 46, 92.
Union Headquarters: Janice Frye, E-mail, 06/15/2006
The Death of Stonewall Jackson: Bill McKelway, "Stonewall's Arm Revisited," *Richmond Times-Dispatch,* January 19, 1992; E.T. Stuart, Letter, November 1931; Janice Frye, E-mail, 09/09/2005.
The Death of Union Major General A. W. Whipple; John Bigelow, *The Campaign of Chancellorsville,* Yale University Press, 1910; park visitor center.
Richmond National Battlefield Park (Richmond)
Lowe's balloon valve: Robert K. Sneden, *Eye of the Storm;* Jubal A. Early, *Narrative of the War Between the States* (Da Capo, 1989); John M. Coski, *Capital Navy* (Savas Beatie, 1996); B.A. Botkin, *A Civil War Treasury*
Cold Harbor: Patricia L. Faust, *Historical Times* (HarperCollins, 1986); Charles C. Carleton, *The Boys of 61* (Boston: Estates and Lauriat); *Our Grandfather,* unsigned, Richmond National Battlefield Park.
Petersburg National Battlefield Park (Petersburg): *Battles and Leaders of the Civil War* (De Vinne Press, 1887), Vol. 4, 545–562.
City Point National Park (Hopewell)
Grant's Headquarters' door: James Blankenship, Petersburg National Battlefield Park, E-mail 08/11/2005.
Sabotage at City Point: Melissa Scott Sinclair, "The South's Headless Hero-Terrorist," *Style,* June 29, 2005; OR, Series 1, Volume 42. Part 1, pp. 954, 955.
Staunton River Battlefield State Park (Clover): National Park Service and Staunton River Battlefield State Park.
Appomattox Court House National Historical Park (Appomattox)
The Appomattox Campaign: files at the park.
The surrender: E.P. Hill, *Fighting for the Confederacy,* pp. 46–47.
The "silent witness": Joe Williams and Ryan Henry, "The Silent Witness," National Park Service Web site.
U.S. Army Quartermaster Museum (Fort Lee)
General Ulysses S. Grant's saddle: U.S. Grant, *The Personal Memories of Ulysses S. Grant,* pp. 420–422; various newspaper clippings, Grant, Markland, and other letters in the Grant saddle file of the museum.
Casemate Museum: *The Morning Press,* March 18, 1905; news release, Fort Monroe, May 10, 1977; *Casemate Chronicle,* May 1977; *Daily News,* May 11, 1977.
Hollywood Cemetery (Richmond): Constance Cary Harrison, "Richmond Scenes in '62," in *Battles and Leaders of the Civil War,* ed. Robert Underwood Johnson and Clarence Clough Buel (De Vinne Press, 1887), Vol. 2, 439–448; Mary H. Mitchell, *Hollywood Cemetery,* Library of Virginia, June 1999; Southern Historical Society Papers; Hollywood Cemetery Web site, www.hollywoodcemetery.org/history.html.

West Virginia

Harpers Ferry National Park (Harpers Ferry): The Winchester Star, July 24, 1984;
The News, Frederick, Maryland, July 18, 1984; Richard Raymond, curator, E-mails, 08/10/2005, 12/10/2005, 06/07/2006.

Wisconsin

The Wisconsin Historical Society (Madison): Text courtesy of the Wisconsin Historical Society's Web page, www.wisconsinhistory.org/.
Wisconsin Veterans Museum (Madison)
Old Abe the war eagle: Abbie Norderhaug, E-mails, 09/01/2005, 09/06/2005, 09/13/2005.
Major Courtland Larkin's mother's poem: Bugle, August 2003.
Capture of Jefferson Davis: Stanley P. Hirshson, *The White Tecumseh* (John Wiley & Sons, 1997); Varina Davis, *Jefferson Davis a Memoir by His Wife* (Nautical & Aviation, 1990); OR, Series 1, Volume 49, Part 1, p. 743.

BIBLIOGRAPHY

Ashmore, Otis. "The Story of the Virginia Banks Funds," *Georgia Historical Quarterly*, Vol. 2, December 1918.

Avery, Isaac. *The History of the State of Georgia*. New York: Brown & Derby, 1881.

Bailey, Ronald. *The Civil War: Forward to Richmond*. Alexandria, Va.: Time Life, 1988.

Battles and Leaders of the Civil War. Vols. 1–4. New York: The Century Company, 1883.

Beers, Henry. *The Confederacy: A Guide to the Archives of the Government of the Confederate States of America*. Washington, D.C.: National Archives, General Services Administration, 1968.

_____. *The Union: A Guide to the Federal Archives Relating to the Civil War*. Washington, D.C.: National Archives, General Services Administration, 1968.

Carleton, Charles C. *The Boys of 61*. Boston: Estates and Lauriat, 1883.

Coski, John M. *Capital Navy*. New York: Savas Beatie, 1996.

Davis, Burke. *The Long Surrender*. New York: Random House, 1985.

Duke, Basil. *Reminiscences of General Basil W. Duke*. Garden City, N.Y: Doubleday, 1911.

Ernst, Kathleen A. *Too Afraid to Cry*. Mechanicsburg, Pa.: Stackpole, 1999.

Faust, Patricia L. *Historical Times*. New York: HarperCollins, 1986.

Grant, Ulysses, *The Personal Memories of Ulysses S. Grant*, New York: Forge, 2002.

Hall, Martin H. *Silbey's New Mexico Campaign*. Albuquerque: University of New Mexico Press, 2000.

Hanna, Alfred J. *Flight into Oblivion*. Richmond, Va.: Johnson, 1938.

Hirshson, Stanley. *The White Tecumseh: A Biography of General William T. Sherman*. New York: John Wiley & Sons, 1997.

Morgan, James Morris. *Recollections of a Rebel Reefer*. Boston: Houghton Mifflin, 1917.

Munden, Kenneth. *The Union: A Guide to the Federal Archives Relating to the Civil War*. Washington, D.C.: National Archives, General Services Administration, 1968.

Parker, William H. *Recollections of a Naval Officer*. New York: C. Scribners' Sons, 1883.

Porter, David. *Incidents of the Civil War*. New York: D. Appleton and Company, 1885.

Porter, Horace. *Campaign with Grant*. New York: The Century Company, 1897.

Sneden, Robert K. *The Eye of the Storm*. New York: Free Press, 2000.

Southern Historical Society. *Southern Historical Society Papers*, 1876–1959, Vols. 5, 9, 10, 12, 21. Richmond, Va.

Wyatt, Edward A. *Charles Campbell: Virginia's "Old Mortality."* Charlottesville, Va.: Historical, 1935.

INDEX

Alabama Department of Archives and History 11
Alexander, Edward Porter 165, 182
Alexander, R.H. 154, 157
Alexander, Ted vii
Alford, Kenneth D. 1
Allen, James 163
Anderson, Robert 113, 114
Andrew Johnson National Historic Site 120
Andrews, James J. 37, 39
Anthony, H.T. 18
Anthony-Taylor-Rand-Ordway-Eaton Collection 18
Antietam, Battle of 68
Antietam National Battlefield 68
Appomattox Court House National Historical Park 180
Arlington House 127
Arthur, Chester A. 149
Atlanta History Center 4; DuBose Civil War Collection 48
Avery, Isaac 90, 91
Avery, Waightstill 90

Bailey, Joseph 202, 203
Baker, Edward L.W. 139, 140
Baldwin, M.S. 130
Barksdale, William 152
Barnard, George N. 46
Barratti, A. 124
Bartow, Francis 142
Baruch, Bernard 134
Baruch, Simon 134
Beale, Jane Howison 153
Beall, Fanny 189
Beattie, Heather D. vii
Beauregard, Pierre G.T. 6, 115, 116, 142, 162, 192
Bee, Barnard 142, 156
Benjamin, Judah P. 23, 24, 57, 139
Bennett, Coleman D. 57
Bennett, Frank T. 106, 108
Bennett, James 92, 95
Bennett, Nancy 92

Bennett Place 91
Benthuysen, Watson Van 56
Berdan, Hiram 21, 22, 158
Beverly, Ezekiel 53
Chief Big Cloud 203
Blackford, W.W. 90
Blackmar, Wilmon W. 31
Blaine, James G. 50
Blane, Peter 65
Blankenship, Jim 172, 175
Blankenship, Mike vii
Bless, John M. 88
Blunt, James 16
Bond, Oliver J. 116
Booth, John Wilkes 10, 27
Borst, Peter B. 72
Boynton, H.V. 40
Brady, John 135
Brady, Mathew 18, 19, 27
Bragg, Braxton H. 7, 8, 13, 14, 40, 42, 118, 119
Breckenridge, John C. 54, 55, 57, 92
Briney, John E. 85, 86
Bromwell, William J. 139
Broward, Helen 33
Brown, John 5, 200
Bryan, Thomas P. 139
Buck, J.C. 135
Buck, Samuel D. 152
Buell, Don Carlos 7, 13, 14
Buford, John 58
Bullis, Charles W. 4, 131
Burgess, Jim vii
Burnside, Ambrose E. 7, 69, 99, 128, 151, 152, 169
Burrell, I.S. 125
Burton, James H. 200
Bush, Larry vii
Butler, Benjamin 4, 109, 168, 190, 191, 192
Butler, James 178
Byers, Samuel H.M. 61, 62

Cairo, U.S.S. 82

Calkins, Chris vii, 1
Call, Richard Keith 32
Cance, Elizabeth 176
Capehart, Henry 31
Carroll, James W. Jr. 85, 86, 87
Carter, Jimmy 39
Casemate Museum 190
Cathey, Boyd D. vii
Chancellorsville Visitors Center 150
Chandler, Thos G. 157
Chatham Manor 150
Chattanooga, Battle of 40
Chickamauga and Chattanooga National Military Park 40
Chief Big Cloud 203
Chilton, Robert H. 88
Citadel Archives and Museum 115
City Point National Park 170
Civil War & Underground Railroad Museum 102, 103
Clark, Micajah 56, 132, 133
Clarke, Blair vii
Clarke, Elaine vii
Clarke, Eleanor vii
Coates, Gayla vii
Cockrell, Francis M. 97, 98
Coleman, Henry Eaton 179
Colgrove, Silas 88
Collins George vii
Cook, Joseph J. 125
Corcoran, William W. 24
Cost, Elizabeth 72
Cropsey, A.J. 63
Curtin, Andrew 100
Curtis, George Washington Parke 127
Custer, Elizabeth 31
Custer, George A. 29, 30, 31, 152
Cyclorama 50

Davis, Jefferson 4, 5, 9–13, 23, 44–56, 82, 85, 93, 123–124, 127, 132–133, 138, 142, 161, 192–194, 206, 207, 210–211

221

Index

Davis, Jefferson Hayes 194
Davis, Theodore R. 49, 92
Davis, Varina 122, 206, 207, 211
Day, William H. 92
DeGress, Francis 51
De Renne, Wymberley J. 133
Dimmock, Charles 195
Disviscour, Jeannine vii
Dog Jack 4, 110, 111, 112
Duckett, T.J. 42
DuBose Collection 49
Duke, Basil 55

Eads, James B. 82
Early, Jubal 8, 9, 90, 112, 151, 152, 164, 168
Eaton, Edward B. 18
Eleanor S. Brockenbrough Library 134
Ellett, Bell and Fox 122, 123
Eppes, Richard 170, 190
Evans, Alice Westmore 172
Evans, Nathan 142
Everett, Edward 100
Ewell, Richard 99, 181

Farinholt, Benjamin 177, 179
Farnsworth, Charles S. 53
Farragut, David Glasgow 67
Ferguson, Champ 65
Ferrero, Edward 169
Foote, Andrew H. 77
Fort Foote Park 74
Fort Pickens 33, 34
Fort Pulaski, Battle for 52
Fort Pulaski National Monument 51
Fort Sumter National Monument 113
45th Infantry Division Museum 96
Fox, Josh vii
Fredericks and Spotsylvania National Military Park 149
Fredericksburg Battlefield Visitors Center 150
French, William H. 69
Frye, Janice vii
Fuller, Bill 37
Fuller, Claude E. 40
Fuller, Zenada O. 40

Galveston, Battle of 125
Gardner, Alexander 18, 19, 27
General 37, 38, 39
Georgia Capitol Museum 45
Gettysburg National Military Park 99
Gilbert, William F. 47, 48
Gisch, John 59
Glasgow, Ellen 194
Glorieta Pass, Battle of 85
Gonzales, Michael, E. vii
Gordon, John B. 182
Graetz, Robert vii
Grant, Fred 188
Grant, Joe 188
Grant, Ulysses S. 4, 6–8, 19, 30–31, 42, 54, 60–61, 80–82, 96, 120, 124, 128, 162–163, 166–170, 173 175, 180–182, 186–189, 190–192
Great Seal of the Confederacy 138
Green, Thomas 125
Gress, George V. 51
Griffin, Donald 199, 200
Griffin, Lucy 144
Grove, Jacob 69
Grove, Julia 69
Gumbrecht, Jack vii
Gunther, Charles F. 183

Halleck, Henry 116
Hanson, Luther D. vii
Harper, Ellis 63, 64
Harpers Ferry National Park 199
Harriot, Thomas 139
Harrison, Burton N. 132, 133
Harrison, Constance Cary 195
Harrover, James D. 53
Hatcher, Rich vii
Hay, John 24
Hayes, Harry 90
Hazen, William B. 116
Hebert, Paul O. 125
Henderson, David E. 154
Henry, Ellen 144
Henry, Judith 144, 145
Herron, Francis 16
Hightower, George 157, 160
Hill, A.P 69, 198
Hill, D.H. 69, 88, 89, 90, 162
Hindman, Thomas 16
Historic Cannonball House 42
Historical Society of Pennsylvania 105
Hoke, Robert F. 71, 74, 88, 109
Hollywood Cemetery 194
Hollywood Memorial Association 196, 197
Homer, Winslow 19, 20, 22, 23
Hood, John Bell 9, 34, 50, 97
Hooker, Joseph 7, 41, 42, 68, 99, 104, 120, 121, 128, 151, 152, 166
Hough, Daniel 113
Howard, Oliver O. 151
Hoyt, James A. 179
Hudson, Charles T. 206
Humphreys, A.A. 163
Hunton, Eppa, Jr. 139
Huston, Joseph M. 109

Ingram, Charles Thomas 96, 97, 98
Ingram, David 96

Jackson, Thomas J. "Stonewall" 6, 7, 69, 88–89, 128, 142, 147, 149 151–152, 154, 156–157, 161, 197
Johnson, Andrew vii, 57, 120, 121, 122, 123
Johnson, Bradley T. 134, 136
Johnston, J. Amber 162
Johnston, Joseph E. 06, 8, 9, 21, 35, 45, 81, 82, 91, 92, 93, 142, 160, 161, 181
Jones, Charles C. 133
Jones, Edward F. 135

Jones, James E. 138
Joyner, Elizabeth vii

Kane, George P. 134, 136
Karne, Ida 206
Kautz, August 177, 179
Kennedy, John F. 134
Kennesaw Mountain Battlefield 45
Kieffer, Abner 166
Kieffer, Luther 166, 168
Kieffer, Theodore 166
Kieffer, William 166
Kludy, Mary Laura vii
Knudsen, Dean vii

LaFollette, Robert 204
Lambousy, Greg vii
Larkin, Courtland 205, 208
Lawton, Alexander R. 71
Lee, Ann Hill 127
Lee, Henry "Light-Horse" 127
Lee, Robert E. 4, 6–8, 19, 27–28, 30–31, 47, 54, 68–69, 71, 88–90, 93, 99–100, 127–128, 130, 132–134, 147–148, 151–152, 161–163, 167–169, 177, 181–182, 185, 187
Lee, W.H.F. "Rooney" 177, 180
Leinicke, Kris vii
Levy, Samuel Y. 47
Libby Prison 140, 141
Library of Congress 18
Lincoln, Abraham 4–8, 10, 22–25, 27, 34, 45, 61, 69–70, 77, 93, 100, 120, 122, 124, 161, 191–192, 197, 203
Lincoln, Robert Todd 182
Lind, Edmund 54
Logan, John A. 50, 51
Longstreet, James 8, 30, 40, 43, 99, 148, 149, 151, 165, 181, 182
Lookout Mountain Battlefield 119
Louisiana State Museum 66
Lowe, Thaddeus 111, 148, 163, 164
Luckie, Cynthia vii
Lyles, George H. 145, 147
Lyon, Nathaniel 6

Madison, Dolly 139
Magruder, John 20, 125, 126
Mahone, William 169
Manassas National Battlefield 141
Mansfield, Joseph 69
Marcy, R.B. 163
Markland, A.H. 187, 188, 189
Marr, John Quincy 136, 137
Martin, David vii
Mary Washington College 152
Mary Willis Library 54
Marye's Height 152
Maryland Historical Society 72
Mason, James 124, 139
Massenburg, Thomas 43, 44, 45
Massey, Fred 44
Mauldin, Bill 96
Maxwell, John 172, 173, 175, 176
McAvoy, Benna 16

Index

McAvoy, Robert 17
McAvoy, William 17
McClellan, George B. 6–8, 20–21, 68–69, 88–90, 128, 147, 149, 152, 159, 160–165 190, 196
McClernand, John A. 81, 82
McCown, Lisa vii
McDaid, Jennifer vii
McDaniel, Zebekiah 172
McDowell, Irvin 6, 141, 142, 148, 151, 159, 161
McElwain, Dorene Buchanan vii
McLean, Lula 182
McLean, Wilmer 30, 31, 142, 143, 182, 185
McMahon, Martin J. 167
McPhail, Donald 4, 177, 178, 179
McPherson, James B. 50, 81, 82
McPherson Farm 100
Meade, George C. 7, 8, 90, 99, 100, 102, 103, 104, 105, 111, 162, 189
Merrimac/Virginia 6, 20, 75
Meyer, Jeff vii
Milne, Heather W. vii
Milton, John 32, 33
Minnesota Historical Society 78
Mitchell, Barton W. 88
Monitor 6, 75
Monroe, James 194
Moore, Marjorie 183
Moore, Otis 173
Moore, Richard 183
Moore, Thomas W.C. 182, 183
Morgan, William 195
Moye, Seaton 65
Mundy, "Sue" 65
Murray, George 157, 159
Museum of Florida History 32
Museum of the Confederacy 134

Napoleon, Louis 46
National Archives 27
National Infantry Museum 53
National Museum of Health and Medicine 25
National Park Service Gulf Islands National Shore 32
Nix, Christian 118, 119
Noderhaug, Abbie vii
North Carolina State Archives 88
Notman, John 194
Nowil, Thomas 63

O'Farrell, Patrick 30, 31
Ogden, David vii
Ojibwa Indians 203
Old Abe 4, 204, 205, 206, 207
Olmstead, Charles H. 47, 52
Ord, Edward O.C. 183, 184
Ordway, Albert 18
Owen, William Miller 152

Parker, Theodore 43
Parker, William H. 54, 55
Pecos National Historical Park 85
Pegram, John 198
Pemberton, John C. 81, 82

Pennsylvania Capitol Preservation Committee 109
Pennypacker, Galusha 109, 110
Perkins, John E. 203
Perry, Madison Starke 32, 33
Perryville and Stone River Battle 13, 118
Petersburg National Battlefield Park 168
Pettigrew, James Johnston 102, 103
Philippoteaux, Paul 101
Pickett, George E. 100, 180, 198
Pickett, John T. 24, 139
Pickett's Charge 101, 104
Pittsford, George Goss 139
Pook, Samuel M. 82
Pope, John 6, 128, 147, 148, 149, 162
Porter, David D. 81, 109, 202, 204
Porter, Fitz-John 53, 148, 149, 164
Porter, Horace 28, 182
Prairie Grove Battlefield State Park 15
Prentice, Joseph R. 120
President Andrew Johnson Collection 122
Price, Willis 44
Pritchard, William E. 189
Pry, Elizabeth 69, 72
Pry, Phillip 69

Ragan, Mark K. 67
Rand, Arnold A. 18
Raymond, Richard vii
Reagan, John H. 55, 56, 206
Red River Campaign 202
Reifsnyder, George W. 194
Renshaw, William B. 125
Reynolds, J.M. 140
Reynolds, William Joeb 13
Richardson, Israel B. 69, 70
Richmond National Battlefield Park 159
Robertson, M.E. 132, 133
Rock Island Arsenal Museum 58
Roosevelt, Theodore 24
Rosecrans, William S. 7, 8, 40, 41, 43, 118, 119
Rosenberg Library 125
Rowe, M.B. 152
Russell, Andrew Joseph 153, 156

Schofield, John M. 9, 149, 180
Scott, Winfield 127
Scurry, William R. 125
Sedgwick, John 69, 151, 152, 159
Selfridge, Thomas O. 24, 82, 139
Semple, James A. 56, 57
Seward, William H., Jr. 77
Sharp, George 183
Sharp, Thomas vii
Sheridan, Michael 185
Sheridan, Philip 9, 30, 31, 112, 180, 187, 196
Sherman, Marshall 78, 79
Sherman, William T. 4, 8–10, 35, 40, 42, 45, 50–51, 61, 81, 82, 92–93, 97, 113, 115, 116, 120, 180, 187, 206
Sibley, Henry Hopkins 85
Simpson County Archives and Museum 63
Skelton, Robert Leonard 177
Slaughter, Montgomery 154
Slaughter, W.L. 154, 157
Slemmer, Adam J. 33, 34
Slidell, John 124
Smith, E. Kirby 10, 93, 98
Smith, Leon 125
Smith, Philemon John 73, 74, 75
Smith, William 137
Smith, William R. 37
Smithsonian Institute 27
Sneden, Robert Knox 4
Soldiers and Sailors National Museum and Memorial 110
Solomon, Steven vii
Southern Museum of Civil War and Locomotive History 37
Spear, Samuel R. 179
Spillman, Nannie 185
Spotsylvania, Battle of 28
Spotsylvania Battlefield 150
Stanley, Vaughan vii
Stanton, E.M. 206
State Historical Society of Iowa 61
Staunton River Battlefield State Park 176
Stephens, John T. 46
Stern, Alfred W. 23
Stickley, Ezra E. 68
Stimson, Henry L. 116
Stokes, Caroline 185
Stoneman, George 10, 42
Stones River National Battlefield 118
Stuart, James E. Brown "J.E.B." 4, 151, 152, 194, 196, 198
Sumner, Edwin V. 69

Tate, Samuel McDowell 91
Taylor, John C. 18
Taylor, Richard 10, 93
Terry, Alfred 109
Thiot, Charles 47
Thomas, Alan vii
Thomas, George H. 8, 9, 40, 41, 42, 44, 119, 187
Thompson, Jacob 24
Thurston, M.J. 148
Tidbal, Edward M. 56, 57
Tompkins, Charles H. 137
Traveller 128
Treadwell, George Curtis 131, 132
Treadwell, George H. 131
Trimble, Isaac 71
Troy, Mary vii
Tyler, John 57, 194
Tyler, Julia 57
Tyler, Letitia "Letty" 57

U.S. Army Quartermaster Museum 185

Vicksburg National Military Park 80
Virginia Historical Society 139

Wade, Jennie 102, 103
Wadsworth, James D. 25
Walker, James 119, 121
Walker, W.H.T. 46
Washburne, Elihu B. 188, 189
Washburne, Hempstead 188
Washburne, Israel 188
Washington, George 127, 138, 139, 148
Washington and Lee University 185

Weaver, Rufus 197
West, Robert M. 179
Wheeler, Jared 71, 73
Whipple, A.W. 157
Whitaker, E.W. 30
White, William H. 139
Whitworth Sharpshooter Rifle 96
Wilderness Battlefield 150
Will, Frances Beall 189
Williams, Joe vii
Williams, Sally Trueheart 126
Willis, Francis T. 54
Wills, David 100

Wilson, James H. 10, 177, 180, 206, 207
Wilson, Leonidas L. 15
Wilson, Woodrow 134
Wisconsin Historical Society 202
Wisconsin Veterans Museum 203
Woods, George 135
Wyon, Allan J. 139
Wyon, J.S. 139

Yates, Jane vii
Yorktown, Battle of 20

www.ingramcontent.com/pod-product-compliance
Lightning Source LLC
Chambersburg PA
CBHW081553300426
44116CB00015B/2869